On the Firing Line

ALSO BY GIL AMELIO AND WILLIAM L. SIMON

Profit from Experience

On the Firing Line
MY 500 DAYS AT APPLE

Gil Amelio and William L. Simon

A HarperBusiness Book
from HarperPerennial

First HarperPerennial edition published 1999.

Designed by Helene Wald Berinsky

The Library of Congress has catalogued the hardcover edition as follows:

Amelio, Gil.
    On the firing line : my 500 days at Apple / Gil Amelio and William L. Simon. — 1st ed.
        p.   cm.
    Includes index.
    ISBN 0-88730-918-6
    1. Amelio, Gil.   2. Executives—United States—Biography.   3. Apple Computer, Inc.—management.   4. Computer industry—United States—Management—Case studies.   I. Simon, William L., 1930–   . II. Title.
    HD9696.C64A8626   1998
    338.7'61004165—dc21   98-15251

ISBN 0-88730-919-4 (pbk.)

99 00 01 02 03 ❖/RRD 10 9 8 7 6 5 4 3 2 1

To Arynne and Charlene

Contents

Preface to the Paperback Edition

"O, how full of briers is this working-day world!"

—Shakespeare

This book, first published in 1998 within months of my "execution," revealed as much about me as it did about the other players on the Apple stage. I was praised in print and in person for my willingness to accept responsibility and blame, yet some commentators and reviewers attacked me personally, not for anything that was in the book but because they didn't like the way I had run Apple. I find that brand of predetermined opinion distasteful whether it's from the far out, the far left, or the far right. And aren't these the same people who demand that precious right of free speech for themselves? Does anyone ever believe there is only one side to any story?

A letter placed on the Amazon.com site from someone using the name "Mr. LowTech" expresses this vividly: "I'm convinced that many missed the point of this endeavor. It doesn't matter if you respect or disrespect Amelio. This is his vantage point. Those that are too close to the picture cannot possibly see it was painted well. They want to attack or defend the book based on their opinion of this man's short stay in "their" world. They are ignoring the candor and visceral sense that the noncomputer person gets from the pages of this well-executed documentary. As a business bio, it is surely destined to become classic."

Just as a soldier returning with wounds or scars or a limp from battle—likely the worst time of his life—can still speak enthusiastically of glorious moments and memorable experiences, so will I remember the many highs and joys of my 500 days at Apple even as I try to massage away remembered pain by involving myself deeply in new work and family pleasures.

Many people wondered why I chose to write this book. My painful experiences were much relieved once translated into worthy lessons for others, and many people have responded with words of appreciation for the lessons gleaned. And from people in business everywhere I continue to receive thanks and praise for allowing them to share this view of my negotiations, battles, frustrations, and successes; a glimpse at what mistakes and misfortunes even a well-experienced corporate leader has had to deal with can be instructive and reassuring.

In the first book Bill Simon and I wrote, *Profit from Experience,* there was a lesson that boils down to "you can't manage what you don't first measure." In other words, set your measurements first and then use that as a yardstick to show what you're achieving. In life, too, one must determine how best to measure performance. I set as my target for measuring recovery a milestone that would assure me I had completely healed from the Apple experience: when my need for reprisal had completely disappeared, only then would I know that recovery was at hand.

When people try to turn the knife and say, "How do you like what the Apple stock is doing under Jobs?," I answer "Thank you." After all, folks, I was the one who had the courage to bring him back to Apple as part of a new, compelling strategy, despite the many warnings not to do business with him, as you will read in these pages. Deep within me I knew that Apple had always reflected the best and the worst of Steve's character. John Sculley, Michael Spindler, and I kept the place going but did not significantly alter the identity of the company. Though I have a lot to be angry about in my relationship with Steve Jobs, I recognize that much about the Apple I loved is tuned to his personality.

The story behind my turnaround efforts is a journey from shabby laptops that caught on fire to reliable and highly dependable machines . . . from a company virtually out of money to a fat $1 billion-plus in the bank that Steve has been able to use for marketing and for following through on the plans my team laid.

It's my contention that people who follow the adventure told in the pages of this book will forever *Think Different* about business and board rooms, about corporations and computers, about jobs and Jobs.

On the Firing Line

1

A Winter's Tale—
I AM HIRED

"What would you think about becoming a member of the Apple board?" The words resonated. I thought, *Yes, I'd be right for Apple!*

The caller was an old friend, but this wasn't social. Strictly business. Tom Friel, a headhunter at Heidrich & Struggles who had been hired to search for another Apple board member, remembered that a few conversations ago I'd shown an interest in taking on one additional board assignment.

Apple seemed a natural, considering my background as a Ph.D. technologist with a number of patents and my reputation as a business leader who had established a notable record for transforming ailing companies. Tom also knew I'd been a Macintosh fan for years, and was used to hearing me rave over the virtues of the Mac.

And Apple as a company holds an extraordinary fascination, virtually achieving the status of a celebrity in its own right. Luc Hatlestad described it in the pages of *Red Herring* magazine as having "a unique power to inspire emotions. . . . It's difficult to imagine any other high-tech company inspiring such heartfelt devotion."

That winter's day in early 1994 when Tom called was at a time when I had brought National Semiconductor from the brink of disaster to showing higher profits than ever. The company had by then progressed to what I call Phase Two of transformation—the less frenetic process of building from strength toward the goal of becoming great.

So my answer was easy. "But Apple's board needs to know that National is an important supplier of theirs. We sell them $25 or $30 million worth of chips a year. They need to be sure that's not going to be a conflict of interest."

Some people claim they can accept rejection easily; I think they're just better actors. Nobody likes to be turned down for something they want. It was uncomfortable when you were in junior high, it's *still* uncomfortable when you're a CEO. So when early winter turned to late spring and still no word from Tom or Apple, I began to wonder.

Then, in June, I was scheduled to cohost the annual dinner for the Silicon Valley chapter of the National Conference of Christians and Jews. This is an organization I've belonged to and supported for a number of years because of its dedication to principles of tolerance and acceptance, standing for values and the kind of follow-through that is fundamental to improving the human condition.

The other cohost that evening was an authentic Silicon Valley legend, A. C. "Mike" Markkula, Jr. As all Apple and high-tech followers know, Mike originally put up the money that launched Apple Computer. He had made a bundle from Intel when the semiconductor industry was still in its infancy and, recognizing the potential, had bankrolled the two Steves with $91,000 out of his own pocket, and arranged and guaranteed a $250,000 line of credit from the Bank of America. As a member of Apple's board since its beginning, Mike had also served as board chairman through most of the company's history. To say he was both powerful and influential is as obvious as saying that Rose Kennedy owned black dresses.

Mike and I were only slightly more than nodding acquaintances. For years our paths had crossed socially, and we seemed interested and involved in some of the same community organizations. I sensed a mutual respect and admiration, so sought out the opportunity at the NCCJ affair to bring up the board position.

Mike looked surprised. "We thought you weren't interested," Mike said, genuinely surprised to find out that I was. It was like the old children's game of Telephone, where a message gets whispered along the line and ends up completely different. Here we were at the highest corporate levels, going through only two or three people, and the message arrived as garbled as at any party of ten-year-olds.

This time Mike carried my message of interest back to Apple's board and got the wheels turning. On my next trip to New York, I was invited to dinner by the two people who formed the board's recruiting committee. We met at a private club, a vestige of an 1800s lifestyle, hidden from most people's eyes—including mine, until that night. An aura of old wealth and unspoken power hangs in the air, accentuated by the dark, highly-polished woods, subdued voices, and the sense that any secret spoken here is entirely safe.

Not that we had any secrets to share. At least not yet. I hadn't known quite what to expect, but this was not an examination of my ideas or even my style. This was not a "What do you think Apple should do now?" session but a getting-to-know-you opportunity, a chance to form an opinion of each other. They wondered if I would fit in with the board so that we could work amicably and productively together; I wanted to see if they could listen to me and to each other with respect and patience.

Frankly, I found both men impressive. Bernie Goldstein, a venture capitalist from Broadview Associates, is a true gentleman—caring and sensitive with a forthright way of getting close without your being aware of what he's doing. As I was to discover, he also has the backbone to become very tough when someone wants to spend company money. Peter Crisp, also a venture capitalist, is a founder and a managing partner at VenRock, a firm that invests Rockefeller money. Soft-spoken and charming, with flawless diction and the wiry build of a long-distance runner, he has an eternal twinkle in the eye that conveys the feeling you're with someone special. Peter had already made up his mind to leave the board on reaching his fifteenth anniversary of membership, then just a few months away, and was eager to find a strong candidate who could join before his time to leave.

At the end of that first meeting I felt not so much interviewed as agreeably entertained. When we parted, Peter and Bernie assured me I would be hearing further—and soon.

I called my wife, Charlene, at the end of the evening to share my impressions. Astute as always, she commented, "Something tells me it's going to take a lot more of your time than you think. Are you sure you want this?" Later I would light on this question as prophetic.

◦   ◦   ◦

The vetting process wasn't over; Apple's then-CEO Michael Spindler wanted to see for himself who this Amelio was. I surmised he had picked up a scent of the board's growing restlessness with the company's performance and probably wanted his own take on whether, as a board member, I might line up against him, contributing to the negative pressure he was already under. The process was beginning to feel a bit like being considered by a fraternity that isn't sure it wants you, but I accepted Michael's invitation to visit.

Spindler was a native of Germany who had also lived in France, and had come to notice by making a notable success of running Apple Europe. John Sculley, the one-time head of Pepsi who was Apple CEO from 1983 to 1993, brought Spindler to work at Apple corporate headquarters. Known for his grueling eighteen-hour workdays, Spindler had been in the right place at the right time when the board ousted Sculley from the CEO job.

Under Sculley, the Apple share of the personal computer market had declined from about 20 percent down to a discouraging 8 percent. The company's fortunes would grow and glow again if market share could be jacked back up to earlier levels. In the waning light of late afternoon, Michael laid out his goal for the company, fully confident that restored levels of greatness were within reach.

The Spindler regime had sent more products to the market, faster and at lower prices. Desperate to drive up volume and regain market share, his team had opened new mass-market distribution channels that put the Macintosh on sale in chain outlets like Circuit City. But this fostered a mass-selling approach by "don't ask questions" clerks. The expression "If your only tool is a hammer, everything looks like a nail" fits the situation—Michael's team was applying a strategy that makes sense in a commodity business, while the Macintosh still depends on a buyer understanding its distinctive qualities. His aggressive stance on a mass-market strategy for Apple turned out to be a negative rather than a positive—in hindsight, probably a big mistake.

Spindler was also in charge when the PowerPC was introduced. The general opinion held that because it was cheaper, faster, and better, it was going to be the foundation on which Apple would make an impressive comeback. The strategy seemed to work big-time—by mid-1994, sales were growing again.

It was a false signal, an unsustainable spike in the curve. Apple marketer Debbie Carlton recalls, "We were trying to attract the first-time buyers, but we got into a lot of outlets where the sales people were okay with TVs and VCRs and sound systems, but really didn't know the Mac. They didn't know what made it better and they didn't know how to sell it."

The smiles around Apple soon looked as jaded as a jack-o'-lantern the week after Halloween. As Michael and I sat together at the tired end of a long day, he shared with me that sales were again very sluggish.

We explored the situation and he outlined his ideas for getting back to the Holy Grail of 20 percent market share. I couldn't help but admire his unflagging enthusiasm and his willingness to examine the dark side of the business. I would later come to recognize in him the Teutonic tendency to look at the most negative side of every challenge, brooding over problems rather than searching for a way to turn crisis into an opportunity.

I remember thinking, *Our personalities are so different, he probably won't want me.*

Give him credit—he wasn't bothered by our differences. I was elected to the board in November 1994, though I didn't actively start until after the holidays, in January 1995, nearly one full year after the first phone query. As things would turn out, it would be just over one year later that I would become Apple's fourth CEO.

o   o   o

Michael sat at the head of the boardroom table looking troubled, and started the meeting with a matter not on the agenda. He asked that the room be cleared of all staff and aides—he would speak only in the presence of board members, in "executive session." From the expression on Michael's face, it was clear to all that the subject wasn't the announcement of welcome news.

I waited for Michael to begin and noticed the tension on the faces of my fellow board members. "We're not making it, the company has to be sold." That was it. Michael had become convinced there was no way to keep Apple independent.

We would soon learn that Joe Graziano—Apple's chief financial officer, who was the other "inside" member of the company's board of directors—was very strongly in the same camp. Perhaps Joe had convinced Michael that the numbers just weren't adding up, or perhaps it was Michael's dour view that tainted the outlook for both of them; I would never know who got that flame ignited.

Over the next few months the camps formed and solidified. Graziano led the initiative to sell to IBM. Markkula bought the idea of selling, but thought the best sale could be made to Sun Microsystems. Spindler was promoting a European sale, to Philips, the Dutch electronics giant.

And my lone voice asked, "Why do we have to sell?" I had been working over the same numbers as the others but saw a different outcome: *Sure, Apple's outmoded hopes and dreams must be dropped, but new workable ones could be substituted.* To me, no way did the numbers add up to a desperation sale.

Perhaps because I had just led National Semiconductor back from losing half a billion dollars to what promised to be a record-breaking year, it looked to me like, *Here we go again.* I anticipated the attitude that the new boy on the board doesn't know all the problems and doesn't have all the answers, but I was experiencing that familiar feeling when faced with a challenge: Don't look for ways around, tackle the problems head on. I wouldn't make it easy for them to throw in the towel.

Powered by Graziano, Apple negotiations with IBM went on for months, but shuffled along like an old man in scuffs. Joe argued that IBM had made some big acquisitions, such as Lotus, and would come to see Apple as a good fit. All we had to do was play our cards right and Lou Gerstner would buy Apple and save the company. What Joe overlooked was IBM's history with acquisitions.

Big Blue has never been comfortable with acquiring other companies, and in this case they inched negotiations forward at an uncomfortable snail's pace. Graziano began to get testy at the board meetings—all he could report was that IBM wasn't responding. He groused at Spindler, accusing him of not pushing hard enough, and then griped at Markkula, complaining he was so interested in the possibilities with

Sun that he was getting in the way of an IBM deal. Graziano wanted with such intensity to sell to IBM that he was unable to see the obstacles were all on IBM's side; he was blaming the wrong people.

My style as a corporate director is to participate more than many others, but I found it hard to get involved during my first months on Apple's board. I genuinely respected all of these people, yet together there didn't seem to be a team rapport. Generally, there's a high that comes when you're pulling together in a common cause—the old Mickey Rooney, "Hey, gang, let's put on a show" excitement that I have come to enjoy when serving on boards. These people were frustrated that the company wasn't successful and they wasted too much mental and motor energy thinking about how to find a buyer. Why waste this talent when it could be applied to building value in the company and improving it?

At one meeting I got steamed up. "Look, let's assume we're successful at selling this company to somebody. What's the first step they'll want to take? Fix the company's problems. Why wait for somebody else to figure that out? Why don't we get started on fixing the problems now? If we sell, the company will be in better shape, the buyer will be happier, and so will we. And if we don't sell, we'll be that much ahead of the game."

Sure, I had their attention . . . but I wasn't getting much in the way of affirmative head nods. I said, "We're not spending enough time at these board meetings talking about what're going to do to fix the damn company." But the board was focused on the problems of getting the company sold, and I wasn't finding the right way of getting my message through.

Perhaps the denial was understandable, given the range and caliber of Apple's problems at that time: lousy product quality; a massive disconnect in market forecasting, so that the company was consistently short of the products in demand while leaving the channels crammed with too many of everything else; high prices that were driving customers away; manufacturing techniques ten years out of date; and major software problems causing frequent computer crashes for users. Adding to that long list of ailments, the hugely profitable Japanese market was leveling off—we could no longer count on increasing Asian revenues to mask the company's other losses.

The pileup of negatives was definitely in our faces.

∘ ∘ ∘

Apple's fiscal year begins October 1, probably so that Christmas falls in the first quarter. Santa Claus has long been kind to computer companies—PC manufacturers must be not far behind greeting card and toy companies when it comes to benefiting from Christmas shoppers. The holiday buying season starts in late October, and in 1995 Apple had soared off to a roaring start for the fiscal year. The numbers were looking sensational. All through the quarter, Michael had been advising board members that the company would make something like $150 million profit for the period.

But the truth lay elsewhere.

The December meeting began with ugly financial news. Now, at almost the end of the quarter, we suddenly heard that although there had been record sales, the company would *lose* money. Apple was selling more and making less. And the loss would be whopping—the quarterly totals would come to $69 million. To say we were stunned would be putting it mildly. Even the board's investment-banker advisors, like the colorful, hard-driving Frank Quattrone, had little to say that improved the mood of board members.

In Michael's defense, he had apparently himself been caught off guard. *Wall Street Journal* reporter Jim Carlton tells the story in his heavily researched 442-page tome, *Apple*. According to Carlton, both Jim Buckley, president of Apple Americas, and his counterpart running Apple Japan, John Floisand, thought Spindler had given his blessings to apply their standard routine of dropping prices to boost sales. They had done it with a vengeance, slashing prices as much as 25 percent. When Spindler found out, he was livid and verbally whipped his two sales lieutenants in front of the full executive staff, demanding, "How could you sell these things for a loss?" Their defense was that they had just been following his orders. Spindler is supposed to have barked back, "I asked you to move the units, not to wrap money around them!"

But always the courageous executive, Spindler had let the blame fall on his own shoulders rather than faulting his lieutenants. Admirable. Yet over and over again, I find that people—even top executives—wait too long before sounding a trouble alert or asking for help. Had Michael reported to the board what had really happened, once I became CEO I would have been alerted to the dangerous Apple sales process of price-cutting and channel-stuffing. Despite his honorable intent, Spindler's report provided us no sense of the underlying problem; I would be left to play Sherlock Holmes in order to find clues and motives behind the disappearance of the Apple profits.

By this time Sun had been making serious overtures. Board meetings started being held every week to further explore the Sun proposals. At one of these meetings, board member Peter Crisp was discouraged by the proceedings. He leaned over and casually said to me, "Gil, have you ever thought about joining Apple over here and helping the company?"

No, I hadn't. I promised to think about it.

I didn't know then, and still don't know, whether Peter had talked to other directors before making that oblique suggestion—or even whether he had been mulling it over beforehand or had instead just been struck with the idea on the spot. Obviously he didn't have the authority to offer me the job, but he had planted the seed.

I left on a prearranged eight-day trip to visit the National Semiconductor plants in Asia. The long arm of the media reached me in remote locations as reporters asked me about rumors that I was being considered by the Apple board to replace Michael Spindler. Clearly someone was feeding inside information; unfortunately the leaks would continue even when the leadership changed. Was it through one of the area associates (which is Apple-speak for "secretary"), or one of the top executives, or one of the board members? Though I have my suspicions, the truth will probably remain a Deep Throat mystery.

At the next board meeting after my return, I told Peter, "I've thought about what a really excellent situation I've got at National. I'm not keen on leaving. But Apple does have a major leadership problem. So, if the board is serious about me taking an active role within the company, I'll seriously entertain the idea."

Over the next two weeks that scenario rapidly played into action.

o   o   o

And the calls came rolling in. I particularly remember Regis McKenna, the PR guru and deal maker who, in the oft-repeated Valley legend, had been talked into helping a fledgling Apple by an arm-twisting Steve Jobs. His promotional efforts had been crucial to the company's success, and the Regis McKenna PR Company had continued as advisor throughout the Jobs, Sculley, and Spindler dynasties. Regis had attended the infamous High Noon shoot-out, the board meeting at which Steve Jobs and John Sculley had each tried to have the other fired. McKenna had sided with Sculley, against his old sidekick Jobs. Now Regis was telling me, "Gil, you're the only guy I know of in this business who has a hope of fixing Apple." I also heard a similar comment from Floyd Kvamme, who in the early years had been the company's first director of sales. Riding high on the flattery, it crossed my mind to wonder if I could get hooked on attention and adulation.

In the hallway during a mid-afternoon break in the continual board meetings to consider the Sun offers, Peter Crisp asked to speak to me privately. He seemed glum, almost somber, as he once again urged me to accept the leadership.

Though caught between a conflict of emotions—fear of the unknown and exhilaration of a new challenge—the time had come to move ahead or put the matter to rest. I replied, "If you come forward with a serious offer, I'll accept."

Peter moved fast to make arrangements. That Sunday afternoon I sat with Mike Markkula at his office in Woodside. The conversation quickly turned to compensation. "What do you have in mind?" I asked.

"Whatever you want."

"Fine. I'll write a wish list and we can go from there."

The next day I faxed him my list. As I assume he anticipated, I intentionally asked for more than I expected to get—including a generous $5 million sign-on bonus and a million shares of stock up front to make me a stockholder.

Mike responded rather rapidly and seemed nonplussed. Instead of negotiating, he merely said, "We can't really do this." I moved the conversation forward into a negotiation mode. Along the way, Mike asked me to draw up a comparison of what I was in line to receive if I stayed at National Semiconductor. The spreadsheet I prepared showed that, provided the company continued to improve its performance record at roughly the same level in a reasonable economy, my contract with National could earn me some $27 million over the next five years.

By nearly anyone's standard, $27 million is a huge amount. But to put the number into perspective, in the five years I had been leading

National, the stock price had increased fourfold (had even at one point reached an eightfold increase) and the market capitalization had increased by some $3.5 billion.

Much as I was motivated to undertake the risky Apple challenge, I knew it had to make financial sense, which meant a compensation package tempting enough to give up the assured situation at National. Finally, in a conversation with Mike—not the time to play coy or be vague—I defined what I had come to see as the three essential elements: "The deal should offer me an increase in salary, it has to be attractive enough to protect my downside, and it has to offer me significant upside."

Translation: The "upside" would be a sizable block of stock options, so that if I did well and the stock picked up, I would be suitably rewarded for my success. Mike accepted this aspect with full understanding of the powerful incentive it holds for any key executive to have a significant ownership position in the company. I offered that the options could vest—that is, come into my control for sale or transfer—gradually over a period of five years, instead of the normal Apple practice of three years. Mike had no problem with this upside arrangement; it would turn out to be the only item to survive all the way through the negotiations.

The "downside" part of the equation meant providing that my family wasn't going to be worse off for me having taken this job. To protect me on the downside, we agreed on a million shares of stock to be received at the outset; even if I were never successful in reviving the company, at least this would replace the money that I would walk away from at National.

On the salary issue, Mike easily agreed to a roughly 30 percent increase over my National salary—from $770,000 to $990,000.

There would also be a sign-on bonus of $5 million.

Once we had a sense we were getting close, Mike brought Peter Crisp into the discussions. The three of us reached an accord that Mike said he would feel comfortable presenting to the board.

It wouldn't turn out to be as easy as that. Not by a long shot.

o   o   o

The next Apple board meeting was to be held in New York on January 31. I flew out as the guest of Mike Markkula aboard his Falcon 900 personal jet. We landed at LaGuardia and headed for the St. Regis, where the board members were staying.

The meeting started at 8:00 A.M., with all the board members present, including Michael Spindler, along with attorneys from Shearman & Sterling, one of the law firms representing Apple, in whose offices we had gathered.

The agenda listed only two items: the deal with Sun and what to do about a new CEO. Short agenda, very long meeting.

Scott McNealy, the dynamic and irrepressible founder/CEO of Sun, had been invited to attend. He arrived with the impressive backup of Larry Sonsini, the number-one attorney in Silicon Valley's most prestigious law firm, Wilson, Sonsini, Goodrich & Rosati. McNealy, who is an impressive thinker and convincing presenter, made a short pitch that showcased all the glowing reasons why it would be great for Apple to align with Sun.

And though I remained convinced that Apple could be saved as an independent company, I was impressed with some of Scott's ideas. I began to waver.

But Apple loyalist that I was and still am, I needed a few more answers. So I asked Scott what to me was one of the two most important questions: "If you buy Apple, are you going to keep the Apple brand name or are you going to drop it?"

Scott's answer: "We haven't really gone into that yet." This ran up a huge red flag for me. In that one response, he undermined a near-perfect presentation. Could it be that this smart, capable business icon was unaware the Apple brand name was something not only worth keeping but worth nurturing and promoting? How could he not have thought about the Apple name—one of the most cherished and valuable of the company's commodities? Something was not right, and for me, Sun was immediately way off base.

But the subject had turned to the number-one issue: Price. Apple was then trading around $28 a share, and the rule of thumb puts a fair price at 20 to 40 percent premium above the market price. I figured we didn't deserve the high end of that premium, because the company was performing so badly, but I certainly thought we'd be at the low-premium end—$33 or $34. Potential buyers try to lowball the price, of course; it seemed reasonable to consider $30 as a floor. I had told myself, *It's got to be at least $30*. And I believe most of the other board members had a number close to that in mind, though I think one or two were eager enough that they would have settled for market price— whatever the stock was trading at that day.

Then Scott McNealy dropped his bombshell: "This is our best offer—we'll pay $23."

I sat there dumbstruck, imagining a scenario: *I'm named CEO, and my first order of business is to go out to all the shareholders and say, "We know your stock is trading at $28, and we know that on average you paid $34 for your shares, but we're going to offer you $23."* I looked at him and said, "Scott, that's impossible. I can't get behind that at all."

If a major company ever sold for dollars a share less than its market value, I never heard about it. We told Scott and Larry we'd be in touch. When the door closed behind them, I said, "I was ready to go with the flow, but this is ridiculous. Forget it!"

The more the board talked, the more negative they came to feel about selling on those terms. Bernie Goldstein was of a different mind and he did, indeed, make a compelling argument: Even though the price had been as high as $50 not long before, at the current $28 the company was in fact overvalued, the price was going to go down, and maybe we ought to take what we could get while the offer was on the table.

At that point another scenario flashed through my mind: *We announce the company is being sold to Sun at $23 a share. Financial analysts and investors immediately deduce that this must represent what the board believes is the true value of the company, and the stock price plummets to that level in a few minutes of trading. And probably keeps on going down, as confidence in the company erodes.*

Since Bernie was point man for the sell-at-any-price camp, I asked him, "How do you get shareholders to accept this?" No answer, so I continued. "They'll think we're asking them to vote against their own best interests. I can't imagine you'll get much support."

By now it was dusk. The fantasy sight of the New York City skyline sparkled outside as the spark went out of our enthusiasm for the Sun deal. It began to look as if everyone had decided. Michael showed little enthusiasm but appeared ready to go along with whatever the board decided. A vote was taken and McNealy's offer was officially turned down.

From the comic Victor Borge I learned that laughter is the shortest distance between two people. Someone made a lighthearted remark and suddenly the board came together as we hadn't in a long time. It stayed that way through dinner, a humble meal hastily brought in to the meeting room by one of New York's many caterers.

o   o   o

It was already evening and the discussion of the CEO situation was only just ready to begin.

Mike Markkula, as chairman, requested an executive session. Michael Spindler must have known what was coming, but it's painful nonetheless. Throughout his life, he had gotten results by working harder than anyone else; now he was being told that hard work wasn't enough. Intensely frustrated that his heroic efforts had brought him to such a moment, Michael rapidly left the room.

The board quickly decided Spindler had to go, and Markkula went out to break the news to him in private.

To his credit, Spindler returned to share with us a few final comments, and it was a less difficult moment than I feared. He managed to be dignified, poignant, and moving, several times saying, "I tried the best I could." In the end there was a respect for this very decent man, even though the fight was out of him.

We then talked about a termination package for him. Peter Crisp and Apple's human resources director had already put together some numbers based on Michael's contract, and the board quickly agreed. I thought that Michael gracefully accepted what I viewed as minimal compensation given the weight of responsibility he had carried. Even so, some reporters would later view it as overgenerous.

o   o   o

I was caught by surprise when it turned out I wasn't the only candidate. Board member Jürgen Hintz had been a Procter & Gamble executive when he joined the Apple board, and he had left to head up a company in France. That hadn't lasted long, and Jürgen had been without work for several months. Now he piped up and said, "I'd like to be considered for the CEO position." Since he was a fellow director, the board felt obligated to consider his bid. I left the room so he could make his pitch and review his qualifications without a sense of the leading competitor judging his every word.

Jürgen then joined me in the lobby of the offices and we made awkward conversation. Since Peter Crisp and Mike Markkula had been urging me to accept the job, I could count on their support. Probably the same with venture capitalist Bernie Goldstein, who had been one of my interviewers before I was accepted on the board.

I was less certain about Franklin Delano Lewis, the head of National Public Radio. A highly capable and gifted man, Del was well experienced in the role of corporate director and well skilled in how to operate at a board level. There's a certain chemistry to the way boards work, which I had already discovered Del to be a master of. We had mostly seen eye-to-eye on board matters, but I had no reading of where he might stand on me as CEO.

Soon Mike Markkula came out to shake my hand: The board had voted to pursue negotiations with me. I had been fairly certain of the outcome, yet the actual moment was tingling.

o   o   o

Opening the discussion in front of the whole board, Mike asked, "The Sun deal is probably dead, but it may not be. They may come back with a richer number. Right now, we just don't know. Would you take this job under those circumstances?"

I said, "Yes, but not if the board is going to accept a price below market. I don't want to be put in that position." They agreed, which for the moment put the final nail into the deal with Sun—or so I thought.

Three hours till midnight. We had been at it for some thirteen hours, with a final area still to be resolved: "Okay, Gil, we're going to offer you the job. What should your compensation package be?" Though I assumed the other members had already been brought up to date on this, I described the terms that Mike and I had settled on.

Once again I was invited out of the room for what I expected to be a rather brief courtesy event. Nearly an hour and a half later, I was finally summoned back. The other directors, thinking we had a deal, began to filter out and head for home or their hotel room, until the only ones remaining were the board's two-man compensation committee, Mike Markkula and Peter Crisp, along with the Shearman & Sterling attorney.

Mike ran down the terms of the offer they had concocted, which was substantially below what I was making at National, and less than Michael had been getting—no downside, no upside, more like upside-down!

I couldn't know whether this was good-faith negotiating—a conscientious board protecting the stockholders by trying to strike the best possible deal for the company—or whether Mike had been strangely silent about the terms he, Peter, and I had arrived at. Who was it that said, "Look at the barriers you encounter only as navigation problems. They are not dead ends but merely detours."?

I was just short of angry; perhaps I should have seen this as a warning sign. Instead I determined to be decisive but not let my annoyance show—tough at 11:00 P.M. So, perhaps with too much emphasis, I said, "No! That won't do." I then patiently went through the same points about salary, upside, and downside, and showed them the spreadsheet I had prepared on my projected earnings at National.

When we stopped for a short break, I got the chance to take Markkula aside. I said, "Mike, I don't want to rain on everyone's parade here, but you know my criteria. Meet those conditions and I'll do it." The others convened once again without me. I decided to clear my mind and try a glass of plain old New York City tap water. A New Yorker by birth, I was still in a few ways a New Yorker, and laughed to myself at how right "Guiliani water" tastes.

Finally—it was nearing midnight—they settled on a more reasonable offer, which was immediately put into the form of a term sheet by the Shearman & Sterling lawyer and typed up by a secretary who had been kept on standby for just such a need. The salary was pegged at the number Mike and I had originally settled on—$990,000, which represented a nominal increase over Spindler's $900,000. The other terms were also in line—a million shares of stock, with restrictions on the sale, and another million of options, plus the $5 million sign-on bonus.

The salary would be augmented by a performance-based bonus. A common pattern for executives, and the tradition at Apple, called for a standard bonus equal to 100 percent of salary, but with possibilities ranging from nothing in the case of poor performance to a maximum of 200 percent. But hoping to provide an added incentive, they had pegged my maximum at 300 percent.

The term sheet would also specify that if another company acquired Apple and wanted me, then I would be obliged to stay on for at least a year, even though I would no longer be the head of an independent company. I wasn't keen on the idea, but agreed because it felt like the right thing to do. If the acquiring company decided they could do without me, then I got an all-in settlement of $10 million.

Did I and do I believe I was worth that much money? The value of a corporate CEO, like the value of an athlete or network anchor, is based on how much it takes to attract one of the handful of people who are qualified for the position. Compared to what a top marketing manager earns, or a sales rep, or, for that matter, a CEO in England, France, or Germany, I would say there isn't any CEO worth the money that a Lou Gerstner, a Michael Eisner, or a Steve Ross gets. And I'd say the same about the earnings of a Michael Jordan and a Dan Rather. But in a highly competitive marketplace, a company, sports team, or television network will pay what it takes to attract talent. Those who can command sky-high incomes benefit from the competition. That's the reality—the old supply and demand at work in a free economy. Is it fair to all the other people who may be working just as hard? No. Is it going to change any time soon? Same answer.

Overall I was well satisfied with the deal. But the next four or five weeks would prove to be highly distressing, giving me an unwelcome view of what life at Apple was going to be like.

o   o   o

Mike Markkula and I finally boarded his plane at 1:00 A.M. for the return to California, unaware that terms of the deal had already been leaked to the press and posted on the Internet.

2

Tight-Fisted Homunculus—
MY CONTRACT GOES THROUGH HELL AND SO DO I

It was the morning after the New York City board meeting marathon—Thursday, February 1—and despite having gotten hardly any sleep, I just couldn't wait to get to work. Somehow I wanted desperately to be in my office, checking out the reality of what had become a fantasy playing out with my eyes open.

Rick Sessions, a National Semiconductor manager, later recalled, "Gil seemed that morning to look twenty years younger, and looked like he was walking on clouds." Though I doubt the story, Rick says that a coworker was walking by in front of the office building and saw me looking out the window. Though I didn't know the man, according to Rick, I waved at him and the man "almost fell over backwards."

I needed a clear head to cope with the first task that morning—a quickly arranged conference call with the National board so I could tell them as gracefully as possible that I was resigning.

A few breaths and onto the next problem—how to pass power along until the National board could select a new CEO. I began writing a to-do list of items to resolve, hoping I could show up at Apple the following morning. The buzzer interrupted my train of thought; my executive assistant, Bonnie Murphy, knew me well enough not to interrupt unless it was important. It was: Apple's inside chief legal counsel, Ed

Stead, was on the phone, his voice as assertive as the buzzer had been.

Without much preamble, he said, "I can't accept the deal you negotiated."

A glorious moment in my career suddenly tasted very sour. Business is based on ethics and integrity; this didn't sound like any version of ethics or integrity within my experience.

I had reached an agreement with two appointed members of the board, in the presence of the company's outside lawyers, and now an Apple staff member takes it on himself to repudiate what the board agreed to. Only at Apple! I would soon know firsthand and painfully that such things really happen at this company.

"Ed," I said, "you don't understand. Based on the term sheet you have in front of you, I just turned in my resignation."

"Well, but I can't accept the deal." Was I hearing right? Exasperating.

"What's the problem? What can't you accept?"

About the only point he didn't complain about was the upside stock options, the performance benefit for succeeding. Of all the issues he raised, my biggest problem was with the initial stock grant, which was my downside protection, the very item that made it financially reasonable for me to walk away from my secure position at National. I insisted my deal had been made with the board, and should stand. We left it that Ed would explore it further and get back to me.

To paraphrase Jean Paul Sartre, some deals begin on the far side of despair.

o   o   o

Over at the Apple corporate offices, a dazed Michael Spindler had called his team together to break the bad news with his typical show of courage and restraint. "Gil is the best man for the job. I wish him the best. I really do." Cindy Simms, his executive assistant who had come to know the very human side of the man, burst into tears.

After the gathering, Cindy and David Seda set about helping Michael stuff his papers and personal belongings into cardboard boxes, a task that would keep all three busy through the weekend. Seda, who carried the title of executive assistant to the president and CEO, had supported John Sculley and would continue to serve under me. Well spoken and of precise mind, David, born in Kenya, occasionally chose to wear a caftan costume from his homeland. He seemed to typify the old Apple spirit of "Do anything, just get the job accomplished, whatever it takes." I would learn much later that despite his brilliant mind and intense work ethic, many Apple employees saw David as part of the problem, suspecting that he "protected" Spindler by himself making many of the decisions and issuing many of the orders that came out bearing the CEO's name.

Sometimes other people's actions are mysterious, leaving possible interpretations of good intentions, bad judgment, or malicious sabotage. Before leaving, Michael Spindler instructed the Apple team negotiating with Sun to spend the whole weekend hammering out final terms of a deal—even though he well knew the board had already received McNealy's "final" offer and turned it down and that I was very much opposed to selling the company, especially in the price range McNealy had in mind. I have high admiration for Michael, but this was a waste of time, and would create one of my first headaches with the press.

By Sunday night, Michael and his cartons were gone. The CEO's office was empty, clean, and dark.

o o o

In Breslau, Poland, over the entrance to the city's oldest synagogue, the inscription reads, "Don't Give Up." Apple, despite what the media doomsayers were writing, was not a war zone, yet I would hold the spirit of that keystone inscription close to me—just in case.

Monday, February 5, 1996. I arrived at Apple's headquarters office complex in Cupertino, then housed in two high-rise buildings known as "City Center Three and Four," to find that my problems had already begun. It was only 8:00 A.M., but the underground parking garage was already full. And Apple, in some matters egalitarian to its core, does not provide reserved parking places for its executives.

I refused to let my brain tally the cost of my time searching for the space I finally found in an out-of-the-way corner spot. It was intended for a compact, but fortunately wide enough for my Cadillac Seville. There are problems and there are annoyances; over time, some annoyances grow into problems, and parking would become one of those for me. No matter how early I arrived in the morning, I would often have a meeting or lunch elsewhere during the day, and return to drive around for five or ten minutes before chancing on someone pulling out.

In the lobby, a one-woman welcoming committee enthusiastically awaited. Claudette Loporto—a fixture at Apple since time out of mind, whose gracious manner is backed up by an amazing ability to remember the names of visitors she hasn't seen for years—swept from behind her counter, raced over, and pumped my hand. She wished me well and expressed her pleasure at my coming to Apple. I said, "Claudette, I'll count on you to keep greeting me with a smile," not knowing how soothing her good-natured greeting would be during the pressures of the months ahead.

In the eighth floor executive suite, I already knew the players on the CEO's personal team, but was frankly baffled about what the hell they all did. At National, Bonnie Murphy had supported me single-handedly. Here, besides Cindy and David, the support team included Angie Pagnillo, Victoria Nielsen, and later, Fran Mottie, and a PR staffer assigned to full-time duty with the CEO who had an office two doors away. What was I supposed to do with them all? It quickly became evident that, quite contrary to initial reaction, they each had more than enough to fill their time, and most of them worked until quite late in the evening.

I've always believed that wisdom dictates a new executive does best to stick with the people he finds in place, at least initially. They know the ropes, who to call to get things done, how to get around barriers— all those necessaries, in other words, that are captured by the phrase about knowing where the skeletons are buried.

In terms of adapting to how I like to work and how I wanted things done, it would have made better sense to bring Bonnie with me from National, and, despite my usual pattern, I had considered doing that. But assured leadership is based on more than just convenience. These people needed bolstering and I needed to show them my trust, so one of my first steps after the hellos was to reassure the group I was not bringing in a team from National and had no plans to replace them.

For a Fortune 500 company, the CEO's office at Apple was rather plain and not very large—about twelve by twenty feet. Like the rest of the executive suite, it had plain white plaster walls, nondescript tan carpeting, boring but decent quality black furniture, and wood-grain tabletops. But the view made up for some of the lack of character, looking out over Silicon Valley to the Santa Cruz mountains in the near distance and the Contra Costa mountains in the far distance to the east (though "mountains" is misleading—each of these outcroppings is more aptly called a ridge of hills).

My new office also had room for a small conference area with two comfortable, office-style chairs. The computer, I was surprised to notice, was a Power Mac 8100 equipped with a video-conferencing camera and microphone, but running at 110 megahertz—comparatively slow even by the standards of the time and not one of Apple's current top models.

What does a new CEO do his first day, his first week?

I spent part of the first day walking around the executive suite, talking to other members of the management team, and part of the first few weeks dropping in on meetings and walking around various parts of the Apple campus, getting a sense of the people and letting them get a sense of me, listening to their enthusiasms and their concerns, beginning to form an impression of the strengths and the weaknesses of the organization.

Kevin Sullivan, the head of human resources under Sculley and Spindler, didn't seem to fit the mold of the other Apple people I'd met. It wasn't just that he was older or that he had a buttoned-down personality; Kevin just didn't radiate the spark, vitality, and hope that permeates the souls of true Apple people. His reception was open and cordial enough, and his years at Apple suggested he knew what he was doing. I concluded that under different circumstances, he and I might have been social friends.

I asked him for an organization chart so I would know who did what, and a layout of the building so if I wanted to drop in on someone, I could get there on my own without having to stop every five minutes and ask for directions.

Satjiv Chahil, the marketing VP whose standard blazer and gray slacks were a classic foil for the color-coordinated turban he wore every day, had been described to me as "dynamic." An apt word for an ebullient man full of imaginative ideas—some of which, I would discover, were less brilliant than others . . . but that's typical of highly creative people. His dedication to the company was matched only by his devotion to show-business celebrities—a combination that would have some short-term upsides but in the longer term would lead Apple into activities that cost time and money, the glamour obscuring what really needed to be done to build a solid business. I saw Chahil's enthusiasm as strong support for team morale. I liked the man and hoped we would work well together.

Morale is an ephemeral quality, especially skittish when company leadership changes. People naturally struggle with fears over whether their jobs are safe and what the new policies will be. These Apple folks were tired of the beating the company had been taking due to declining market share and gross margins. And the layoff of 1,300 people started by Michael Spindler was still in progress. Clearly they needed to begin hearing some welcome news as fast as possible.

So I instructed Satjiv to get some positive momentum going. "I want a press release every day on something positive—a new product, a customer placing a large order, a new concept or an idea about the future from one of our Apple Fellows. Something going out every day." I wanted his staff working on that until he had a pipeline spewing out upbeat releases. That was, I think, the first business assignment I gave to any of the executives.

The corporate rumor mill was already at work. Perhaps because Cindy was answering the phone "Dr. Amelio's office" (the title is based on my Ph.D. in solid-state physics from Georgia Tech), word started going around that I wanted to be spoken to using that formal manner of address. Previous CEOs of Apple had been addressed as Steve, John, and Michael; a break with that tradition was being perceived as cause for alarm. And, in fact, the question came up at one of my first drop-in meetings.

It's not my style to confront people with Steve Jobs–style questions like, "What do you do around here that's good for the company?" I find this arrogant. Instead, I like to find out what people view as their recent successes for the company. I've learned the hard way that true success comes from doing more of what's right rather than trying desperately to change everything being done wrong.

One of the meetings I arranged to attend that first week was an operations-review session of Apple's interactive media group. Kai-Fu Lee, who headed the group, introduced me. When I asked for questions, a manager named Howard Green shot his hand up; like so many of the Apple managers, Howard is a bright guy with a strong educational background (Cornell undergraduate, Stanford MBA). He asked, "What do we have to do in the first 100 days?" The question was in a way prophetic: It was the first time anyone had mentioned that time frame, which has become traditional in American politics as a landmark for the press to measure the achievements of a new president. Perhaps the question stuck with me; it would become a land mine.

Since this was a product group, they were probably anticipating a product-oriented or engineering-oriented reply. But my answer to Howard was "Get the cash flow going." They had to hear that basic truth, because it was the first order of priority. No company can operate without cash, and I knew from reports to the board that the situation was approaching critical. Michael Eisner had issued an edict early in his career at Disney that every unit would become revenue generating; he was also making the point that cash was king. That wisdom was even more valid for the cash-strapped Apple.

Word got back to me later that the group had picked up on my use of the term "process"—it was already becoming clear that I'm a process person. But the group had also concluded I didn't yet know which gears and levers to push at Apple. Hardly surprising at the time; what was surprising was how long that would take and how difficult it would be.

At one of the informal drop-in sessions, somebody gathered up enough courage to ask me a question that was apparently a burden on everyone's mind. It was about my suit and tie and the rumor that my clothing style was a symbol of a tough Amelio regime. I guess my white shirt is boring enough to be appropriate for a CEO, especially since CEOs spend so much of their time meeting with major customers, bankers, and other squares from outside the company. John Sculley, it seems, transitioned from suits to casual attire (though he never made it to the Jobs level of shorts and surfer sandals). Someone informed me that "even the very European, very traditional Michael Spindler rarely wore a suit." My style had apparently generated a panicky rumor, "Oh my God, we're being invaded by guys in suits."

Apple people believe firmly that nobody ever got a worthwhile idea wearing a shirt and tie. I made an effort to reassure that a new dress code would not be part of the changes. But that was not to be the end of the fashion furor.

My own eye-opener about clothing styles came a little later when I encountered a young Apple engineer who was wearing two days of beard, and a *dress*. Though I made it a point not to comment, the story flashed through the company that I had asked, "Is this a dress-down day?" and had been told, "No, he's dressed *up*." At least the Apple sense of humor was intact. And I could hardly wait to tell Charlene how I'd kept my cool.

Following the visit to Kai-Fu's group, I got a letter from Dave Nagel, the senior VP of research and engineering, that said something like, "I want to thank you for making your tour over here in R&D. You saved at least a dozen resignations I know about." No small matter, since the brain drain of brilliant people was a severe problem. In particular, the departure of genius engineers always meant they were taking away not only their talent but their history and knowledge of the project they had been working on, which a replacement would not be able to duplicate in months, if ever.

My first day wouldn't be over until 10:00 P.M. A board of directors meeting was scheduled at 5:00; it would resume the next morning for another hour and a half. Sun Microsystems continued to ply us with variations on their buyout offer, but with a price still far below market. Their deal still made no sense to me, and I wouldn't sell Apple stock-holders down the river. But I felt we had an obligation to listen.

o   o   o

As a board member, I had complained repeatedly that Apple had no clear corporate strategy, no statement of direction that could be used as a basis for deciding which businesses the company should be in and which not, which markets we should be pursuing and which ignoring. Apparently, Apple had *never* had an official statement of strategy— which inevitably means that every executive, and most managers, design their own versions. Everyone pursues their own goals, rowing frantical-ly, but each pulling in a different direction. Definitely not a recommend-ed formula for success.

As a board member, I could complain; now it was up to me to set the course. My first choice was to preside over decisions made by the executive team.

Launching that effort, on Wednesday I met with Apple's VP of cor-porate development, Doug Solomon, and outside consultant Mike

Townsend. I had first met Mike on taking over a failing division of Rockwell International in Newport Beach, California, thirteen years earlier. It turned out he had a genuine talent for plotting strategy, which he's been doing ever since. Mike left Rockwell about the same time I did and resurrected his consulting business. Though his company, Decision Analysis, is now based in Oregon, he's always made himself available when I need him.

The task for Doug and Mike would require them to find a strategy that made sense for the company and would be acceptable to the management team. I had no illusions it would be easy; in fact, it was to provide one of the most painful lessons in the dysfunctional Apple culture at its most powerful and most destructive.

o   o   o

Michael Spindler had held weekly meetings of the "Apple Leadership Team," the top management, and I stayed with the practice. The first such gathering, held at 11:30 A.M. on day number three in the large conference room a few steps from my office (known as the "board room" because it was so often used for board meetings), proved to be a huge surprise in several ways. The session was packed—a crowd of eighteen to twenty that included executives, senior managers, and even support people. This was definitely not a tight session of the CEO with his direct reports, but an assembly. I know how natural it is to want to be included in high-level meetings, but this crowd was not what we needed when discussing policy and strategy.

Later, I would recall my first sessions with the senior managers at that Rockwell division. I had called for a business review, giving each manager time to present the situation in his own division or area. It took all day, and when they were finished—around 10:00 P.M., I stood up and said, "This company is losing $2 million a month, and for the last fourteen hours, I've listened to reports that are filled with nothing but good news." That was the culture: The previous management hadn't wanted to hear bad news, so sweep the problems under the rug. No wonder they had gotten into such a mess.

Now here I was at the corresponding first Apple meeting. Different culture, but judging from the behaviors on exhibit, every bit as destructive. The executives had been alerted that the first part of each meeting would be devoted to a major topic, announced in advance, which they were to come prepared to discuss. Then each senior VP was to give a prepared talk, no longer than five minutes, summarizing what was going on in their area, what the critical issues were, the status of problems and what are they doing about it. We would all get a feel for what was happening throughout the company.

Wasn't it Lord Chesterfield who added at the end of a letter to his son that he was sorry to have written such a long letter, but didn't have time to write a shorter one? Boiling data and issues down to a few minutes is tougher than being given thirty minutes or an hour for a full presentation. You have to spend a lot of time thinking about how you're going to get across everything that's important in a mere five minutes.

When time came for that part of the meeting, I was stunned to discover that *no one* had come prepared. The senior management of a Fortune 500 company, and not one of these executives had spent any time getting ready to share a report with the rest of the team. What was I to make of this? The answer, I think, was that every one of the VPs considered their domain as their own responsibility and had no serious interest in letting others address the issues in their area. Again, "I'm rowing as fast as I can. I don't have time to tell you where I'm heading."

My reputation describes me as a calm executive, one who can manage without resorting to anger. It's a style that comes naturally to me, just as true outside the office as in. But on rare occasions, anger is in order to make a point. Another incident at that first management meeting brought me close to that, in a way that was actually quite unfair to the person involved.

Apple had been without a CFO for months (another action item on my crowded list of top-priority issues), and Controller Jeanne Seeley had somehow been managing her own job and juggling the CFO duties, as well.

During the meeting, I asked Jeanne to gather certain financial information and provide me with a detailed analysis of the cost of each product, broken into fixed and variable costs. "We've never assembled that data," she said.

That's fundamental information every manager should have. I said so, and said I wanted it.

"It'll take a few weeks," she said.

I replied in a tone of voice nobody in the room could mistake. I said I never again wanted to hear from anyone that information I asked for would take anything like that long to deliver.

Later I would find out it wasn't incompetence, bad organization, or bad management that Jeanne was struggling with, but, of all things, out-of-date information systems. Financial data was being collected on one set of systems in each of the sales regions, processed on different systems at the Apple offices in Austin, Texas, and reports generated by an entirely different computer. The three types used different software, and none could communicate or transfer data with the others. We were a computer company with out-of-date systems and a massive computer headache. An international firm had been brought in to create a uniform business system throughout Apple, but it was an effort of years that was still mostly in the planning stages. The price tag, several hundred million dollars, would prove too expensive; the project would be canceled before it had ever achieved much. What a waste. But at least I found a chance to apologize to Jeanne.

o o o

Due in part to Spindler's last stand—the instructions that had kept the Apple negotiating team at work with Sun over the previous weekend—the reporters continued to describe Apple as still for sale; employees felt undermined and insecure.

The pressure was coming from the other side, as well. Even after Apple's board had said "Thanks, but no thanks," Sun's champion CFO, Bill Raduchel, continued to try to find a way to put the deal together. He wouldn't let go for two reasons: He thought Apple was an apt fit for Sun at a fantastic bargain price, and he also knew his boss, Scott McNealy, seriously wanted to get his hands on Apple. The Sun board wouldn't agree to raise the ante, but Raduchel, an extraordinary negotiator, kept looking for any other sweetener he could figure out to try to make the deal attractive for us.

So in addition to the hours-long board meetings on my first Monday and Tuesday, there was a conference-call meeting on Wednesday, as we listened to various iterations of Raduchel's overtures. But it was eating up time I needed for taking the reins.

It had to come to an end so I could get on with the job. I gave instructions that a press release was to be issued saying, "This company is not for sale." The release was drafted and routinely sent to Legal for review. They had a complaint that seemed to me strictly a PR matter, with no legal implications at all: "Apple never responds to rumor."

I insisted. We finally settled on a compromise. The press release would be issued, but it would contain the statement "Although Apple does not respond to rumor, . . . " Ugh!

o   o   o

Ed Stead had been busy talking to board members, rattling cages by insisting that the term sheet with me wasn't a contract and wasn't binding, and that the deal they worked out could lead to stockholder suits. Those are scare words; board members can be spooked when a threat of legal liability is in the air. The directors were already uncomfortable at the state of the company, and Ed had them picturing endless lawsuits and constant appearances in court.

Peter Crisp, a man of integrity, wanted to stick by the deal, and I believe Mike Markkula was prepared to go to bat for me, as well. But Ed kept after the board about "the term sheet is just a guideline, and that guideline isn't acceptable to Apple. We'll have to negotiate something else." He cracked the door open and some jittery people rushed through it. I was amazed at how easily the other board members found it to set aside the word of their colleagues, still their consciences, and abandon the agreement that had been made.

My position was, "I accepted this job based on the agreement, I resigned my other job based on it, you guys have got to make me whole on this." But the message wasn't getting through. I hired Greg Gallo, from the Palo Alto law firm of Gray, Cary, Ware & Freeman, and told him, "Just do what you've got to do, but get this contract settled." Imagine having to hire an attorney to work out the details on a job you're already doing.

o   o   o

The PR departments at my previous companies continually struggled to be noticed by the business press. At Apple, calls from TV units and media people asking for one-on-one interviews had been flooding in from the time my appointment was announced, before I even arrived.

To relieve the pressure, I agreed to a press conference and some one-on-ones for Friday of the second week.

Two hundred reporters and seven television crews showed up, including all three major networks, PBS, CNBC, CNN, and National Public Radio.

Among the reporters who were scheduled for one-on-ones was Louise Kehoe from London's *Financial Times*. She and I had known each other through a couple of lifetimes before Apple, and, leave it to Louise, she asked the most thought-provoking question of the day: "What can I say to our readers to explain why Apple is relevant?"

Tough question. Using a term that a Brit would especially appreciate, I answered that we were the "loyal opposition," the alternative—the platform alternative, the solution-alternative way to get into personal computing in the modern era, and that made us very relevant.

Though spur-of-the-moment, it was an answer I would continue to use. Louise, I'm afraid, didn't find it compelling enough. She wrote instead that with Apple's market share as low as it was, the company wasn't going to have major impact on the world. Not the understanding that I hoped for.

Most of the other media pieces were essentially neutral. There was no wild enthusiasm and only a little in the way of harsh criticism. Peter Burrows of *Business Week*, who would always appear on the lookout for a way of getting into print at my expense, was one of those who had already written critically about my compensation. Peter's story ran under the headline "An Insanely Great Paycheck" and included a photo captioned "Gil's Gelt."

Some reporters weighed me against Steve Jobs and rated me low on the charisma scale. This is comparable to saying that Eisenhower wasn't as effective on television as John Kennedy. Like Eisenhower, I'm a good administrator and an organized thinker; like Kennedy, Steve captivates audiences. But to make the point in print is not much above *National Enquirer* journalism.

I was criticized for my hairstyle, the way I dress, and because I'm not thin enough (though by comparison to Michael Spindler, I'm Twiggy-shaped).

The press had become acutely negative on Apple because of the battle that had been raging between my predecessor and the media. I wanted to start moving the relationship back to a healthier place and told the reporters I'd try my best to be more available. From then on, my schedule included one-on-one interviews almost every week and larger events about once a quarter, where I'd just make myself available to a round table or in Town Hall format.

Some executives (again I think of Michael Eisner) are successful yet almost reclusive in terms of appearances, rarely showing up at a press conference to do anything more than read a prepared statement. The Eisners just don't allow themselves to get sucked into the vortex. I used to wonder, *Why is Eisner so reclusive? Why isn't he more visible? Disney is such a wonderful company, why doesn't he talk about it?* My view has changed: I think now that he was simply more aware than I of the dangers lurking just beyond the edge of the spotlight.

When Lou Gerstner faced the media on taking over at IBM, he tried to make the case that "I don't have all the answers yet, I'm working hard on them. When I have answers, I'll tell you about 'em." I tried a similar tack, but dug a hole for myself when I said something about "This is only day ten of my first hundred days."

I had inadvertently planted the idea that there was going to be a hundred-day speech, or a hundred-day event, a promise that would rapidly take on a life of its own, carrying with it the inference of problems solved and solutions in place by the 100-day mark.

It was symptomatic of how the press can drive your agenda and would prove a painful headache in the making.

o   o   o

Greg Gallo, the attorney I had hired to work out the contract problems for me, soon became exasperated. He sounded more fed up than I had ever heard him. "This is the best I'm going to be able to get for us," he said. "We can't do any better than this." Ed Stead, tight-fisted homunculus, had worn him down.

"This," it turned out, meant a set of terms far less favorable to me than the deal that the board's compensation committee, Peter Crisp and Bernie Goldstein, had originally agreed to. The worst of the package Greg had been able to arrange lay in a slashing of my downside protection. Instead of a million shares of stock up front to compensate for what I had walked away from at National, I would earn the shares over a five-year period—200,000 a year. But with strings: They would be tied to a performance measure and awarded only if the performance met criteria to be set by the board. If the company didn't improve quickly enough, I could get nothing. Ed Stead had insisted that this was the only way these shares could be treated as tax deductible by the company.

The $5 million sign-on bonus had also been gutted. This, too, was to be paid over the five years of the contract. The final compromise improved on that a little, and had it both ways: The amount would be earned at $1 million a year for five years. These payments would be credited against $5 million that I would receive up front, paid in the form of a loan. That is, I would get the $5 million initially, but only as a loan on which I had to pay interest; I would be considered to have earned it only at the rate of $1 million a year. If for any reason I didn't stay the full five years, I would owe Apple back the "unearned" portion.

This package of annual income and long-term opportunity put me at about the seventy-fifth percentile of people running companies the approximate size of Apple. Above average, but by no means near the top of the list.

Still a rich package. But instead of being covered for what I left behind at National, the downside was now dependent on my staying for five years, and on the company's success. The downside had gone from some $27 million more or less assured at National to virtually zero.

The Apple lawyers had also put in a clause that I had never seen in any agreement: The entire contract was subject to shareholder approval at the next stockholder meeting . . . which would not take place until February 1997, a year away. If the shareholders rejected it, I would be right back to square one, would have worked the whole year with little more than my salary to show, some fraction of what I could have accumulated had I stayed at National.

At that moment, I was ready to tell Apple to go pound sand; perhaps I could reconvene the National board and say, "I've changed my mind."

But Mike restored my confidence in dealing with Apple people. I told him, "Mike, I'm not trying to hold the company up, but this contract doesn't really meet my minimum concerns for protecting me. I may have to pull the plug on this whole thing. I'd be out of a job, but I may just have to do it."

We kicked it around and Mike said, "I'll make a private deal with you that is not to be told to anyone. If the company fails to come through on your downside protection, then I will pay you the remaining stock out of my own pocket for the downside."

That was an incredibly generous offer and seemed to provide a way out of a difficult situation for Apple and for me. His only concern was that if word leaked out about this private deal, then the company would have all the more reason not to honor the original terms with me. I've respected his request for secrecy until now, when it no longer matters.

I said, "Mike, do you mind if I write this down—you'll keep a copy and I'll keep a copy. A memo for the record, and we'll be the only two people with copies." He agreed.

I wrote it down the same evening, faxed it to him, got back a couple of minor changes, and sent him a final draft. It wasn't signed, but despite the sour experience with the board, I had complete confidence in Mike's word. By then I was so consumed with the issues at Apple that the contract wasn't something I wanted to spend any more time on.

I've always believed that when people strike a deal and shake hands on it (in this case more than figuratively, more even than an actual handshake, since it was put down in writing), people of honor stand by the deal. You can always sit down later and say, "I want to reconsider the terms with you," but if the other person says, "I don't want to make those changes, I want to stick with the original terms," then you cannot in good conscience insist. This has nothing to do with who could prevail in court, but with traditional notions of honor. Apple's outside counsel was present on that Wednesday night and raised no alarms; the final board approval was to be a mere formality. I think they had a moral obligation to stand by the agreement; what a disappointment they were to me. I was left still wondering if I had done the right thing in resigning from National.

This whole contract episode had been a contest for control. If Ed Stead could veto anything the CEO did, he would position the legal department to wield far greater power than I believe is proper for a technology company. *Okay, Ed,* I said to myself, *if you want to play . . .*

Ed was just my first Apple experience of the power in-fighting that employees describe as "too much politics." I was no novice at corporate power playing, but I was an innocent compared to what I would soon find. My eyes were about to be opened wide.

3

Borrowers and Lenders—
SOLVING THE CASH CRUNCH

Most people at one time or another experience the pressure and worry of running out of cash, with credit cards maxed out and barely enough in the bank to pay the rent and utility bills. If that's never happened to you, congratulations, but you certainly know people who have suffered through hard times—even if they don't like to admit it.

Apple was in that miserable predicament, and it was clearly the number-one problem demanding attention. Not long before I began, Apple's then-treasurer, Mary Ann Cusenza, had rung the alarm at a board meeting. The company had enough money to continue running for a while, she'd said, but at the rate of the present slide, Apple would be out of money somewhere around May. That shook the board members . . . but nothing had been done. The clock was still ticking, the slide hadn't gotten any less steep, and a solution was nowhere in sight.

The CFO position had been vacant for five months, and I wanted that post filled as soon as possible. In a meeting with former BofA vice chairman Lew Coleman on day two, I had asked, "Would you be willing to become Apple's CFO, even if just for a year while we get back on our feet?" He turned down the offer for a reason I couldn't argue with. "I'm a banker," he said. "Running a corporate finance organization doesn't fit where I want to go." But he generously offered, "As a friend,

I'll give whatever advice and counsel I can and be a sounding board for you."

I accepted on the spot and leveled with him. "The company has a severe cash flow problem. We have $500 million in the bank, and loans coming due in April for $150 million."

"That won't leave enough reserves for a company of this size."

"Exactly. And I need some advice on what we should be doing."

Lew asked me to set him up with key people in the finance group and held lengthy individual sessions over a period of four days with Treasurer Jane Risser, Controller Jeanne Seeley, MIS director Joe Riera, and several others. His report was far worse than I had anticipated— one of those clouds that defies the promise of a silver lining.

"You've got to treat the cash flow problem like a near crisis," he said. "This isn't just an idle caution, you could really run out of money very soon if you don't do something." I could see he was worried for me, and no wonder. I was as scared as I had ever been of a business situation and felt as if I had just boarded the Titanic.

But I waited, knowing Lew would be prepared for more than just bringing bad news. He would also have advice to offer based on his wisdom and experience, and what he had learned from his input sessions.

"You've got to go to work aggressively on reducing inventories to free up some cash," he said. "But to get out from under the sword, you've got to try to renegotiate the bank debt."

"With the condition Apple is in, will they listen?"

"They'll listen, but you may not like their answers," he said. And referring to our loans from Japanese banks that would soon be falling due, he added, "You've got to do everything you can to convince the bankers to roll over those notes."

Lew and I pulled together a presentation which we hoped would convince our Japanese lenders that Apple remained worthy of their confidence, and they should extend our $150 million loan for a year. Through the next few weeks, I would find myself grateful that Lew Coleman had insisted I focus on renegotiating the bank loan. Given the number of alligators snapping at my backside, this one crucial item might not have received my full attention in time to stave off disaster.

I needed a CFO like Lew. I needed executives who could see problems and suggest solutions. I needed the alligators to stop snapping.

◦ ◦ ◦

In the early days of transforming an ailing organization—whether it's a whole company or a division, plant, or workgroup—every meeting must involve tackling another crisis and solving it. There's no time for anything else and too much talk won't get the spiral turned around.

Fortunately, not all the crisis meetings are downers. In my second week, I dined at the Plumed Horse restaurant in the nearby Yuppie village of Saratoga with one of Hollywood's best-known movers and shakers, Jeff Berg. He arrived impeccably and impressively turned out, looking very Hollywood. My irrepressible, starstruck VP of marketing, Satjiv Chahil, had set up this meeting and assured me I would have fun talking to Berg, who is CEO and chairman of the blockbuster talent agency International Creative Management, ICM. Berg is much admired for putting together some of the biggest deals in the movie business—a little easier, perhaps, when you're also the agent for A-list stars like Tom Cruise, Harrison Ford, and John Travolta.

What most people didn't know, though, became evident in the first few minutes of conversation: Berg is no shallow 15-percenter. It turns out that he holds a degree with honors in English from UC Berkeley and serves on the boards of several universities. He's one of those Los Angeles people who can be an absorbing conversationalist *without* indulging in Hollywood gossip and anecdote. Satjiv was right; this was a man whose company I would seek for any reason. This was business, but it was also a blast.

I was impressed with Berg's knowledge of Apple; he surprised me with his sanguine comments on issues he thought I should keep in mind to make the company successful—continuing to improve the technology while developing the user experience. He pushed hard, as well, on the idea of industrial design—making our products sexy looking. This was a notion I gravitated to quickly, because I agreed totally: A computer that's great looking is a real plus in the marketplace. (In accepting the idea, I was unknowingly paying homage to one of the wiser of Steve Jobs's approaches.)

A worthy list. But I was trying to save evenings and weekends whenever possible for being with family, and I confess sitting with Berg and beginning to wonder, "What am I doing here?"

It soon became clear. Powerful as Jeff was in Hollywood, he had felt for some time as if he was playing second fiddle to superagent Michael Ovitz and had been delighted when Ovitz left the agency business to become a key executive at Disney. But a Jeff Berg isn't satisfied with being the biggest agent in town; he was looking for ways to expand the agency business. There are just so many A-list actors in Hollywood, just so many pictures produced each year, and even if your company is doing a huge share of the deal-making, there's still a finite limit to how big you can grow.

So Jeff had set his sights wider, and his gaze had fallen upon corporate America. Apple Computer—with its glamour image, currently tarnished, and its much-appreciated "computer for the rest of us" value system, currently in disarray—looked like a perfect fit.

Jeff and Satjiv had worked out a business deal: ICM was to help improve Apple's soured image. Jeff could do a face-lift and turn a has-been into a superstar again. Frank Sinatra made a comeback, why couldn't the Mac?

The fee was Rodeo Drive prices—$1 million a year.

That was just ICM's take. Product placement costs and all other expenses were additional. And the contract was already signed.

Another example that there were a lot of dimensions to Apple Computer that went far beyond what I could have anticipated.

∘ ∘ ∘

Even a walk down the corridor of the executive digs felt like an experience fraught with challenge: In each of the offices near mine toiled some key executive I was just coming to know, wrestling with problems that would only gradually be revealed to me. I wondered what caged alligators they would let loose at me on some future date. These were professionals who smiled graciously when I stopped by, while obviously hoping I wouldn't ask any challenging questions or sound as if I was checking up, making demands, or showing dissatisfaction.

There is always that uncertainty when a new boss takes over. *Am I going to get fired or demoted? Will I be embarrassed or humiliated?* It's far worse, of course, when the company is in trouble: There's more than enough blame to hand around.

While I focused on the top priority items in the first two weeks—

liquidity, finding a CFO, and initiating an effort to define the company's strategy—there still remained the nearly overwhelming task of trying to get a handle on the entire $10 billion operation. My calendar was loaded with half-hour and hour sessions held all over the company. I worked my way through getting-to-know-you meetings in which my primary agenda was really getting-to-know-your-problems. And without being too brusque or leaning too heavily, I needed to dig for more crucial information: getting-to-know-the-things-you're-trying-to-hide.

The company's new VP of developer relations, Heidi Roizen, had started the same day I did. I found her easy to talk to—a proficient and articulate communicator. As the CEO of a small clip-art software company, TMaker, she had profited handsomely at a young age when the company was sold. She had then taken time to start a family (career #2) and was now rejoining the business world.

Heidi was bringing experience, contacts, and experienced judgment to her role at Apple, and I preferred to ignore the mention that she had once been a girlfriend of Steve Jobs and that some ill will may have lingered between them. That had nothing to do with the situation at Apple. I'd leave the gossip for others to ponder.

Her job running Developer Relations was absolutely critical to the company's future. Computer users always want the latest, hottest software. But with Apple's market share plummeting and the press writing about companies shifting from Macintosh to Windows, we were in danger that software developers might decide the market size didn't justify their continuing to create new software and upgrades for the Mac. If we ever lost the allegiance of the developers, we'd lose the whole shebang.

Wooing the developers had always been a function taken seriously at Apple, and Heidi would be heading up a $75-million-a-year organization that kept 300 people busy explaining, training, hand-holding, and cheerleading. Apple "evangelists," as they're called, had always been chosen from among the best and the brightest, and the company was relying on them. They needed a strong and effective leader.

We talked about her view of the challenges and what direction she had in mind for keeping the developers committed to the Mac. I stressed the importance of her role and assured her that my door would always be open; I wanted to hear from her whenever she encountered problems that might need my attention or assistance.

In my first strategy meeting with Human Resources VP Kevin Sullivan, I recounted my 1980s Rockwell turnaround, my first corporate lifesaving experience. "I told the leadership that the place to start was not with the factory, not with the engineering, not with the marketing, but with the people. And I think the same rule probably applies at Apple."

Sure, I told him, there were giant-sized problems in every area, in all of the disciplines, but the key to solving them rested with the Apple people. Troubled organizations have a serious morale problem, one of the key symptoms and sometimes also one of the major contributing factors. In Apple's case, the people problems were compounded by an alarming brain-drain and vacancies in several high-level positions. I told Kevin, "I want your help in bringing aboard talented people. If you find good people there are no openings for, create a position." I believe that my people-philosophy blew right over him.

Kevin also promised to provide a one-page summary of the executive compensation packages. I was concerned about the rate of departures and wanted to make sure that compensation wasn't a main reason that top people were leaving. (Kevin's one-pager would reveal that some senior managers had stock options that were way under water—when the stock is perched around 25, an option price of 53 does not give the person any incentive for staying. And when pressures are intense, devotion to the company loses its potency as a strong enough reason to stay.)

Another subject Kevin and I reviewed was Apple University, the corporate training organization. They were doing a satisfactory job of teaching accounting skills and the like, but a lousy job of developing management skills to help people turn into effective leaders of their organizations. From the very first, I had been getting e-mail from employees describing Apple middle managers as "amateurs with no management training," well meaning, dedicated people who "didn't know what they were doing." So one of the first assignments I gave Kevin was to redefine the role of Apple University.

I met with Guerrino De Luca, who was successfully running our software subsidiary company, Claris, one of Apple's few success stories. Their FileMakerPro had grabbed market share as a very popular database, and ClarisWorks, which combines word processing, spreadsheet, and other applications into a single package, had been a bestseller, out-running its competition at the low end.

One of the ideas I was wrestling with was whether to pull together all Apple software into one large organization. I was exploring the bene-fits of marrying the successful Claris to Apple's in-house division that was, with notably less success, developing the Macintosh system soft-ware. I eventually decided not to do that. Many times since then I've thought perhaps the decision might have been a mistake: We might have been better off if I'd moved quickly to put those software opera-tions together.

And then I had meetings with key players outside Apple. Regis McKenna responded to a call and came in to talk so I could share my concerns about the company's image problem, the perception that "the ship is sinking." I expected that Regis's PR genius and Apple knowledge would produce some groundbreaking ideas on what we might be able to do to improve that image. Regis did, as Regis always does, come back with some excellent projects and themes.

But since he had already made the decision to redirect his company away from public relations and into marketing, he was not in a position to take on Apple's image problems as our PR agency. I was surprised and maybe a bit hurt, and I would have to look elsewhere.

One of the early calls I had received was from Gary Tooker, the CEO of Motorola, whose company was involved in the "AIM" alliance, which also included IBM—an alliance that was vital to Apple. Motorola was the source of our processor chips and a lot of the other silicon going into our computers, and they were our largest supplier. But Michael Spindler apparently never had time for them, and Tooker had never been granted a meeting with any high-level Apple executive. I just shook my head in disbelief and arranged a meeting. He brought in his head of semiconductors, Tommy George, and took the opportunity to say, "We want to build a better relationship between Motorola and Apple. Motorola wants to pledge whatever support you need." Tooker found ways to elegantly express all those things that any heads-up com-pany says to its best customers. I hoped Kevin Sullivan was looking for men like this to join Apple.

Any astute company—at least, those in technology areas—also says to its customers, "Let us know what you're designing, what functions you'd like your products to have, what's on your wish list, so we can try to create materials that fill your needs." The impression I got from this discussion was that Motorola had never received much detailed information or feedback from Apple. No real give-and-take, no back-and-forth dialog, so they had much of the time been guessing at what Apple wanted. Gary is too wise and smooth to be critical of anyone, but it was clear he felt that Motorola had been pretty well ignored. He was both pleased and relieved that someone was finally listening, and I saw this relationship as a problem that could easily be fixed.

Another call went to Don Macleod, who had been National Semiconductor's CFO since I had appointed him to that job five years earlier. During my term as an Apple board member, I had become aware that the company's financial systems weren't providing appropriate or timely indicators of how the business was really doing. I knew that management often didn't recognize when a new disaster was about to strike until the very last minute. I explained this to Donnie and extracted his promise to work with some Apple people I would send over to him. I wanted him to help us establish a completely new metrics system—something he had done at National with remarkable success.

Donnie brought a laugh when he reminded me that a consultant who had worked with him in developing the National approach had formerly worked in Finance at Apple. They had used the Apple approach in creating the National Semiconductor model; now, the techniques were being trucked back in to bolster Apple. Another indication that our once-great company had lost its way.

A team of Apple people showed up on Macleod's doorstep four days after my conversation with him; one item, at least, was moving ahead with the kind of speed that the situation demanded.

o   o   o

From where I sat, a number of items seemed to be falling into place. But I would learn much later that consultant Mike Townsend, hard at work on strategic planning, had told a mutual friend, "This might be the shortest honeymoon in Gil's career."

The relationship between CEO and the top managers at Apple was different and stranger than anything I had ever encountered or even heard about. I would meet with one of the vice presidents and we would discuss a particular problem and what needed to be done. We'd agree on a course of action.

And nothing would happen. *Nothing.* It was as if the conversation had never taken place. No follow-through . . . no explanations . . . no reports. And these were the top executives of the company. Did Spindler experience this? Did Sculley? How long had this been going on?

Someone once disdainfully described the U.S. president as a flea on the back of an elephant—the bureaucracy guided the beast, ignoring instructions from the order-giver at the top.

I remembered back when I took over my first sick organization, as its third president in three years. The executives assumed I would be gone as quickly as my predecessors, and largely ignored me. I had used an extreme technique I refer to as "shooting one of the lead buffaloes," which manages to get people's attention. Would I need my buffalo gun again?

The media prefers to treat the CEO of Apple like a film star, and Apple people enjoy having a media phenomenon in the top position of their company. But it seems to me that Apple management treats their CEO like an airhead celebrity—an icon who is supposed to represent the company in the press and at public forums, but is not to be trusted or respected for the making of business decisions. Were podium skills more valued by Apple people than business acumen? I dread to think this could become the accepted view in business, just as it's become the view in politics.

I was fighting to do my job, when process and follow-through should be the mantras of any manager. I was used to managers who made things happen; the two of you would agree, "We've got a problem here," and the manager would understand his job was to go fix it. Then I was accustomed to a cloud of dust and lots of activity.

At Apple, what I got instead were critiques, second guesses, and opinions, but no fixing of the problems.

An example: On the product side, what concerned me most in the early days was the too-frequent crashes and lockups that were giving users a bad experience and the Macintosh a bad name. After all, Apple's whole reason for being was to create a user experience that is easier and more friendly. Apple has always said to users, "You don't have to be a techno-nerd, you can sit down at the machine and do useful work right away. And the computer will be stable and reliable—it won't crash on you, it won't lose or garble your data." That had been implicit in the promise Steve Jobs made from the very beginning, so poignantly captured by the much-repeated phrase "the machine for the rest of us."

Now it was no longer true. "Apple users are frustrated," I said to Dave Nagel. Dave understood; we both knew it was dangerous for Apple to drift away from the original ideals. The company reputation and market share were suffering because of it, and we had to focus hard on giving that user experience back to our customers as quickly as possible.

Dave reacted as if totally unaware there were any problems.

I said, "I'm an intensive user of Macintosh products. If I sit down at the computer and get an undesirable result, I know there's something that needs to be fixed." Could it be that this was the first time he'd ever heard the words "customer" and "problems" connected with our products? It was as if he'd never used a Mac, which obviously couldn't be true.

What was I to make of this? It seemed to me that an Apple executive who is a diligent user and observer would have had a lightbulb go on a long time ago and started an intensive effort to get things back on track. It's not as if we were building nuclear turbines or a control system for the Space Shuttle, where you made the item but never got to use it. Everybody at a PC company uses their products every single day. You've got to be blind not to see a problem.

Dave agreed with everything I said. I felt reassured and confidently turned to other matters. Two weeks later, in a conversation with Dave's head of software operations, Ike Nassi, I casually mentioned, "Dave and I had a conversation a couple of weeks ago about the stability problems. What's the progress?" Ike didn't know what I was talking about. This was the first time he'd heard of the conversation.

Apparently it just wasn't inherent in an Apple executive to leave a meeting with the CEO, immediately gather his/her direct reports, and tell them, "*This* is what we need to do."

At that point, I said to myself, *My instructions to Dave Nagel didn't go anywhere. I'll work directly with Ike.* Once again I went through a list of questions and comments on improvements I wanted made in the software.

Again nothing happened. I moved further down the line, to Mitch Allen, the working-level manager running the project for our next-generation operating system, Copland. Mitch, I discovered—at three degrees of separation from the CEO's office—was making all the important decisions for the crucial Copland software. He was a highly capable man, but definitely not qualified to be making top-level decisions that would impact the entire corporation.

Dave and Ike, two very genuine and smart executives, were responding to action items only on a theoretical plane, but not taking the kind of decisive, hands-on action that was absolutely essential for getting the company back on track.

The conclusion I came to was that both were really professors at heart, perhaps with an eye on going back to the campus after gaining experience in industry. It frustrated me that they weren't getting the job done; something would have to change.

o   o   o

The MacWorld conferences gather together an attendance of Apple loyalists, developers, industry analysts, and enough press to cover a presidential visit. Three times a year—in Boston, San Francisco, and Tokyo—tens of thousands of ardent fans crowd in with a fervor equal to what I imagine a Trekkie convention must generate.

Tokyo is included in the MacWorld city list because the Japanese are ardent and passionate Macintosh fans—the MacWorld there draws, incredibly, about 170,000 people. The leading historical explanation, I assume, is that the design of a computer to handle an alphabet-based language, plus the number, punctuation, and symbols, was child's play compared to the challenges of a language based on ideographs. For a long time, this proved an insurmountable barrier, until the creation of a graphically-based computer, the Macintosh. It wasn't until thirty months after the Mac was introduced that Apple knocked down the barrier and showed the Japanese a Macintosh running the company's new KanjiTalk operating system. It was as if a two-year-old American baby had just learned to write in a difficult foreign language. That country's businesses and consumers could hardly get enough Macs, and Japan became one of Apple's most lucrative markets. MacWorld Tokyo regularly fills the largest auditorium in the country.

MacWorld attendees always expect to hear what's new and what's ahead directly from the Apple CEO. In 1996, MacWorld Tokyo was written in boldface type in the calendar for my third week on the job. Talk about an awkward time to travel halfway around the world. But there was never a choice of *not* going, which would have been seen as an insult by the Japanese, and probably interpreted as hiding, or worse, by an already critical—and increasingly hostile—American press.

In Tokyo I candidly revealed my thoughts about the problems I found at Apple, along the lines of what I had been saying to the Apple management team. The Japanese responded to my forthrightness with an enthusiasm that reinforced my intuition, the sense that our customers had sized up the problems the same way I had and were delighted that the Apple CEO was owning up to them. I was highly encouraged at the prospect of talking to audiences eager for the truth and loyal enough to back me while I fixed the problems.

In one sense, MacWorld Tokyo couldn't have come at a more convenient time: It afforded an opportunity for me to meet in person with senior executives from the three Japanese banks that were part of the lending group on our $150 million loan.

We gathered in a meeting room of the Imperial Hotel—six of them and, accompanying me, the head of Apple Japan, Harada-san, a staffer from Apple's treasury organization, and an interpreter. My pitch emphasized the successful history of my reign at National Semiconductor—the one-foot-in-the-grave condition when I arrived there, the tough financial controls I was putting in place, and the success that had been achieved. *Profit from Experience* had been published in Japan, and I suspected they had read in those pages the details of my National Semiconductor experience.

In essence I was putting my own credibility on the line. My basic message was, "I need your help. In the past, I've done other transformations successfully."

The bankers asked all the expected questions about how long until we would be back into the black, what gave me confidence that the steps I was taking would make it happen, and the rest. In the traditional model of Japanese businessmen, and of bankers everywhere, they remained pokerfaced. I left without a clue about whether they would extend our loan. How long would it be before we had an answer? Weeks, more than likely. And if they said no, what then?

I returned to the United States with blessings from our Japanese customers and partners, raves from the press, and an overload of uncertainty. In just these few days in Tokyo, the roller coaster had reached a crest . . . and then left my stomach churning.

4

A Tempest and a Brave New World—
SOME BAD TIMES AND GOOD

"That man is brain-dead."

It was a remark that belied my reputation for not exhibiting anger, a remark of the kind I never expected to hear myself make. Only a few weeks into the job, I was already frustrated beyond the pale with the unbudging recalcitrance of Apple executives. My patience was being stretched far beyond comfort levels and I saw a definite change taking place in my moods and my reactions (not helped any by adding pounds due to lack of exercise. I had even taken to using stairs instead of elevator, but with little result beyond startling the occasional employee who encountered me there in passing).

My frustration came in part from the too-common experience of executives who had agreed to a specific course of action but would then renege. The attitude was, "I agreed, but that doesn't mean I have to do anything about it." I remember thinking, *This isn't some backward country, this is Silicon Valley, 1996.*

The sense of urgency I had discovered lacking in Dave Nagel and Ike Nassi wasn't confined to them—they simply typified the frustrating combination of intelligence with "I'll do it my way" that was a leading dysfunctional aspect of the Apple culture. I was encountering it wherever I looked.

One of the basics I expect to take for granted is that once I have buy-in from a senior manager or a working group, the project moves forward from that point unless there's a later agreement to shift direction. In the case of Apple, it simply didn't work like that, and this dysfunctional style would have to change. The relationship between the CEO and the management of the company was different than anything I had experienced before, and that came home to me in full color at my first executive off-site.

At other companies I had limited executive sessions to top managers, but for this first Apple session, I decided to include a number of "influencers" like the legendary Guy Kawasaki, who enjoyed a broad-based support throughout the ranks of Apple and in the world of Apple fans and developers. Over the years, this type of off-site had proven a powerful tool for me to get a company's top managers to agree on goals. The agenda would include defining the company's core businesses and setting an approximate timetable of expectations for the year ahead.

Unlike many of the familiar corporate turnaround solutions, my approach to restoring an ailing company back to functional strength does not rely on a series of flamboyant decisions made independently as each new challenge arises, but on a well-defined *process*. I've tried to make clear my distinction between a turnaround and a transformation, two approaches that to me are as distinctly different as a fad diet from a long-term healthy eating plan. And the transformation process isn't one that needs to be designed from scratch for every company, but has a group of essential elements in common, which are tailored and reordered to fit the particular set of ailments being faced. Perhaps I have never been forceful enough when articulating the differences between a solid transformation process and the typical turnaround method, and too few people, it seems, have grasped the distinction.

All this may sound stuffy or dogmatic; it's my way of saying that, while each corporate transformation is in some ways unique, there is in fact an underlying process I've developed through my management years for carrying out transformation and restoring health—a process Bill Simon and I detailed in *Profit from Experience*. At the risk of over-simplifying, I'll say here only that the process revolves around financial issues, business practices, and people issues, and includes elements such as achieving financial stability first, creating a vision that defines success, learning what the end customer values and delivering that, and establishing metrics in order to "measure your way to excellence." (This is, obviously, a short and rather arbitrary list of items, meant only to give the flavor.)

As the executives and selected others gathered at the first off-site early in March at the stately, traditional Claremont Resort Hotel in nearby Oakland, I had every expectation of getting them teamed up behind the transformation process I had been setting into action. Where at Rockwell I'd found the managers avoiding bad news, at National Semiconductor no one seemed to be focusing on the all-important gross margins. At Apple, I was to find something altogether different, something not uncommon but entirely new to my experience.

Everyone arrived at the off-site having been notified of the agenda and the goal, so I expected some heated debate from sharp managers with different viewpoints and different experiences. And I had steeled myself for a concerted resistance that would challenge me to earn my leadership stripes. I watched for their openness to each other's ideas. I waited to see a sense of solidarity and togetherness, a sense of a feistiness that in essence would say to the new CEO, "We'll think this through together and together we'll reach a decision, and then we'll sign up to make things begin moving the way we agree they should." I was ready and waiting.

None of it happened.

The group met each item on the agenda with a cool distance. The lack of connectedness between the players was both shocking and frustrating. Even on an issue as fundamental as what the core business should be, I had no success in getting them to reach any agreement. How could they, when they were splintered into hostile camps with each person weighing the benefit to his or her own team and goals?

Each group within the company—U.S. Sales, Engineering, Marketing, and so forth—had its own agenda. This is what's termed the "silo mentality"—executives making decisions based on whether an idea was right for their own division or group, and the company be damned. That's not unique to Apple, of course, but here it had been honed to a fine art. Some call it politics, others admire it as a productive corporate in-fighting. In my view, it's an outgrowth of managers who are not yet able to think like corporate executives.

Most people prefer doing something because they *want* to and not because they *have* to; I've learned to suggest rather than order. But here, I was being humored—I'd open the next agenda item—about the operating system or marketing or product mix—and people would listen attentively and offer a few comments. Yet in moments, the conversation would be back again to whatever they had been haggling over before—unwilling to think for the company rather than for their own territories.

Jim Buckley, president of Apple Americas, had brought four of his key people—the sales managers of each area, the frontline leaders who are in direct contact with customers. These people generate revenues and in a very real sense know better than anyone else what's working and what's not. On the other hand, as could be expected, their viewpoint is focused on sales—*short-term* issues—while I was struggling to get the group focused on the *long* term: Survival.

When a company is in trouble, there's a conflict between what must be done to keep the cash coming in versus how the company needs to change in order to stay in business. Sales teams are primarily concerned with the issues to do with moving product out the door; this meeting was called to focus on staying in business. Are the two primary issues connected? Of course they are. But there's more to the company than one area, and an executive team needs to be concerned with the broad, longer-range challenges.

For example, we had been talking about the need to simplify the product line, which at that point offered many different models and variations replacing one another at such a rapid pace that no sales rep, store, or customer could keep track. We had to simplify rapidly and drastically. But Jim Buckley wasn't having any. His attitude was "If a customer wants it, we have to build it," which is a painful variation of "If you build it, they will come" . . . except that what we were really building was confusion. Customers came to buy and left bewildered. And the cost of inventory and of maintaining these many products in the distribution channel was deflating our profit margins.

Buckley is a likable man, and I admired what he had achieved over his years at Apple. But on this point he was adamant, playing, I decided, to the audience of his four district managers. And he began to argue beyond adamant to the point of stonewalling the discussion.

Buckley was the ultimate sales guy and it permeated his essence, yet

I've come to know that when the emotions fight the brain, the emotions *always* win. Buckley's emotions are sales-oriented, and he couldn't get his executive intellect working with the program of transforming Apple.

It was under the strain of this confrontation that, in an aside to members of my personal team during a break, I unfortunately let off steam by calling Buckley "brain-dead."

With guidance from me, the executives at the off-site set up a few task teams to address specific issues like developing a road map for entry-level products and formulating a strategy for "crossing the chasm"—keeping the business afloat until new products and programs begin to take hold. I couldn't help thinking that when politicians want to delay taking action, they form a committee to study the problem; I hoped our task teams would be more than a delaying tactic.

But beyond the formation of task teams, the two-day off-site accomplished almost nothing except proving to me that my perception of Apple executive conflict was on target. How would I resolve this fundamental, critical problem?

o　o　o

Marketing chieftain Satjiv Chahil came in and asked, "How would you like to see Apple featured in the next Tom Cruise movie?"

Thinking, *What's not to like,* I said, "I'd love it—what's the deal?"

Apple was to provide a Mac laptop to be used in the movie. When I asked how much more it would cost us, he said, "It's not going to cost us anything." That seemed too easy and too cheap. A few more questions brought out that we would have to commit to run an ad campaign based around the use of the PowerBook in the movie. Fair enough.

"How much will we have to spend?"

"About $5 million."

We had $190 million allocated to advertising for the year, and this sounded like an effective way to use some of it, so I gave Satjiv a green light.

He came back a while later and said, "I can't go ahead. I don't have the money allocated in my budget."

I said, impatiently, "I've given you the authority to spend the money. Do it."

"I can't. It's in Jim Buckley's budget, and Buckley thinks this whole

Mission Impossible idea is a waste. He won't release the $5 million to me."

I couldn't understand what was going on. If Satjiv was in charge of advertising, why would Buckley have control of the advertising budget? It didn't make sense.

Cindy got Jim on the phone and I told him, "I want to go forward with this *Mission Impossible* campaign and I've given Satjiv authorization to do it." He said he'd be right over to talk to me.

Buckley got to Cupertino from the Apple Americas offices in the nearby town of Campbell in a blink. He appeared at my door and roared in.

"This is a waste of money," he said, "and it's not going to do anything for us."

After giving him a chance to offer his views and let off some steam, I explained my thinking. "It really looks to me like something well worth doing, and I've made the decision to go ahead." He took the opportunity to blast me with a full measure of disagreement, even saying something that made me blink: "You can't do this."

Then, without giving in, he began to back off. This incident should have been an early warning sign, but I unfortunately chose to overlook it.

o　o　o

Steve Jobs had not been exactly running up a series of successes following his departure from Apple. His computer company NeXT, funded in part by Ross Perot, had created an impressively advanced desktop machine, but could never find enough buyers. He had eventually been forced to shut down production and concentrate on the software business. His movie company Pixar won high praise for the innovative, imaginative *Toy Story*, but Steve revealed that under his contract with Disney, he did not expect Pixar to make an appreciable profit on any of their first several productions.

Still, he had every reason to believe he would earn recognition from the movie industry to match the praise the critics had heaped on his movie. But when the Oscar nominations were announced, the name *Toy Story* was nowhere to be found.

Steve was used to bright lights and media attention; he thrived on it. Somehow the halo of success appeared to have slipped—things just didn't seem to be going his way.

o   o   o

When a company is running smoothly and the executive management team is capable of handling the everyday crises, the CEO can take time for the kind of public appearances that enhance the image of the company. For me, that time was still a long way off. Yet restoring confidence in the company was an essential, a top priority.

Besides MacWorld in Tokyo, in February I also traveled to the CeBit Conference in Germany and the Seybold Seminar in Boston. At CeBit, the world's largest office convention, the competition for press attention is fierce. David Seda was almost embarrassed to tell me that at the same time I was scheduled to hold our press conference, thirty others would be going on simultaneously.

That meant I had traveled to Germany to present to a very small group of people.

"Only about a hundred or fewer," David guessed.

In fact, the press interest in Apple was staggering: 360 eager reporters showed up with perceptive questions and a positive interest focused around variations of "When will Apple get better?" Seda returned with his confidence restored and later described that "Even Gil was impressed." And he was correct—I was definitely impressed, encouraged, and delighted with the time I had allotted to the European press.

But my appearance at Seybold proved to be quite a different experience. An annual gathering of senior people in the publishing community, these regularly scheduled seminars are designed to show off the latest technologies, products, and trends in publishing. And since the Macintosh has been uniquely successful in winning allegiance from people in this industry, it's always been important for the company to put on a major showing at Seybold.

I decided to keep my remarks informal, using just a few notes—a method that's more comfortable for me than speaking from a formal written text. What I'd left out of my decision-making calculations was that the appearance of an Apple CEO is a media event. I could no longer just share candid but casual views about what we were doing, where we were going, how we were going to get there. The audience responded to my off-the-cuff style and hung on every word I said, leaving me struck by how dedicated the publishing community was to the

Macintosh. But the reporters were not ready to grant me the same latitude.

It has always seemed to me there was a tacit and honorable agreement covering a situation when a speaker doesn't read from a prepared text. Reporters, I assumed, recognize the informality, understand it, and make allowances for statements that might not come out exactly as the speaker meant them. I expected that members of the media would not literally quote me word for word, but would listen for the thrust and report on the ideas I intended to convey.

Wrong. My statements were used out of context; much of what appeared in the news was not at all what I had intended. After Seybold I began to evolve from my own casual, trusting style to one of calculated preparation and distinct distance. I resented sorely the fact that I was coerced into becoming highly sensitized about the way I spoke— especially to representatives of the media.

Charlene urged me not to overreact, not to change the essence of who I am. Her advice was hard to follow when the Apple PR professionals were urging major style changes. Still in my first month, the roller coaster was again picking up speed.

o   o   o

When Apple's CFO had left months before, Michael Spindler had started the search for a replacement, and had settled on Fred Anderson, a Californian then working on the East Coast. For some reason—perhaps Michael's sense that his tenure was coming to an end—the matter had been left hanging. Although board member Bernie Goldstein touted Anderson very highly to me, I was reluctant to put someone I didn't know into such a key post.

Weeks had gone by and I hadn't made any progress, so I asked our executive recruiters to line up some candidates for me to meet with while back East—Anderson among them. Leaving the Seybold conference, I shuttled down to JFK and did the interviews in a meeting room at the airport.

In a situation like this, everything is compressed. Apple had been without a CFO for so long, and the cash situation was so desperate, that I couldn't put the decision off any longer. I had to act quickly, even though disaster can lie in that direction.

How do you size up a candidate for a crucial position in a short space of time? For me, an answer lies in getting a feel for how people handle themselves. This is one of those situations where instinct and experience play a big role, though I knew all too well that even the most experienced among us have made serious mistakes in selecting people.

All three candidates were impressive and eminently qualified, but from the very first I felt totally comfortable with Fred. An easygoing man with an all-American look and a friendly smile, he was obviously bright, he was successful, and his personable communication style brought to the table a comfortable give-and-take—a rare quality and one that would be especially valuable to Apple, since a major challenge for our CFO would be dealing with bankers and the investment community.

His background was encouraging, as well. He had worked for SDS, a computer company that Xerox bought. He was also highly respected by the financial community and had many close contacts there. And when I asked, "What's your assessment of the problems at Apple? What we would have to do together?" he responded with a lucid assessment; his thinking paralleled mine. It was clear he had done some homework in preparation for the meeting and we were reading the situation in a similar way. I decided after the one meeting that he was the man for the job. Within forty-eight hours, I made him an offer; he agreed to report a month later, at the end of March.

o　o　o

What report was the press giving the outside world about changes at Apple? At the end of my first month—one-third of the way into the 100-day measurement point of my success—the image-shaping effort seemed to be in complete disarray, left to people who either had no time to respond or no experience in dealing with the press on strategic matters. A newspaper reporter facing a deadline in hours might not get a call returned for two or three days. *San Francisco Chronicle* columnist Herb Greenberg complained in print that the "bunker mentality" of Apple PR hadn't changed, and pointed out that the company never issued a press release explaining my compensation package, leaving the press to jump to their own conclusions from documents filed with the government. Greenberg wanted to hear the company's explanation of the facts, so he called Ed Stead. But, the article said, "His response? I don't know. I'm still waiting for him to return my call."

So press people felt they were being treated with high-handed dis-respect by the company—an attitude that had been building at Apple for years. It shouldn't have been surprising that some of the reporters reflected back in their stories the high-handed treatment they were get-ting from Apple PR.

The press was now regularly attacking me for my compensation package, for things I said, for not moving fast enough. Some people claim to handle negative press without feeling infuriated, but I don't believe that; I believe they're just better at masking their feelings.

A more effective way of dealing with the press is to think in terms, not of communications, but of relationships. I would have done better to build strong relationships with a few members of the media who would listen to the full story before writing their pieces. Not that this would stop personal criticism any more than pleas for privacy stop the paparazzi, but the important aspect is making sure that a comprehen-sive story about company strategy gets explained to a selection of reporters willing to listen. I had no way to balance the negative image that was rapidly escalating.

Apple's PR organization was made up of solid, competent commu-nicators who weren't building relationships. What's more, too many of them were not on a par intellectually with the top-caliber journalists assigned to cover Apple. I take the blame for my failure to recognize the lack and make changes, fast.

Perhaps, too, I should have been more guarded in my public state-ments, or even more aggressive. Alan Markow, the astute PR man who I had brought in to National Semiconductor as VP of Communications, told friends, "Unless Apple lets reporters see that Gil is in there slaying dragons, some of the reporters are going to start writing 'Is Apple Dying?' stories." His prediction turned out to be prophetic, but didn't reach me until much later.

o   o   o

To be candid, there was plenty the press had every right to criticize us for and were smart enough to nail us on.

Knowledgeable insiders had long been complaining that Apple had some of the best market research in the United States, but no one had paid any attention to it in years. Whether that was valid or not, the fact was we were doing an abysmal job of deciding how many of each product to produce.

Case in point: The disastrous Christmas past, 1995, had been one of Apple's worst ever, leaving the company with tons of unsold "iron" (the industry slang for hardware). Meanwhile we had recently introduced a new Power Macintosh, the Model 5215, in the same all-in-one design that Steve Jobs had hatched for the original Mac. The 5215 had been conceived as a product for the education market, but we couldn't make them fast enough. Even the employees' store, housed in what was then the R&D complex on De Anza Boulevard in Cupertino, couldn't get the 5215; they were forced to tell eager employees there would be a wait of weeks before orders could be filled.

And problems cropped up in unexpected places. For probably the first time in Apple's history, there were major conflicts between new Macintoshes and Apple's own software. As a result, the brand new Mac 7200s didn't work—customers who bought those units took to screaming at the salespeople; businesses and universities that had made quantity purchases were especially incensed and had every right to be.

One Apple manager had been given an earful of abuse from a friend who ran a professional training institute, teaching publishing and multimedia skills; his classrooms were filled with people sitting in front of 7200s that were playing dumb. His frustration was generously shared with anyone who would listen—the press included.

The invincible Apple people continued to work harder than ever, feeling overwhelmed and emotionally drained by the amount of effort enhanced by a daily diet of frustration. I understood how they felt, because I shared those same feelings. But valued people were still leaving in droves, not entirely surprising considering the atmosphere at Apple—and that the employees, engineers in particular, frequently got four or five headhunter calls *a day*. Apple talent was considered highly prized, and the company was a prime hunting ground for recruiters.

A consultant leveled with me, "Say whatever you want about how Apple culture tainted the work style of Apple people, but wherever I go, the really valuable players are Apple people—they are the outstanding winners and workers all over the Valley. Everybody knows it and everyone wants them." To companies all over the world, being an Apple alumnus or alumna meant even more than a Harvard MBA. Yet the drain was hurting badly; would we be able to slow the loss of irreplaceable people?

◦ ◦ ◦

The "communications meeting," or all-employee meeting, now widespread in business, had always been an Apple ritual. (One of the very early employees, Steve Acers, remembers his first one, held at a Marriott Hotel near the original Apple offices. "We were all sitting around on the floor, and near me there were these two guys in Birkenstocks and field jackets. I asked, "Who the hell are they?" The kid next to me said, "Shhh—that's Steve Jobs and Woz.")

My first comm meeting fell on a Tuesday morning late in March. This would be the initial opportunity for most employees to see me in person, and I wanted it to be as casual and friendly as I could make it. Getting dressed that morning, I chose a sweater and tossed aside the jacket and tie I'd originally decided to wear. *This is right for going to meet with friends—these folks are neither customers nor bankers, I thought.*

To keep the setting unstructured, I had decided on a stool and small table. That was all I thought necessary for easy, relaxed conversation with the Apple people. I would speak from a few cards I had prepared with bullet points of what I wanted to cover.

Among the points I had listed were:

> Strategic planning
> Communication
> Attitude
> Morale
> Execution, follow-through, and process
> Focus
> Customers do not know who Apple is—they are lost
> Our customers are constantly asking me, "Apple, what is your business direction, and are you able to stick to that direction longer than two months?"
> What is Apple's overall vision?
> What is Apple doing to retain the great people we have?

I felt confident until walking into the Flint Center in San Jose, where these meetings were traditionally held—a large theater with the audience set back an uncomfortable distance from the stage. I knew immediately that it would be difficult if not impossible to establish strong, personal contact. On the other hand, the site was large enough to accommodate the Cupertino-area employees, and I couldn't fault my support team as I felt prone to do at that moment.

Apple people all over the world would also be included. Employees at locations as remote as Ireland and Singapore would be watching a real-time relay via satellite TV. I wanted every Apple person to look me in the eye to see that I meant business. But it was going to be a bigger challenge than I bargained for.

∘ ∘ ∘

Backstage, the makeup lady pats and powders, and I discover I'm feeling more nervous about going on in front of this crowd than I had expected. It's almost time. I'm standing in the wings waiting for my cue. In the audience, someone has brought a huge multicolored beach ball. People pass it overhead, hand to hand. Then they start bouncing it. They waft it from one side of the auditorium to the other. People are hooting and clapping, laughing and calling out, and it's getting louder, and noisier, and more raucous.

I stand there wondering, How am I ever going to get the attention of this crowd? And just then I hear my introduction.

I walk onstage and my first line comes out, unrehearsed and unplanned: "Hello, boys and girls."

The audience goes wild—laughter, applause, cheers. It couldn't have been better if a team of Letterman's writers had crafted my opening line.

∘ ∘ ∘

That beach ball affair had put the audience into a lighthearted mood, and I had caught their wildness on the crest. They began with laughter and applause and stayed in a wonderfully receptive mood throughout the rest of the session. I only wish other aspects of my history at Apple had been as thoroughly successful as that one meeting, where everyone seemed to feel good about themselves and the others gathered with them.

When that special sound of anticipatory quiet reached out to me on the stage, I began with a painful statement that informally expressed my state of mind. "Boy, have we got ourselves in a fix!" Obvious agreement with that statement began as a rumble that exploded into relieved laughter when I announced, "This is not a speech, just us having a talk. I didn't think you'd want me to spend that much time writing a speech, with so much else to do."

More laughter and applause, a signal to stay real and honest and far away from the typical pep-talk stuff of communications meetings. I wasn't into that motivational BS, and these people wouldn't stand for it.

I acknowledged the many e-mails they had been sending. "The volume now is getting to the point where it's hard to keep up, so if it's a few days before I respond, I hope you'll understand." Even so, I encouraged them to continue: "Communication has got to go in both directions. It's not just me standing here talking to you. It's you communicating with me and together deciding what's the right thing to do."

I reminded them that Apple people had built a company brand name with something like 87 percent unaided recognition around the world, a feat achieved by only a handful of other companies like Coca-Cola, McDonald's, and Disney.

Deep down I'm a teacher at heart—I had originally thought I would use my Ph.D., backed by a little industry experience, to become a professor at an important university, and I use sessions like this to give some subtle (I hope) business lessons. In that vein, I was open in sharing my observations about the problems and what I thought we needed to do in a number of areas.

On product design, I told them, "We've allowed Apple products to get overly complex. That's a big factor in our problems with quality, and it's impacting our profitability, too. We're actually selling some machines below our cost—below what we paid just for the bill of materials."

I described this futile business practice as "a dollar-exporting machine," which brought an appreciative laugh. Many of them understood full well what I was saying and had for a long time been aware of this self-defeating practice. The applause meant they were relieved and pleased that management was finally getting it.

Then I laced into the subject of collaboration, which seemed to me a very large problem at Apple. "We don't live in an era any longer where we can play John Wayne and carry the whole day ourselves, not in today's technologically complex world. There's virtually nothing this company can do of significance if we go the way completely alone. We've got to depend on the work that went before, work done by other great people. So why don't we just embrace the notion of collaboration.

"On the Macintosh, if you want to do file sharing, you've got to go through three different control panels. Why? And then I always do the steps in the wrong order, and a message pops up, 'You have to make Appletalk active before you. . . .'"

The response showed they knew very well from their own experience exactly what I was talking about.

"Sometimes I think you can see the org-chart of this company in that computer." I expected to explain that metaphor, but their reaction assured me they definitely understood: These people had long been aware of design teams that simply hadn't been talking to each other.

Moving on a little later to the subject of the financials, I said, "Business isn't good, and it's not going to be good for a while until we build a heck of a lot more value into our products. We've got to get break-even down to about $9 billion. Now, what levers have got to be pulled to do that? Well, fundamentally there are two: Cost—the infrastructure cost of the company—and gross margins." The professor within me was having a blast, and these folks were accepting Amelio in the role of professor as well as CEO.

"It's a lot more fun and much less worry about costs when a company has higher gross margins. But there's a hard truth about gross margins: The only way you get them is from customers, who use purchasing dollars as votes. So gross margin is a direct measure of how much we're satisfying our customers."

A slide I had designed came on at this point, showing our revenues, expenses, and margins for the quarter just ended. Pointing out that the numbers were after tax, which makes them look smaller, I said, "Our tax rate is about 37 percent, so all of you with calculators out there, divide by 0.63, and that will tell you what the write-down was and what the pretax loss was, which is how we should be looking at ourselves. We shouldn't be depending on Uncle Sam to pay part of the bill."

Our real cost for the write-down, I said, was about a billion-one and "that's just got a few more zeroes than I'm comfortable with." My forthright admission brought another appreciative response.

They should have been wondering at this point about how we were going to squeeze dollars out of our product cost. "We know market prices are going to keep coming down," I said. "Apple already gets a small premium for our great machines relative to Windows platforms, and we should. We deserve it. But with our current products, we're not going to get more than a modest premium, and so we'd better do something about that. We've got to take a hard look at our architecture and evolve it in an intelligent way so that we can steal some of the thunder from our competition."

I was on a roll, everything was clicking. I had been nervous about not being able to fill the time—at National, the CEO had always been given a half-hour at employee meetings, but Apple had always allocated a full hour, and I was sure I wouldn't be able to talk that long. Yet when I checked the clock that had been mounted at the footlights for me, I found the hour almost gone. I was stunned—only ten minutes left to cover what was to me the most important topic.

"I'm getting short on time, but I won't leave here without covering one last item—something that's most important to me. The topic is you—the people of this company." I explained that I had left it for last because I wanted them to take away my view that corporate success is essentially about people, relationships, and how we work together.

I said that I wanted many advantages for Apple people—that they needed and deserved to be respected with information and communication. I expressed my views on expanding their education and keeping them updated and current in a world moving rapidly forward. "I want you to be empowered to act and make events happen, to be recognized for the accomplishments of the past and treated as equals by being held accountable for the things you haven't done." (This very fatherly attitude, surprisingly, got a round of enthusiastic applause.) "And I want you rewarded accordingly."

And then I headed into the toughest subject at all—the brain drain. "The fact is that we're losing too many talented people. So here's your assignment: If you know a good person who's 'loose in the socket,' get them to stay. Get all your friends and gang up on them. And if you know a good person who's left the company, bring them back. They're welcome. Let's get that pride back. Let's be proud of what we do."

Then, despite the time crunch, it was time for questions.

By telephone from the headquarters of Apple USA in Campbell, a customer relations person asked, "What can be done to create a synergy of cooperation between the various areas of Apple, such as Product Marketing, Engineering, and Customer Support?" If I had paid a shill, it couldn't have been a more perfect question.

I gestured to the executive team and said, "These guys don't know it yet, but when bonus time comes for the executives, there's going to be a single scorecard. Everyone is going to get a bonus at the same rate to be sure we're all in this together. If some try to get ahead by pulling others down, they're just going to be shooting themselves in the foot." More affirmative nods and applause.

I told another questioner, "The one thing I think Bill Gates and his people do better than we do is that they follow through. They're like an army marching. I don't think their technology is that strong, except for the stuff they stole from us, but they're like bulldogs. They get onto something and they never let it go. We have to get some of that."

The final question wasn't a question, and it wasn't a plant. A young man named Jordan Matson, with a job title cryptic to anyone not in this industry—development tools evangelist—stood up to say, "I'm a little infamous for a question I asked at the shareholders' meeting, and I want to say that today I got the answer. The question was 'Does the executive management of Apple Computer value the employees?' And the answer I got today was 'Yes,' and I want to thank you for that." The audience endorsed the sentiment with applause. Jordan, wherever you are today, I hope the Apple experience was challenging and rewarding despite the many traumas.

For an upbeat conclusion, I wrapped by showing the rough cut of a new Apple *Mission Impossible* television commercial featuring Tom Cruise—the first time he had ever agreed to appear in a TV ad. The meeting was over; the audience awarded me one of those inspiring Apple moments: a standing ovation. I was told later that it hadn't happened at an all-Apple event since the day Steve Jobs introduced the Macintosh.

In most of life, image is a vain issue to be concerned with. But for any leader—in politics, business, the family, the classroom, church, community service—image seems to impact whether people will follow with enthusiasm or merely because they're *required* to. The power of believability and sincerity added up to an image that was attractive to the people of Apple. I needed that, I wanted that, and was delighted to have made it happen.

There was much erosion over time to the connectedness I established with the Apple people that day, but some of it would hold fast. When I left seventeen months later, I was to get letters from employees saying, for example, "Gil, you told us where you wanted us to go, and it's beginning to work." And, "We're just starting to understand how powerful it can be."

Someone (it must have been Satjiv—who else but Satjiv!) counted that I had been interrupted by applause and appreciative laughter forty-one times. A heady, satisfying experience, exhilarating, creating the sense that Apple people were willing to give up the traditional Apple ways of doing business that had led to the current predicament, that they were eager to fall into step and be guided by me. That impression would prove dangerously misleading.

5

Measure for Measure—
WE HAMMER OUT A STRATEGY

This White Paper is a strategic framework. You might wish to think of it as the top couple of layers for a company-wide strategic plan which doesn't yet exist. While it has been written quickly and is a working document, it sets forth the basic direction, strategies, priorities and the like for Apple Computer over the next few years. It is a framework providing a structure for future detail and implementations.

—*Preamble to the Apple strategy White Paper, April, 1996*

"This company is confused about where it should go, and has been for years." Mike Markkula was Apple's board member closest to the operations of the company, so his critical assessment was a bold admission.

In this conversation months before I became CEO, I said to Mike, "We sit around at these board meetings and hear presentations from management about, 'We want to do *this* project, we're going to launch *that* new product or feature,' and each one seems to be a stand-alone idea."

"I know exactly what you mean," Mike said. "And it gets us nowhere."

In another conversation, Mike used an acronym he had coined himself to describe where he thought the company should be heading with its operating system strategy: Caos, which stood for something like "Computer-Agreeable Operating System." He meant an operating system that would fit in better with the rest of the world of computing. But he pronounced the term "chaos." It would come to seem an especially apt description for Apple's overall corporate strategy.

During those first weeks, on my walk-arounds and conversations, I wanted to get a handle on how well Apple executives and senior managers understood the company's strategy and direction. Most of the executives had no coherent answer; those who did usually had a version focused on their own chunk of the business. Jim Buckley interpreted corporate strategy in terms of sales, merchandising, and channel partners. Dave Nagel talked about software design. People in manufacturing focused on lowering costs and achieving shorter production cycle times. In R&D, many of the projects were not synchronized into a product road map nor related to any direction the company might take.

It's a serious danger signal of a troubled organization—whether a work group or entire company—when the managers or the executives hold far differing views of the direction and strategy. Even Doug Solomon, the brilliant Ph.D. who held the title of senior VP, corporate development, would soon be straining under the additional duties I had recently given him of leading the strategic planning effort for the company.

My walkabouts into Apple's outback revealed a serious lack of understanding of how the company made its profit. As for organization, the charts I was shown at presentations seemed to have no bearing on how responsibilities were distributed. I could find no one to satisfactorily explain the wisdom behind the structure of the corporate organization.

Here was the silo mentality at work: It was as if we were structured into medieval fiefdoms. Walls had been built that seemed impenetrable. At the same time, there were no checks and balances to eliminate overlap, and I found many groups farming the same crops. I recognized the problem but had other pressing concerns that would have to come first.

The secret of being miserable, according to George Bernard Shaw, is having enough leisure time to bother about whether you're happy or not. Fortunately I didn't have enough time to be miserable, could think about nothing other than Apple—most urgent, solving our liquidity problems and creating a strategy that we could all get behind, one that would become the basis for every decision made throughout the company.

Ever since I had arrived, employees had been in effect saying, "Tell me where the hill is that you want me to take so I can go do it." When the head of their group and their vice president didn't know which hill to point to, or even where it was, that had to spell big trouble.

And that's what strategy is all about: It's figuring out the location, direction, and priorities. Basic strategy defines, "That's the hill we've got to take and here's the way we're going to do it."

The strategic planning process was my way of throwing the ball onto the playing field. The real game was about to begin. I would stay in charge as coach, giving overall directions, calling the shots, and closely reviewing the decisions and results. The day-to-day work of developing strategy was to be a combined effort, run by Doug Solomon, with most of the writing and much of the thinking to come from outside strategy consultant Mike Townsend. We intentionally kept the team very small.

A member of Doug's team who contributed mightily both in shaping concepts and writing text for the paper was a woman whose initials, LJB, were on her car's license plates—usually parked in an early-arriver's space when I drove in and still there after I pulled out. Linda Brown's intelligence partnered with her creative right brain; she used them brilliantly together. With a title of senior manager, corporate development, her position down the line kept her closer to the actual work levels of the company, so she was able to offer possibilities that others of us, in the exclusive surroundings of the executive suite, just couldn't see. Somewhere Linda had learned to phrase her ideas in probing questions that I found productive, insightful, and thoroughly helpful.

Doug and Mike and the others were immediately forged into a get-things-done team. I knew they would be bringing different concepts to the table and hoped that would produce a useful friction.

o   o   o

When I shared my concerns over a lack of clear strategy with the board and reported on the project I had initiated, naturally they asked, "How fast will you get it done?"

"A big-picture strategic plan, not too many details—the thirty-thousand-foot view of the landscape—will probably be completed in a couple of weeks."

To back up that commitment, I told Mike Townsend, "The first deliverable is to be done in two weeks. I want a quick synopsis of the strategy that Apple people could use for guidance while we flesh out a full White Paper in greater detail." (The term "White Paper" is, I think, adopted from statecraft and describes an authoritative report on some major issue; the White Paper would provide the blueprint for all the detailed strategy decisions that would follow, and so would provide the fundamental definition of where we needed to go.)

But when Mike had the two-week version ready, it was primarily useful only in making me realize that to be of real value, the strategy statement would need to be a lot longer than I had thought. Too many conclusions were dependent on other related issues. A logical decision about point A couldn't be made until we thought through and decided on points B, C, D, and E. So even an acceptable first-pass version didn't materialize in the promised "couple of weeks," and it wouldn't happen even in a month.

There's a story about a young and eager new hire who worked very late to make a good impression. One evening, as he was on the way out, the CEO stuck his head out of a door and asked the young man for help. Gesturing to the shredding machine, the CEO asked, "Do you know how to work this thing?" The young man said, "Yes," and the CEO passed him a document. As he fed it into the machine, the CEO said, "I only need one copy." Despite the best of intentions, some plans just don't work out the way we intended.

My two-week promise to the board for a quick look would evolve into a forty-page White Paper that would take two months to develop. Even more than before, I was left trying to figure out why everything at Apple felt like bench-pressing 500 pounds. Developing a strategy shouldn't have been such a damn frustrating exercise; I had set strategies in place many times before without the sweat and pain that would be experienced before this one was done.

○　○　○

Where do you start a process like this? At National, I had begun at my desk, where I put together a few ideas of my own to update the existing strategy document. When the members of National's management team met at our first off-site, we were able to use my draft as a jumping-off point for designing a vision statement and as the framework for revising the strategic plan. By the end of four days, the elements were in place and the project well started.

At Apple that approach was out of the question. First of all, there was no existing plan to revise, so the effort would have to start from ground zero. And the self-interested mentalities of the executives created an atmosphere of confrontation rather than cooperation.

To kick off, I gave the strategy team directions: The new framework should focus our efforts on areas where we could be #1, #2, or at least #3. (No acknowledgment is necessary to Jack Welch for this notion, which was nothing new at Apple. John Sculley tried the same thing and Michael Spindler had issued nearly identical orders. The needed follow-through had always been lacking; I was confident I could supply that.)

As another starting point, I wanted the team to use research on the company's performance in the past. Apple's people, I had observed, always wanted to charge ahead. Admirable, except that in the past this had traditionally meant that nobody wanted to bother seeing what research had already been done.

To be sure Doug got the backing he needed, I told the executives, "We have a team assigned to draft a strategic framework for the company. But I want everyone's thinking to be considered before the final White Paper is written. Be sure you get your ideas to Doug so your views can be represented." They were informed of the short deadline, and I reinforced the importance of this project by explaining my commitment to the board.

They listened politely, but did nothing.

Doug sent Linda Brown to follow up with each of the senior executives and also with a handful of other influencers. She repeated my message, "We're moving forward on a strategic plan, what are your thoughts, what ideas do you have to contribute, what do you think should be included?" And she would also ask for examples of mission statements and strategic plans that had been done in the past. "If you have ever written some strategy for your area, could you please share it with us?"

My disappointment was great; virtually no one contributed any documents or even any thoughts to Linda, Doug, or me.

So 90 or 95 percent of the White Paper represented my thinking and the team's.

o   o   o

Some of the valuable input we managed to collect came from unexpected quarters. Early in March, Charlene and I attended a charity affair to raise money for the Tech Museum. At my table were two former Apple employees—Linda Lawrence, now a senior VP at Netscape, and her one-time boss at Apple, Kirk Loevener, who was at the time a VP at Silicon Graphics.

Linda mentioned that when at Apple she had done an intensive study on customers and the installed base. It had been an expensive project that had produced a lot of information on what Apple users wanted to see in our products. But "nobody was ever interested in looking at it," she said. I asked to see a copy, and she arranged to get it to me. Her data provided the background understanding I had been wanting and needing.

I don't believe the Apple leadership were stonewalling; it's just that strategy is concerned with the future, and over so many years of changes and redeployments, these people, accustomed to the veneer of emergencies, could find no heart or time in their calendars for thinking beyond next month's products, next month's programs. Too many Apple people, I concluded, live only in the present and are so wrapped up in the present, so totally engrossed in fighting today's battles, that they live unaware of the past and the future. All today, no yesterday, no tomorrow. They weren't stonewalling on the strategy; the strategy dealt with tomorrow, and there was no time in their calendar for tomorrow.

o   o   o

Over the years, Apple people had established friendships with reporters, and many members of Silicon Valley's fourth estate considered themselves Apple insiders. When the company's worldwide communications system, AppleLink, was operating, Apple encouraged a warm, inclusive, one-large-family aura with vendors, educators, and the press—a style that contributed to Apple's greatness.

The flip side of that togetherness with the press evolved into troubles of monumental proportions for an ailing company needing some calm and quiet in which to recuperate.

When other companies have internal struggles, few outside the company care, while the slightest vibration within Apple was considered newsworthy, even headline-worthy. In many ways Apple people abused the press, using them to win power struggles within the company, get better jobs, or take revenge by feeding information that would support a personal cause or vendetta. Any Apple internal friction became widespread Silicon Valley news—understandable but unconscionable.

I much prefer an open company, but I reacted to the Apple persona and soon assumed that anything not under padlock would become public knowledge. What could be done to prevent the strategy work-in-progress from being discussed in the press before we could determine what the long-term goals of the company should be? This highly sensitive information could be of enormous value to a competitor, giving as large an advantage to other companies as knowledge of our new technology.

And when you're considering options, you look at a lot of ideas that on analysis don't make much sense. If any of these leak before you've rejected them, you will look silly, or downright stupid.

So arrangements were made to provide the strategy team a secure room to work in—a long, narrow, windowless chamber directly across from the executive offices that came to be known as the "War Room." As further protection against leaks, Doug Solomon had the only key—no one could go to work until he got there to unlock the door. He stoically bore the brunt of this, even when people started calling him "paranoid" about security.

In the process of being so tight on security, some of the senior executives decided the planning team was taking pleasure in *not* listening to them. Linda Brown was trying to extract input from each of the executives, without success, but when one of them wandered over to the War Room, he or she was turned away. The concern was real: The walls and table were covered with sheets of paper headlined with a bold statement of an idea or position. Most of these would ultimately be rejected, but the whole process could be undermined if one executive caught a headline of something that might adversely affect his area and decided to do his best to torpedo the whole effort. Dave Nagel tried to come in and was turned away; so were Jim Buckley, Kevin Sullivan, and evangelist Guy Kawasaki. They had passed up the opportunity to contribute and weren't welcome just so they could find out what was going on.

o   o   o

At one strategy session, I was asked how National Semiconductor had coped with its giant competitor, Intel—a polite way of asking, "Do you have a plan for surviving against Microsoft?"

"We did it by competitive positioning. We looked at what Intel was in and went after places where they weren't. When the Microsoft train comes down the tracks, we aren't going to stand there with our arms outstretched. We're going to stand alongside the track and as the train comes past, we're going to find something we can grab, and swing aboard."

But the truth was that for Apple at the time, Microsoft wasn't the problem; our problems lay in only two main areas: the marketplace and internal dysfunction. Our biggest challenge was the one Pogo had identified: We have met the enemy and they are us.

o   o   o

In the middle of this effort, I received more painful evidence of how much interest the public seems to hold over the inner workings of Apple.

I firmly believe that grass-roots employees have the keenest perception of what's really going on in an organization. On a Thursday afternoon, about twenty employees gathered with me in the board room for a "coffee-klatch" session—a technique I've long used as a way of hearing the views, suggestions, and complaints of those who work where the rubber meets the road. The rules are: just me and them, with no other executives present; no transcription is made; and everything said remains in complete confidence—"Nothing leaves the room."

During this first coffee klatch at Apple, I used an analogy in answering a question about perceived value as a basis for pricing. I said something like, "When I need a flashlight, the product I choose is always a Maglite. Their flashlights cost more, but you know it's going to be reliable and long-lasting. When the electricity goes out, you know the Maglite is going to work." In other words, if you want to succeed with a consumer product, the buying public must perceive it as a good value with respect to cost. You can only charge more and increase your margins if the buyer perceives that you've built in something that makes it worth more than the competitive products. So quality and reliability need to be built in from day one.

One of the participants of the session was so taken with the analogy that he couldn't contain himself from sharing it with Guy Kawasaki, who thought it worthy enough to include in his popular electronic newsletter, *EvangaList* (which he was still producing for Apple at the time I left). Both men were intent on helping me gain stature within the Apple community. But the story backfired.

The press picked it up in a nanosecond, which wasn't in itself so terrible, except—hungry for any scraps of news on Apple strategy—they wrote that Gil Amelio had decided to chase after premium pricing, which would mean providing improved features so we could charge higher prices . . . leading almost inevitably to lower sales. Didn't he know, the articles asked, that Sculley had tried the same tactic and failed?

The entire executive staff, ignoring the organized public relations damage-control efforts, spent much of the next day on the phone talking to reporters about what happened, what was really said, what was meant, what the implications were, and doing that which in the political world is called "spin doctoring." Not at all what executives should be doing. They succeeded in fanning the flames that kept the incorrect news hot for days.

I had known from the get-go that Guy's action had been well intentioned, but he graciously apologized. It was another illustration for both of us—for all of us—that a press lens would remain focused for constant close-ups of the company.

David Seda, reflecting on the incident, recounted a more painful problem Michael Spindler had suffered. At a meeting with the twelve members of his executive management team—the top executives of the company—Spindler had detailed the sensitive negotiations under way with a Japanese partner unhappy over their Apple relationship. Within four hours, Spindler's outline of Apple's position reached Japan, which in the end cost the company heavily. "We wrote them a check for $10 million," Seda told me. At least the Maglite episode didn't end with us needing to write a check to anyone, but how do you adequately measure the damage of a small but far-reaching leak like this?

o　o　o

The strategic planning team had been working even longer hours than the Apple standard. One section, on market sizing, financial models, and the business model, was completed in a marathon twenty-four-hour session. Extensively long hours were beginning to be the norm for these folks, so when I heard that a $16 voucher submitted for middle-of-the-night pizza had been turned down by someone in accounting, who had been told to cut expenditures, I could only groan. Time to recall the advice to "suffer fools gladly."

Three areas of conflict were tearing at their work and at times dividing the team against themselves. One was the question of whether Apple should be continuing to pursue the *enterprise* market. Doug and Mike Townsend, as well as many employees and members of the press, believed Apple had flat out lost the interest of business computer users and management information services directors who make most of the computer purchase decisions. We had heard from many quarters that to continue chasing after the business market was a waste of valuable resources.

It was originally John Sculley who fixed the marketing sights on winning front-door acceptance and entrée for Apple by corporations worldwide. Despite years of rejection and frustration, a large contingent continued to fervently argue that Apple had to win and maintain a position in corporate America. This logic held that if the business world became 100 percent Windows, it would only be a matter of time before everything else went that way and Apple would be left trudging down a road to a dead end.

I sided with these enterprise supporters, but even my closest advisors strongly disagreed. This debate raged throughout the company, and, from what I was told, had been a popular lunchtime subject for some years. I still think that anyone who really understands the PC market realizes that if the use of a Mac can't be justified in a business setting, then it's nearly impossible to justify it in most other settings. This argument would have to be settled in the strategic plan.

I had expected the strategy planning process to be a challenge, but despite the cerebral team I had chosen, it soon became a bloody battle-field. Even Mike Townsend, usually cool and laid back, began fighting on several fronts simultaneously as he struggled to define markets where Apple could excel or continue to excel. Mike later recalled, "Apple apparently had struggled with this for a long time, and it was happening all over again. I was frustrated beyond my limit."

Every time a decision was made that we could not afford to stay in a particular line of business, an internal campaign would be mounted to reverse the decision. The team would agree on a list of focus areas, and the next day someone would say, "Wait, you can't shut *this* business down—it's bringing in a billion dollars a year."

When I'd try to point out that the market didn't fit any of the focus areas we'd agreed on, or warn that something wasn't sustainable or the business was going to disappear, no one would listen. Nobody would agree to give anything up.

Focus is essential. But a company in trouble can't afford to give up businesses producing attractive profits and margins. Both statements are true, yet only one of these courses can be followed at any given time. Which would it be? We needed a King Solomon to divide this baby and settle disputes; Doug, though brilliant, was a Solomon in last name only.

Another issue that had polarized the company into two camps was the thorny question of the place Apple could find in a world dominated by the Windows operating system. The strategic team had to untangle that barbed issue, but it began to look as difficult to resolve as a messy divorce.

My position was, "The Microsoft guys have won the battle, but the war is not over, and they haven't won the war." In other words, there's now a *de facto* standard in personal computers. So what do we do? We design our future-generation operating systems so they work with Win-dows but still feel like a Mac, look like a Mac, and work like a Mac. We win both ways: We're able to give users the winning, satisfying Mac experience, yet also give them the ability to use their computer to run Windows applications.

My view was also held by many Apple people, but was countered by the strongly held, loudly voiced opinion that considers Microsoft "the evil empire," not to be trusted, dealt with, or given an inch of ground. This opinion was not expressed just within the company but also among Apple users, customers, critics, and media commentators. Even now, the same volatile debate still rages within Apple and wherever techies meet.

The brilliance of the Rhapsody operating system would in time bring the promise of finally bridging that gap and resolving the antagonism. But that's getting ahead of the story; more on Rhapsody much later.

o   o   o

We concluded a full draft of the White Paper on April 10, about two months after launching the effort. This was version 4.0, and it had grown to forty-five pages from the two- or three-page original version I had initially thought we could do. It now carried the title, "At the Crossroads: A Strategic Framework for a Renewed Apple." Even this version for distribution had still been plagued by areas of disagreement between Mike Townsend and Doug Solomon's strategy team. The team had prevailed by the simple expedient of writing the final draft.

And that was what I presented to the board on April 13. I was nonplussed to find it receiving only mild enthusiasm, a level of approval that suggested only, "This is a solid piece of work and probably moving us in the right direction." I wasn't sure all the board members really understood the implications of the plan. That shouldn't have surprised me, but I was disappointed by their cautious responses.

I'm not certain even now that on April 13 I fully appreciated all the far-reaching implications and ramifications of the plan. Some of the decisions had built-in repercussions that would reveal themselves as time went on. For example, if you decide that education is a key market, then that needs to be backed up by software development, a dedicated sales force, the ability to price competitively for that marketplace, and so on. It would have been innocent just to say, "Apple's been successful in the education market, we should continue to focus on that." Decisions within the White Paper would be like pebbles thrown into a pond. What shores those ever-widening ripples would eventually reach was more than any of us could fully predict.

Although contained in their praise, the board at least gave their assurance of standing behind the plan. As I came out of the meeting, my associate Cindy saw my smile, assumed the session had gone well, and gave me a high-five. *Someone,* at least, thought things were going right.

On the other hand, later that same day, Kai-Fu Lee, VP of interactive media, announced his intention to leave and join Silicon Graphics. A world-class expert in speech recognition, Kai-Fu was considered one of the top two people in Apple engineering. We were continuing to lose valuable talent at an undiminished rate, and Kevin Sullivan could not find the necessary means to stem the tide. He, and the other managers as well, seemed unable to say or do what was necessary to get people to stay.

David Seda calculated that I had been spending 30 percent of my time with employees, yet my e-mail from employees was telling me, "You haven't been out and around enough." Whatever I was doing, it apparently wasn't having much impact on the departure rate or morale.

I was able to impact that problem for a time by starting a series of e-mail letters to employees that I called "ReachOut"—for that's exactly what I was hoping to do. These messages were crafted with a personal touch, a human touch, hoping to let people know that I was, indeed, sensitive to the issues on their minds and that I really did care about them, even if they weren't seeing enough of me at some Apple facilities.

The ReachOut messages were my way of clinging to the incredible rapport I had established at the first communications meeting, and they hit a very responsive chord. But only for a while. Despite the many expressions of appreciation I received for them, the ReachOuts dwindled as more pressing issues demanded my attention, and I agreed to let the writing be taken over by Apple PR. The warmth and human quality was immediately lost. In hindsight, I regret allowing this to happen, since the messages were a decided favorite of employees and had been truly successful as a way of sharing my concerns, gaining support, and building morale.

o   o   o

Just stamping a White Paper "Confidential" wouldn't have had much impact. Around Apple, "Confidential" was typically interpreted as "Spe-

cial Delivery to the Press." So the White Paper included a first paragraph that almost begged employees to use discretion; the language was
unusual for a corporate document: "Leaks of documents like this to the
outside world steal from Apple the benefits there may be in surprise. It
also sets us up to look like idiots when someone gets hold of a basic
idea or takes part of the strategy out of its appropriate context. Each of
us has a serious *personal* stake in keeping this document and its con-
tents private. Please help."

This innovative approach worked: Little of the White Paper's positions or ideas reached the pages of newspapers and magazines.

The main sections of the White Paper were devoted to a mission
statement and strategic vision, a set of strategic principles, a section that
reviewed Apple's past performance ("Looking at Reality"), and "Looking
to the Convergent Future," on where we intended to go. The most
extensive part of the document went into details on the new Apple
business model, dealing with critical issues like the core markets and
target markets we would focus on, the phases for putting the plan into
operation, how the company would need to be restructured to carry out
the plan effectively, and the anticipated short-term and longer-term
impacts on revenues and costs. The paper even included a risky candid
(and accurate) prediction that "This strategy may result in a drop in
Apple's unit and dollar sales volume" and (less accurate, fortunately)
"may impact the availability of investment funds."

It's been said that a problem accurately stated is a problem half
solved. Well, we had said it. The other half would be a great deal harder.

∘   ∘   ∘

You can't run a business just on theory or strategy. I would definitely
need to build some heavy-duty momentum. The framework had to be
adopted everywhere, used throughout the company—a concerted
follow-through effort that had never happened before at Apple. To
begin, I held a meeting for about fifty people at the director and manager level, so they could hear the concepts of the White Paper directly
from me, with an explanation of what was expected of them.

Once again I had set myself up to be frustrated; I still hadn't learned
that by expecting the best from Apple leaders, I was leaving myself wide
open for disappointment.

Here was Apple's new CEO, who was going to be talking about the new strategic plan, the new direction for the company. Surely my office staff would be kept busy turning away people clamoring to be included.

Wrong. Some people who were specifically invited didn't even bother to show up. Maybe they figured, *We keep changing CEOs, this too shall pass.* I saw empty seats and was disappointed—even mystified. But that was only the beginning.

One of the strengths of the White Paper, I thought, was that a lot of data had been pulled together and boiled down to show how poorly the company had done in the past. Presenting that hard information in black and white would surely wake people up like an icy shower. I wanted these managers to know the extent to which we hadn't done well and needed to think about what we had to do better.

Yes, I know that the best way to lose a friend is to give him some advice for his own good. In a similar way, the "Looking at Reality" section of the White Paper, although intended as a motivational tool, lost me their support.

What I expected was that each middle manager would take this document, read it carefully, and then put some heavy-duty thought into designing the tactical plans for his or her unit that would light a rocket. I needed them to ask: "How does this apply to my group? Can I implement this both in spirit and in substance so my people can be aligned to the effort of the corporation?"

Instead, these managers read the report, handed out copies to their people, and then put it in a drawer. The sum total of their support began and ended with passing out copies. As individuals, beyond finding fault with it, they weren't willing to think about it and they weren't even going to discuss the new strategies at their meetings. This vital document was treated with as little attention as a New Yorker pays to the siren of a police car.

I was beyond anger at this lack of support. The most immediate impact I could see was on such a superficial level that it was almost laughable—people took some of the phrases out of it and made them part of the culture. The document called on Apple people to create products that would offer "distinctly superior user value," a phrase I admired because it contained the rhythm and flavor of Steve Jobs's famous description of Apple's "insanely great products." The phrase caught on, and almost overnight we began to hear people talking about "DSUVs"—satisfying, as far as I was concerned, only in demonstrating that some folks had at least read the document.

I would actually have felt better if the leadership had expressed their annoyance and disagreed with the strategic decisions, resisting because they were unwilling to buy into my new directions. But that wasn't the case at all; shoulder-shrugging is hard to respond to.

What was their problem? Did these brilliant and experienced Apple people now expect a detailed marching plan? Were they waiting for the thinking to be done for them? I would have expected them to be demeaned if issued tactical orders in the style of Step One, Step Two, Step Three. . . .

It appeared we had a major problem in the middle-management ranks. Their attitude was, "Gee, this is a nice paper, but it doesn't tell me what I'm supposed to do." These were people fully capable of designing and planning the work that would support our new strategy. They learned how in the best schools, and most were well experienced. And they were neither lazy nor recalcitrant.

I concluded they had never been asked to think at this level. Instead, they wanted to be handled in one of two ways. Either they wanted you to do the thinking and then tell them precisely what they should do—or they didn't want you to bother them at all, they wanted to be left alone to do whatever the hell they thought happened to need doing today.

In any well functioning organization, the managers would have each analyzed the White Paper and carefully thought out a list of three or five or ten goals for their own group in line with the goals of the Paper. Then they would have called their people together and said, "Here are the new goals for the group, and here's how they support the new goals of Apple. Now we need to plan the specific things we're going to do in order to move in this new direction." And they would have prodded, cajoled, cracked the whip as necessary to make sure everybody was falling into line.

Could they have demanded that kind of shift in work processes without trodding on the freedom of action and independence that were among Apple's greatest strengths? I would have been lying to myself if I had answered with an unequivocal *yes*. Asked individually, any Apple person would quickly acknowledge that changes were needed, but now it was time to start changing, and . . . nothing. It was becoming evident that without some remaking of Apple attitudes and style, we were not going to get the company onto a healthier course.

o   o   o

At a large, successful corporation that operates in the traditional model—a Hewlett Packard or a Xerox—a corporate personality has developed over time, and managers share an understanding about how to operate and how to work up to the expectation levels of their leadership. At Apple, each manager had run up a pirate flag that was flapping in the breeze: the counterculture at work, independents shunning the rigors and disciplines of tradition and rules. They were hard put to know what to deliver in response to my request for, "Give me the process."

Employees want to see their company succeed, want to see projects succeed, want to take the right action. They want to taste the sweet fruits of victory. Apple people hadn't been getting much chance to do that for a long time.

Eliza Doolittle, in Shaw's *Pygmalion* (and in *My Fair Lady*), was neither stupid nor contrary, she just hadn't learned any better. No one had ever expected more of her or trained her until Henry Higgins came along. Her humble place in life was caused by neither low intelligence nor malice; she needed to be taught. In the majority of cases, that was also true of the people of Apple.

At times I reread the White Paper and find that I'm still pleased with what we achieved. I believe the document is as clear and effective a plan for Apple today as it was when we wrote it.

There is an overriding lesson here for managers at every level: As soon as you are in a position where you have a measure of strategic responsibility, you need to be spending some portion of your time getting away from the tactical to think about corporate strategy and how you translate it into action for your group. If you're doing that, you're fulfilling the proper role of a manager.

I hadn't yet figured out how to get the people of Apple to begin the process of translating goals into actions.

6

Tragedy of Errors—
MY MISTAKES BEGIN TO PILE UP

Terry Crane, vice president of our education business, reached me by phone in an excited state. She had just found out about a Governors' Conference on Education that IBM's Lou Gerstner had put together. "We've got to get an invite to this thing, Gil," she said. "Apple's got to be there, you've got to be there."

Education has traditionally been one of the strengths of Apple, and Terry was right: This was too important to be shut out of, and I couldn't imagine anyone even wanting to have a conference on education without Apple being present. According to Terry, each governor was entitled to bring one businessman with him. I would have to move rapidly.

The CEO of Apple, I had discovered, could reach virtually anybody on the phone. If the call wasn't put right through, the other person would call back shortly. But Governor Pete Wilson and I had known each other for some time and would have taken my call in any case. When I told him the situation, he said, "I just invited somebody else to represent us. Why don't you call the conference back and see if there's a governor who doesn't have anybody to go with him."

Which is how I came to be at Gerstner's conference at the Palisades in New York wearing a name badge that said, in large letters, "SOUTH DAKOTA." I'm not sure why Ted Waitte, the CEO of Gateway 2000, wasn't there; perhaps education isn't as key a market for Gateway, and probably education is not so compelling a topic for him as it is for me.

I give Lou Gerstner a lot of credit. He had made the conference highly relevant, so that something like forty-four of the governors turned up, an amazing percentage. And President Clinton flew in to deliver the keynote.

Dr. Crane found out that rooms were being set up to showcase IBM's education story with displays and demos to demonstrate how their computers were able to offer worthy solutions for the education market. So our event marketing team leaned on the conference management: "If you've got demo rooms for IBM, then you're obliged to provide demo space for Apple." Probably they were concerned that we could make it look like they were just staging the conference as a sales ploy, a self-serving event, rather than a real concern for the quality of education. Lou Gerstner would not have appreciated that. The IBM people agreed.

The space we were assigned was only about one-tenth the size of the IBM room, but Apple stole the show. Instead of having stodgy, graying sales executives in drab-colored suits, we did something truly attention-getting: the Macintosh demo stations were run by schoolchildren from the inner city—some from across the river in Newark and some flown in for the occasion from Tennessee, with their teachers to chaperone. The kids absolutely bubbled with enthusiasm about what they could do with their computers and how easy it was to learn on a Mac. Their enthusiasm was infectious and everyone at the conference tried to gather around to see these children at work. Instead of boasting about what Apple computers could do, we translated the demos into how the young people could learn. IBM was feature driven; Apple concentrated on benefits. As I observed the difference between the demos, I realized that people were seeing the Apple advantage played out right before their eyes. How could this essence be translated into every aspect of what we were doing?

The conference reached some useful conclusions. The political hot potato was a proposal to support the concept of nationwide standards testing, not very popular with any governor who might have reason to fear providing ammunition to opponents if his state ranked near the bottom. Nonetheless, the proposal passed.

Apple went on to have improved sales through the summer and an especially strong year with sales to education. I'd like to think our showing at the conference may have had a bearing on those results, one of the all-too-few bright spots in our sales records of this period.

o o o

The wise man says it's not worth worrying about events you can't control. I had made my best effort to convince the Japanese bankers about extending our loan, and couldn't control the results beyond that.

But how could I keep from worrying? The $150 million was due in April unless extended. It was already April and still no answer.

Finally, barely a week before the due date, the response arrived. They said both yes and no. Yes, they would roll the loans over; no, they would not give us a one-year extension. We would have only six months to get back on our feet. But that was enough breathing space for the moment. The immediate pressure was lifted, and just in the nick of time.

o o o

By April, Apple's army of soldiers was still uncertain which way to jump about the Gil Amelio leadership. They were beginning to pick up their pace marching behind my leadership, but people continued turning in their dog tags at an accelerating rate. Battlefield promotions became routine. A typical reflection of the uncertainty was an e-mail sent out by director Carlos Montalvo, who, soon after this communication, was promoted to the post of vice president of the interactive group. His message found its way to me through a respected Apple consultant.

Carlos graded my performance as "looking and sounding patriarchal without becoming patronizing"; he and the people he'd talked to sized me up as understanding Apple's business and they were "impressed with what Gil is doing."

But he forthrightly urged that I needed to respond to what he called the number-one unanswered question across the company. Writing that I needed to announce "What Apple would *stop* doing," he described employees as being horrified that with 2,500 fewer people, the company would continue aggressively pursuing every line of business: Newton, Publishing, Media Authoring, Servers, Pippin, Imaging, Consumer, K-12, PowerBooks, Copland, OpenDoc, Internet. Carlos warned that if the company continued on a course of doing everything, "it would be Spindler all over again."

The number-two Montalvo concern was that I might, rather than shut down or sell off sub-par elements of the business, do "the Washington thing . . . i.e., cut back everything by 15 percent."

I agreed with this perceptive young man's take on both fronts. The net effects of being unfocused, I've long been convinced, are confusion, waste, and frustration. Fuzzy strategies and programs prevent a company from reaching industry leadership. I was still not nearly as focused as I wanted to be; I would continue to deserve low grades on *focus* until I made and announced clear decisions.

Two months on the job and I was being loudly applauded for some actions and booed for others. I couldn't help recalling a remark of the late Roberto Goizueta, CEO of Coca-Cola: "I'm sleeping like a baby—I wake up every two hours crying."

∘   ∘   ∘

For well over a year, the stock options received by almost all Apple employees had been essentially worthless—the price the employee would have to spend to buy a share was much higher than the current price of the stock. I wanted to improve the program, hoping to slow the departure rate.

Our stock-option specialist, Lisa Ceglia, devised a new option plan based on a program I had used successfully at National Semiconductor. With board approval, the new arrangement was announced in mid-April.

The plan brought employees a mixed blessing. It repriced the options to near the market price (good news). But vesting would start over (bad news). Vesting in this situation would entitle an employee to purchase a certain percentage of the shares granted them at the option price, each year over the vesting period—typically several years. Used as another tool for saying, "Stick around," it effectively tells the employee, "Here's a reward for your dedicated service, but you only get it if you stay; leave too soon and you only get part of the reward, or none at all."

The amount of the reward is, of course, directly related to how well the stock price does, which aligns the employee's interest with the shareholder's.

Most shareholders, though, don't like to see a company lower its employee stock-option price, because it's against their own interests. So requiring the vesting period to start over would, I hoped, take the sting out for shareholders.

I suggested that the new arrangement be announced as a plan-in-work, and that we ask for comments and suggestions before activating it. Although we were able to incorporate the few practical suggestions that were offered in good faith, the vast number of responses were acrimonious complaints and accusations.

Howard Green, who was then acting VP of the interactive media group, wrote: "Employees presently feel there is little to no upside for remaining loyal to this company. We have no profit sharing, bonuses are significantly lower due to company performance, and now there is less stock being issued. When you add it all up, it's a significant reduction in compensation." In his view, the "risk-to-return ratio" had become out of kilter with the rest of Silicon Valley because the danger of job loss in the ongoing cutbacks wasn't balanced by the kind of handsome rewards that might be possible by joining the right startup. He reiterated how difficult it had become to attract top talent and he ominously reminded me of a fact I had been living with every moment of every day: "All of our assets have feet."

This was one of the many times that I picked up double signals from Apple people who professed a fierce company loyalty but wouldn't support any plan that didn't put them—as individuals—at the very top of every priority list. They refused to accept that Apple wasn't yet in the financial position to redesign a stock program that would be impressively better for all employees. Sure, they needed to be convinced that I would keep their interests in mind, but I also needed to bring this ailing company back to health. Those twin top priorities couldn't always fit together; it became a most excruciating balancing act.

I had made a solid business decision about options that could also sit comfortably on my conscience. The board agreed, but Apple employees distanced from me. I was fast becoming disillusioned by their expression of love for the company, because they were unwilling to let me back it up with action. I began to question, *Was it me or was it them?*

o   o   o

Why is life punctuated with petty annoyances that drop in at the worst possible times? While on a holiday with Charlene before starting at Apple, a washing-machine water hose had broken, flooding the entire first floor of our Los Altos house. Repairs couldn't begin until the house had thoroughly dried out. Weeks went by, with little improvement. To speed things up, the contractor brought in huge fans and heaters to dry the floors, with large tubes running into the walls to dry them out, as well.

When they turned all those fans on, we felt like we were in a subway tunnel with trains constantly roaring past. We had to eat all our meals out and live upstairs, but still couldn't escape the din. That went on for a month before the house was dry enough for the repairs to begin. Certainly not conducive for getting any work done at home.

o   o   o

There are those who would say that business leaders should be able to ignore the emotional part of complaints—disapproval, disappointment, and dislike from their employees and even from customers—to hear it like background noise and ignore the static as though it didn't exist. It's true that no matter what is done or how carefully a product is manufactured, there will always be people who phone or write to complain and blame. A chief executive is most often advised to shut down his concern for individuals, just as doctors are taught to treat diseases and not patients. I would resist; I was determined not to treat customers as background noise.

Although I agree that complaints are inevitable whether a company produces angel food cake or locomotives, I believe that complaints can provide an invaluable guide. Most people seem to know and are able to express what they *don't* want or what they *don't* like, rather than what they do want—the negative rather than the positive. So over the years I've forced myself to develop a keen ability to extract from the negative the kernels of useful advice.

But customer complaints that were coming into Apple were of a very different and disturbing character. Almost from day one, the feedback from the marketplace had a stridency that made the skin crawl. And that intensity would soon increase.

Letters about the same problem, when received from people in many parts of the country, in different industries, in different walks of life, are evidence of a problem about to mushroom into a disaster. These complaining customers were not part of some organized letter-writing campaign; it was clear that I was onto something needing serious investigation—and I had better get to the bottom as fast as I could.

I had begun to realize how widespread problems were throughout the company. In manufacturing, we were carrying way too much inventory, our cycle time was too slow, we had high rework rates. In distribution, we were terrible about meeting delivery commitments—people would sometimes wait for months to get a machine they should have had in a matter of days. And so on, across the whole company.

What mystified me was why I wasn't hearing about major problems from my executives. They should have been coming to me saying, "Gil, there's a serious issue here that needs your attention." Why was I learning about Apple problems primarily from disgruntled customers?

I came to recognize the fault lay not with the individual executives, but with the culture. They had learned over the years to view the CEO as a person who went out and made speeches, and left them alone to run (or ruin) the company. God forbid the CEO should try to make a real business decision that they hadn't cooked up and put on his plate. I believe they had come to the conclusion that an Apple CEO was just another user-friendly icon—a figurehead who shouldn't interfere with hard business decisions that one of them hadn't initiated.

Problems are solvable. That's what people do much of their time at work—solve problems. Hearing forthrightly about what was happening would have been reassuring, even enjoyable. Instead we were playing a childish game of hide-and-seek. I had been at Apple for months and the real work hadn't yet begun; we were still shadowboxing.

Only very gradually were they beginning to understand that I was a different breed of CEO—one to whom they could bring problems, a CEO who intended to get and stay close to the action.

I've learned the hard way that changes don't happen overnight . . . but it may well be that I was far too patient. Telling myself I would hang in there and lead them toward change, I was hanging myself and didn't know it.

◦　◦　◦

The word was out that communications sent to me in confidence would not get back to the sender's manager or appear as a black mark in personnel records. Keeping my word on this required four or five hours every evening as my e-mail rapidly swelled to gargantuan proportions. The extra payoff for Apple was that employees could without fear raise flags on important issues that I couldn't seem to learn from my executives.

Newton was a prime example. This hand-held device—the category is called "personal digital assistant," or PDA—had suffered a rocky history. Introduced in 1993 before the bugs had been worked out, the early Newtons were so unreliable at handwriting recognition that they were a subject of jokes for late-night talk show hosts. Although Newton technology had vastly improved since then, sales had never ignited.

CEO Michael Spindler and his senior managers had worked with the consulting firm of McKinsey and Company to come up with a plan they hoped would save Apple. One of the recommendations McKinsey had made involved the Newton project. Their advice amounted to "sell it or close it down"—an opinion that retained a secure hold on the minds of the people around me.

My e-mail, though, brought messages from a number of employees to say that Newton was being treated as a stepchild but was really better than it was getting credit for. That was enough to make me hesitate on following the McKinsey advice until I had done some checking of my own. What I learned convinced me that while there was much work still needed, Newton had the potential to be a winning product.

Experience has taught me that perseverance is often the essential ingredient in success. When you're on the way to introducing a new product or a new technology, there are lots of moments along the way when you despair, but could succeed if you persevered—rather like not giving up on a marriage at the first argument. On the highway to success, there are a lot of exits, and it's tempting to take one when the going gets tough.

A prime example in my career involved the charge-coupled device, or CCD, on which I'm coholder of the basic patent. The CCD is the basic element at the heart of the home video camera, fax machines, and other optical sensing devices. In the late 1970s, U.S. companies got impatient when the technology didn't lead to an overnight miracle, while the Japanese companies stuck with it and turned it into a huge, global success story.

My investigation into the Newton convinced me it was a wonderful technology that had been brought out too early and positioned incorrectly. I decided not to cancel it.

Months later, shortly before I left Apple, the Newton group introduced a hot new product, the MessagePad 2000, which was what Newton should have been in the first place. Keeping the Newton alive had been costing Apple some $15 million a quarter—money we could have used effectively for other endeavors or for keeping more employees on the payroll. But now, with the MessagePad 2000, Newton was breaking even and poised to be a money-earner for the company.

So Apple gained a new, successful revenue source, but lost the opportunity of other projects the funds could have been used for. Had I made the correct decision?

Newton was a tough call.

o   o   o

In the spring of 1996, we were getting ready to introduce a much-touted product called Pippin, which had been developed as a way of broadening the company's base beyond PCs into the arena of games. Pippin was a game machine used with a TV, which sounds like a copycat of the Nintendo idea, but the Pippin had what was supposed to be a big advantage: the CD-ROM that carried the game you wanted to play also had on it the Pippin's operating system software, a scaled-down version of the Mac OS. So Pippin didn't need the extensive memory capacity that would ordinarily be required for devices with such stunning graphics. Though pricey, it could be produced at a much lower cost than even the lowest-end PC. That was the theory; the reality wouldn't come close.

Pippin was being driven by marketing VP Satjiv Chahil, who came at this product with a games orientation as a result of his years as a marketing manager in Japan. It turned out that this left us standing in the station, because Pippin had all the workings to be a phenomenal Internet device. This may not be the worst but it is surely the saddest of all the Apple stories: Pippin could have been the first, best, and least expensive Internet computer on the market—the solution that allows technology-resistant users to sit in their living rooms and surf the Web on their television sets. And the displays would have had the appealing look and feel and ease of use that causes people to fall in love with the Macintosh. How smart we are when looking back over our shoulders.

Pippin was launched in Japan in June 1996 and sold something like 20,000 units at the starting bell, which had everybody smiling. It sure looked as if we had a big winner. Finally Apple was getting the positive press that was sorely needed; a strong Pippin win could give the company some real stature in a whole new product category.

Over the next four or five months, we sold a grand total of 5,000 more Pippins. For a company the size of Apple, that's a dribble, with revenues at the noise level, barely large enough to be discerned on the income statement.

When time came for the U.S. launch in November, word had already drifted back that Pippin was a tainted product, and it was doomed. I realized too late that Pippin was in a middle ground—too expensive for a game machine when you could buy a Sega for $200 and have a choice of a zillion titles . . . but costly enough that for several hundred more, you could buy a full-fledged computer and use it for playing games and doing all those other productivity things besides.

Satjiv didn't see it; I didn't see it. If anybody at Apple brought it to my attention, I missed the point completely. After the fact, of course, *everyone* saw it.

Not long afterward I read suggestions in the press that Pippin should be repositioned as an Internet box. Journalists and industry commentators were seeing what we had missed. By then, it was too late—others were ready ahead of us to go after what promises to be a huge and lucrative market.

In the end, Pippin just faded away, another missed opportunity.

○　○　○

Spring, the season of rebirth and renewal. Spring of 1996 at Apple was, instead, a season of horror stories. On the positive side, new CFO Fred

Anderson was now on board, able to join me in the urgent, near desperate push to win control over the company's continuing severe cash problems. Meanwhile one other issue was taking an inordinate, disproportionate share of my time: Copland.

Copland was slated to be our next-generation operating system software. Why should the CEO of a giant company not only involve himself in such a technical issue, but spend time on it to the exclusion of other urgent matters?

Apple had been saying for months that the much delayed Copland would be revealed at the World Wide Developers Conference in May, when the 4,000 loyal software developers attending would each be handed a set of disks containing the program in its "beta" version—a not-yet-ready-for-prime-time release, standard in the software industry, that still contains bugs and problems, but can be used by programmers for developing their own software.

As our head of developer relations, the Developers Conference would be put on by Heidi Roizen and her "evangelists." She well understood without any word from me that keeping the developers happy was critical. In early May Heidi came to me and said, "The Copland guys are not going to be ready, and we better not wait 'til the last minute to tell the developers."

"That's terrible news," I said. "But frankly, I've been expecting it. What do you suggest?"

"If we announce right now that Copland isn't going to be ready, we might help the situation." A preconference announcement wouldn't solve the problem—but at least by lowering expectations, we could put a lid on the disappointment.

"You can't just say it's delayed. What can we give as the new date?"

Heidi did more digging, and based on what she found, we agreed on announcing a delay of another two and a half months—to near the end of July.

Whatever else they're great at, software developers are notorious failures at accurately predicting when a particular stage of development will be completed. Everyone in the industry accepts software schedules as highly unreliable. So this slippage was disappointing, but would not be viewed as a disaster.

Nevertheless, I continued to experience uncomfortable warnings about the project and started asking software bosses Ike Nassi and Mitch Allen, head of the Copland project, for their scheduling data— the critical path modeling or whatever technique they were using to manage the project. At first it didn't register as possible, but neither Allen nor Nassi had any data or projections to show me. I wondered how they came up with the forecast they had given Heidi. Were they just pulling dates out of thin air?

I asked, "What did you base the July date on?"

It was based, they said, on the rate at which bugs—errors in the software code—were found and fixed, an approach that's based on the observation that as you get closer to the end of a project, you find fewer and fewer bugs. And they had had enough experience using the approach, they assured me, to be able to predict accurately.

A quote attributed to Albert Einstein describes insanity as "doing the same thing in the same way and expecting a different outcome."

Their previous prediction, based on the same bug-count method, had been May, and they hadn't mentioned anything about missing that date until Heidi had begun asking. Possibly their method was reliable for doing an upgrade to an existing program. But for a totally new piece of software for which the technical approach was fundamentally untried, it seemed to me a very dubious proposition indeed. My credibility was being tested, as was Heidi's.

Mac fans believed Copland was the operating system that could save Apple. But with continued slippage, we weren't being successful in supporting that hope. The press had begun to describe Copland as "too little, too late."

Why was the operating system so important? To answer, I have to go back fifteen years to the days when Steve Jobs had snared a project hatched by a computer hobbyist turned Apple engineer, Jef Raskin, that gave birth to the original Macintosh. Steve saw it as the insanely great machine that would sell for under $1,000 and be so intuitive that a beginner could set it up and use it—the machine that would ultimately give rise to the "for the rest of us" slogan.

To make the Macintosh wonderful but inexpensive demanded many compromises—compromises that would have a critical impact on the Apple of my reign, a decade and a half later. It's a technical point, but worth appreciating. The ideal calls for "partitioning" the computer's memory—putting the operating system, which tells the computer what to do and how to do it, in one assigned, protected area of memory, and settling the applications—the word processing programs and spreadsheet programs, etc.—in separate areas.

With this arrangement, if the word processing program runs into a problem and stops working, the user restarts the troublesome program; everything else keeps running fine. But without partitioning, if one program locks up or crashes, everything else is effected; the computer has to be shut down and restarted, and in the process, any work that hadn't been saved to disk is lost.

Steve Jobs's problem was that partitioning would have required more code in the operating system, requiring a larger memory and a bigger power supply, in turn probably requiring a larger box. Of course, the price would need to go up, and the schedule would slip. So Steve was projecting a domino effect that would take him further and further away from his dream machine; it probably took him a nanosecond to make the decision.

For the original Macintosh, smaller, cheaper, but with no memory partitioning was undoubtedly the smart choice—even though people like me, who stood in a line on the street to buy one of those first Macs, found them very unstable, crashing all the time and causing many frustrating moments. But after a couple of years, when most of the bugs were eliminated, the Mac became more stable than any other PC of the time.

Today's Macintosh operating systems, twenty or thirty or forty times larger than the 128 kilobytes of the one in the original Mac, are as big as the software used in the telephone system to control all the phone traffic of the United States. Yet memory protection had never been added.

The scientist part of me said it was only a matter of time before the level of complexity got so big that "chaos theory" would take over, as in *Jurassic Park,* and minor blips would cause unpredictable results, making the computers unusable.

Despite all the reasons for at last incorporating full memory protection, the Copland team had decided not to include it—a decision urged by marketing and sales people, for whom any new operating system that couldn't run on every Macintosh, no matter how ancient a machine, was breaking faith with Mac owners. Instead the Copland team had devised a pseudo protection scheme, which in truth left the problem basically uncorrected. It became devastatingly clear to me that sales was controlling technology, based on their short-term thinking.

Stability is exceedingly important. When new users work up enough courage to sit down at a computer, if the machine freezes or crashes, they're tempted to say, "I must have done something wrong, I'll never learn," and abandon the effort. All the more likely if the computer is a Mac, with its reputation for being so easy to use.

So in essence I agreed with what the press was saying: a day late and a dollar short. At this point we had 500 people working on Copland, we had already spent hundreds of millions of dollars on it, and it was not going to solve our biggest problem: stability. Instead of helping revive Apple and bring it back to prosperity, Copland in fact had the potential of doing exactly the opposite, of being such a disappointment that when it finally came out, people would try it and say, "Apple will never get this right," and abandon the platform totally.

With each step of my Copland investigation, I had more questions. How are fundamental decisions being made? Who are the influencers and what are their motives? Is Apple a technology company or a marketing company?

A decision on Copland would require yet another tough call.

o   o   o

According to famed college football coach Paul "Bear" Bryant, "If anything goes bad, *I* did it. If anything goes semi-good, then *we* did it. If anything goes real good, then *you* did it."

Reporting Apple's quarterly results in April 1996 has to rank as one of the most dreadful experiences of my business life. I would take the hit and a hard one it would be.

The burden of the Christmas miscalculations just before I arrived dragged along with me like Scrooge's chains; I was forced to face the ghosts of Apple's past, and they had come back to haunt me. Spindler had been thoroughly convinced that Apple's salvation—if it wasn't to come from selling the company—would be accomplished by pushing huge quantities of product into the marketplace, enough to gain a 20 percent market share. If successful, his strategy would have repositioned Apple as a vigorous player, and it would also prove the triumph of his business acumen and leadership. With the best of intentions, Spindler put his blessings on the directive to manufacture large quantities of merchandise rapidly and to focus on low-end products for the first-time computer buyer. The result was computers the market didn't want, computers that had been built to a lower quality standard. This inferior quality excess merchandise was crammed into warehouses; now I needed to write it off.

The write-off was inevitable; the question was how much. When I first faced this dilemma, CFO Fred Anderson had yet to report. The finance organization had lost hordes of people, and I would have to rely on Jeanne Seeley, the corporate controller who was also trying to handle the CFO duties, and Jane Riser, who was filling in as acting treasurer (but who would perform so well that she would later be appointed treasurer in her own right).

One of my very first assignments had been to the two of them: "You and your teams need to attack this problem of what we have that no longer has value, what we should write off, how much we should write off, and what kind of reserves we should take."

Both women were competent professionals; both were tremendously overburdened. It was unfair to expect them to handle problems for which they lacked experience. To complicate matters, under their intense work pressures, they were not working as well together as they might have in a more normal situation.

The floodwaters inched up gradually. Every day or so I'd get a report from the finance people, "We found some more stuff to write off," until I began to dread their appearance at my office door. The totals increased alarmingly, and I fell into the habit of checking my watch and the calendar, longing desperately for the day to arrive when we could finally close the books.

Fred Anderson's arrival to take up his job as CFO had come late in the quarter, too late to be much help during the hunt for write-offs. My request once he started was for "as conservative a judgment as was absolutely legitimate." I was already beginning to fear a number in the hundreds of millions, which is a huge amount of money to take as a write-off. I never expected a figure as gargantuan as we would arrive at.

A nagging thought, prayer-like, kept coming back: *My God, this must be going too far. There's got to be some worthwhile stuff in what we're proposing to write off.* No help came from heaven; I would have to face the music, and it would be more like Wagner than Mozart.

o   o   o

The law relative to corporate write-offs has changed dramatically. Before about five years ago, management could make a decision with only the stockholders looking over their shoulders. If a company had one business line that seemed to have a high probability of failure, they could just take a deduction against the profits from the rest of the business.

Then the SEC decided this was being used as a way for companies to prop up future earnings or avoid paying taxes, that while in some cases it's prudent for a company to take worthless assets off its books, some companies were abusing the practice. As a result, the rules became much more restrictive.

The principle here is that inventories being written off are no longer worth what they originally cost the company. Normally, product coming out of the factory is, until sold, carried on the books for what it cost to make. But that's not always valid. We had a warehouse full of product that Apple built for eager Christmas shoppers who never showed up. The computers were being carried on the books for what it cost to build them . . . but if nobody wants them, what's the real value? It's whatever you may be able to unload them for, or, worst case, the scrap value. So you take a write-off, reducing the value of the goods from what you were carrying them at, to a realistic estimate of what you're really likely to get. (To accountants, this rule is known as "the lower of cost or market.")

Wall Street understands write-offs. But they don't like to see them quarter after quarter—that makes the company look bad, it makes the management look bad, it conveys an image of continuing crisis, and it gives investors the jitters. So when you're in a situation like Apple's, you want to take all the write-offs you need to, all at once, and get it behind you.

In our case, though, it wasn't so straightforward. I wanted to do this all at once so it wouldn't hang on to haunt and hurt us later . . . yet the total grew larger and larger.

One day I sat at a board meeting, which I will remember too vividly all the rest of my life, and said, "I'm about to tell you the toughest thing I ever had to tell anybody."

And then I swallowed hard and got it out: "We need to write off about a billion dollars."

They were stunned into silence. Very little news at these meetings had been anything but depressing in some time, yet this was a whole different magnitude. I went on, "We've been over the numbers, I've been over them personally, and they're all valid. It's my recommendation that the board accept this and let us go forward with it."

It's really hard to look at yourself in the mirror and say, *I'm about to write off a billion dollars.* How much effort on the part of how many human beings does that represent? One hell of a lot. And you're saying, *"I'm going to throw it all away."* It's emotionally draining to deal with such an enormous number, to stand up before the public and your employees and your board and say, *"Trust me, this is the right step to take."*

The board didn't like it, but I helped them understand the necessity, and they finally gave their approval.

The official press release on April 17 announced the after-tax amount of loss as $740 million, which came to $5.99 per share. It was a devastating number, especially when compared to the announced results in the same quarter of the preceding year—$73 million net profit.

Our press release also included the news that Apple would be "redeploying" 2,800 people (the Silicon Valley euphemism for letting people go). The 1,300 reduction number that Spindler had announced in January would be more than doubled. Nearly 3,000 people to be disappointed and disillusioned by the company they had served. I had decided years ago not to describe people and employees as bodies or head count—a typically crass habit in business environments. Referring to them as people humanizes the situation and reminds me of my responsibilities to these people and their families. The use of statistics or depersonalized terminology allows leaders to hide their heads in the sand. Layoffs are not redeployments in my book, and I regretted the term being used by our PR people.

Fortunately, media coverage of the announcement was balanced and fair. Lawrence Fisher wrote in the *New York Times* that it seemed unlikely the news would "restore confidence in the struggling computer maker," but "some analysts had been expecting far more drastic cuts." He also noted, however, that Apple shares edged up in after-hours trading following the report.

∘　∘　∘

I deeply believe that before you kick off a sexy marketing and sales program, you better have solid products to offer. Through this early period, I focused much of my thinking on the necessary foundations that could provide more reliable products—quality control, product design, product packaging, manufacturing—the elements that create products which will attract people to buy and become part of a loyal customer base. We needed to do these things and do them right, before it would make sense to go all out on a sales and marketing effort.

We were spending $190 million dollars a year on advertising, Jeff Berg was driving hard to get the Macintosh prominently featured in other movies like *Mission Impossible,* and Satjiv Chahil was creatively conjuring brilliant schemes to get Apple and Mac in front of people at music concerts, Web events, and through a myriad of other ingenious ways. But the products had never been lower on the quality/reliability scale. To be perfectly frank, the Apple products being manufactured and shipped during my early days were dreadful, not worth shouting about, certainly not worth spending huge sums to advertise and promote.

If you spend big bucks on advertising, and the advertising stimulates demand but the products then disappoint buyers, those customers may never come back—you may lose them forever. It was my judgment that we needed to clean up the snags with the products first. When we had products we were really proud of, then we could launch advertising that would shout it from the rooftops. In the meantime we'd continue to advertise, of course, but at a significantly reduced volume.

Not everyone at Apple or within the Mac community saw it that way. One contingent struck out at me with complaints that "Apple's advertising stinks, you guys are not getting your message heard, people don't know what you stand for anymore, you really gotta get the word out, you gotta get a lot more hype going."

The other contingent, not nearly as vocal, agreed with the tack that you don't stimulate demand for products that are likely to disappoint.

Another example of a continuing series of battles between the short-term and long-term teams.

It was another tough call, but I decided to slash the advertising budget by nearly one-third, to $135 million.

Given the scope of problems I was dealing with, the decision on advertising looks relatively minor. In fact, advertising became the central issue that would fourteen months later put me on the firing line and lead to my fall.

7

Two Gentlemen in Redmond—
I CALL ON BILL GATES

We were airborne by 6:30, without a cloud in the early morning sky. It was Wednesday of my sixth week, and our destination was Redmond, Washington. Heidi Roizen, David Seda, and I knew that the people of Apple, when they heard of the trip, would be uncomfortable about Gil Amelio reaching out to Bill Gates. And they would probably not like any accord that might be reached.

Michael Spindler had considered Microsoft the enemy and had never had a meeting with Gates. As far as I know, the two never even spoke on the phone. I was sensitive to how widespread that animosity was among Apple people, but couldn't ignore the many positive reasons for our company getting on closer terms with Microsoft. In any industry where one company is King of the Jungle, turning your back probably hurts them only a little, but may hurt you in devastating ways.

Microsoft earns a gross profit of $200 or $300 million a year on software for the Macintosh, so has an interest in seeing Apple survive. On our side, we had even more to gain by mending fences. Any computer is essentially only as valuable as the software available for it. Microsoft had consistently introduced new or upgraded applications for the Macintosh a year or so after the Windows versions, and the Mac versions consistently ran slower than the Windows counterparts. I wanted to see that situation change.

Bill Gates and I had first met when Microsoft and National Semiconductor joined forces back in 1994 to codevelop a telephone with a computer chip inside that would store phone number lists, place calls at predetermined times, and perform other useful bits of chip magic. Although the product never made it to the marketplace, the joint effort had provided a chance for the two of us to meet.

One of my early action items as Apple's CEO had been to call Bill Gates: "I'd like to get together and see how we can cooperate."

He said, "Great, but you don't have to come up to Redmond. I get down there often and I can save you the trip." It was gracious of him, and although we each intended to make it happen as soon as possible, our administrators couldn't arrange a time slot that worked for us both. So I had scheduled this trip to Redmond rather than put the meeting off any longer. My Citation II business jet made flights like this one very convenient—although the plane would soon became a cause célèbre, generating nonsensical sensationalist gossip.

o   o   o

Executives of major companies have traveled by corporate aircraft since the Ford Motor Company and others began the practice back near the dawn of commercial aviation in 1925, two years before the Lindbergh flight. Shareholders and financial analysts support the economics of travel by chartered or company-owned aircraft because it makes financial good sense. Do the arithmetic: Multiply an executive's hourly earnings by the additional time he or she would spend making the same trip by commercial airline, then add the further savings of the two or three other company personnel who so frequently also need to attend the same meeting or conference.

Apple executives had been traveling for years on jet aircraft chartered from ACM Aviation, a company owned by Apple's sometime board chairman, Mike Markkula. This fact has, I believe, never been published before, but there's nothing unethical about it. Apple paid Mike's company current going rates for the aircraft, the same as it would have paid to any other executive-jet charter service.

However, I already owned the Citation. There was no longer a need for using Mike's planes, since Apple executives could now make business trips on my aircraft at a *lower* cost to the company. And I ordered a cutback on executive travel, so executives were using my aircraft less than they had been using Markkula's.

Although we successfully reduced management travel costs, I was to receive a barrage of criticism from the press. The *New York Times* said that "Amelio, an amateur [*sic!*] pilot, also arranged to have Apple lease his private airplane for business." And the *San Jose Mercury News* version was that "Amelio has another company in his life—Aero Ventures, of which he is the sole owner. Apple pays Aero $1,695 an hour—that amounted to more than $100,000 in a few months last year—for use of an Aero plane."

Newspaper and magazine stories repeated the accusations so often that Apple employees began to become disgruntled, believing that the deal on my airplane was lining my pockets while gouging the company when in fact at the price I charged Apple, I needed to subsidize the operating expenses heavily out of my own pocket. The highly misleading press stories acted like dropping a rock through a glass roof, shattering morale on its way. I couldn't help but stifle my annoyance and wish they would ask for details so they could tell the complete story.

The fact is that people accepted the version of reality presented by the media, and I believe this is what happens in virtually all situations where we are not in a position to gather the facts ourselves. We form our own impressions—through television—of whether we think a particular presidential candidate is honest and forthright, outgoing and believable, or something else. But the press—broadly including less independent sources such as, say, a union newsletter, a company's employee magazine, a paper published by our church or temple, etc.— may strongly shape our opinions on matters like whether the candidate's voting record, couplings with other-than-spouse, smoking pot with or without inhaling, hiring illegal aliens, and other such acts are valid grounds for rejecting them.

I've never believed the argument that the press only reports the news and leaves opinions to the editorial page. I think that as soon as a writer (journalists and historians included) indulges in the use of adjectives and adverbs, they've entered a territory in which it's virtually impossible to write without the story being colored by their own prejudices, beliefs, assumptions, experiences, and ambitions. There are not enough colorless, neutral modifiers in the language for anyone to be able to write a paragraph of copy that isn't influenced by opinion. And if you doubt this, just read carefully any paragraph of news from your favorite paper (including the *Wall Street Journal* or *New York Times*) or record and play back the presentation of a story on the evening news. If you can't tell the reporter's attitude, you haven't been paying attention.

Thankfully I haven't come away from the Apple experience with a paranoid perspective of an evil, out-to-get-me press. On the contrary, I put a heavy burden of responsibility on the rest of us. I don't believe we as individuals do anywhere near an adequate job of evaluating what we hear and read, nor do we seek more facts. It takes rugged determination to sort out our feelings and make up our minds without prejudice. And a level-headed evaluation process is far more difficult when some very large proportion of reporters see an event from the same perspective. This is not, as media bashers would have it, some sort of conspiracy. The fact is that many media professionals have similar backgrounds and approach the news from a similar perspective. That they frequently arrive at similar conclusions should not be a surprise.

All of us have at least one deep-seated insecurity; the misleading stories about my jet stabbed right at the heart of my basic values of truth, intelligence, and honor. But my optimistic personality would soon seize control and again it would be a wonderful morning with an opportunity to make a difference.

o   o   o

I flew as pilot-in-command that morning, with a frequent flight companion, professional pilot Ken Ambrose, in the right seat. I enjoy flying the Citation II, a seven-passenger, twin-engine business plane that is the world's most popular jet aircraft. It's incredibly easy to fly, but takes so much of the work out that a pilot has to fight against developing bad habits and getting lazy about watching the gauges.

We walked into the Microsoft headquarters building at 8:45, with plenty of time to spare for our nine o'clock meeting. I was quite surprised when, five minutes later, a young woman came in to announce, "Mr. Gates will see you now."

No one would have expected a busy CEO to be ready early, but Bill was already seated in the conference room waiting for us, and I was struck by his very open and warm welcome. He bounded out of his chair and lunged forward to shake my hand. "Gee, Gil, it's great to see you again, and congratulations on your new assignment at Apple." With the kind of forthright graciousness I would expect of a friend, he uttered the social platitudes of, "I'm really looking forward to us working well together," and so on.

No introduction was needed for my associates. Bill and David had met before, and Heidi was an old friend, even included among a small inner core of buddies who had gone with Bill on an African safari and other similar escapades. I had brought her to this meeting as Apple's leader of developer relations, since we were there to speak to Bill in his capacity as someone who writes software for the Mac.

David was along strictly because I wanted someone taking notes of the decisions that were made and didn't want to be diverted from the conversation by doing it myself. I knew David had a far different set of responsibilities when he worked for Spindler. My instructions were that he was to listen 99 percent of the time, speak 1 percent of the time, and record a valuable set of notes. David had previously made it clear that he was negative on this whole notion of getting closer to Microsoft, but, loyal staffer, he nonetheless supported me in the effort.

I opened with a little preamble, recapping the purpose of the meeting, along the lines of, "Let's find ways to do great things together." And I stated a goal that contained an all-too-familiar complaint of Macintosh users. "We want our mutual customers to have the experience that when they run Microsoft products on the Macintosh, the software runs as well as it does on a Windows machine."

Bill said, "I want to talk about that, but first I prepared a presentation that I'd like to give."

With that he stood up and went through a thirty-minute pitch, complete with colored flip charts on the history of the relationship between Apple and Microsoft. The first image to hit the screen was a photo of himself with Steve Jobs back in those early days when they were both about twenty-two years old, full of hopes and aspirations and dreams. And then he recounted all of the Apple-Microsoft milestones along the way, some good times, some bad. It was, I thought, a heartfelt reviewing of an eventful past. So far, this was more like home movies than a business presentation, but it certainly lifted my spirits.

Bill talked on at some length about how important Apple had been to Microsoft in the early days, how important Apple had been to the growth of his company, and the extremely warm relationship that had gone sour. Finally, he talked about his strong desire to see the relationship improve. I was thinking, *I want to see it improve, you want to see it improve, we'll surely be able to do something.*

As he continued to talk, I became quite sure that the business charts had been put together by Bill himself. This wasn't a presentation that some staff person had handed him five minutes before we arrived. He had organized it, designed the visuals, and was in full ownership of the ideas.

An underlying theme kept recurring throughout his talk: He was pained by the way the relationship between Apple and Microsoft had taken a nosedive after such a soaring start. He expressed hope that with me as leader we could once again revert to a positive association. Bill was not ashamed of the link between his emotions and intellect. I was pleased at that, because nothing is more off-putting to me than an intellect completely divorced from feelings. Just as he has often been described, I was seeing a total person.

As he was wrapping up, I wondered if he would put out his hand, say "Nice seeing you," and leave the rest of the session for us and his people. But he didn't. When he finished, he sat down and patiently took part in the remainder of the meeting.

One of the other Microsoft presenters was then cued to talk about the financials. I observed the relationship between Bill and his people and admired the respect with which he was treated. But he was brusque at times, even harsh. Bill sometimes makes an offhand remark that's very blunt and his people are embarrassed when he does it in front of others. Yet his behaviors are accepted as part of the whole. His people seem to live with it; I could perceive no hostility.

The gist of the financial presentation was "Our revenues for Macintosh products are slowly declining and our profit is declining. This is not a good situation, we need to get it turned around, and we want to work with you in trying to find a way."

"We can do that," I responded. "But if you want to see volume grow and profits grow on your Macintosh products, you're going to have to improve the user experience." They knew perfectly well what I was talk-ing about. With the operating speeds of computers today, users expect any routine action to happen instantaneously. Yet for a Mac user, launching a Microsoft product was an exercise in patience. To open Microsoft Excel on a Macintosh took twenty seconds. Word 6.0 was even worse, something like thirty-five seconds, which for a user can seem like an eternity. However, on a Windows machine, users could launch in the blink of an eye.

"Our performance on the Mac can't be better because of the way we write our applications. We do the Windows version first, then base the Mac version on that. So the Mac versions will never be as optimized as the Windows versions."

I said to Bill, "If that approach isn't giving you the results you want, maybe you should consider a different approach."

Gates said, "Our new version of the Internet Explorer is just coming out, and you're right—that's exactly what we did. The first version of Internet Explorer was actually done on the Mac before it was done in Windows." He insisted that the Mac version was an excellent product and would provide an outstanding user experience.

"I'm glad to hear it," I said. *I would see it before I would believe it.* "Now you need to go back and do the same for Word and Excel and PowerPoint."

Gates is an impressively tough negotiator, so I pressed the point. "I want to have a gentlemen's agreement that you'll go back and clean up these performance problems." I held my breath.

Bill said, "I agree with you. You're right and we at Microsoft have to go in and clean up the applications."

This is going well, I thought. A sudden quiet descended while a deli-catessen lunch was wheeled in and set up. For several moments no one seemed to have anything to say. Then over lunch, between bites, we explored other areas of possible cooperation on a fairly technical level—such as whether there was some cooperation we could do with object linking and imbedding.

At the time, although Java was coming up, it wasn't yet really important and was never mentioned—a sign of how fast the landscape changes in high tech. If the meeting had been held a mere twelve weeks later, Java would have been spotlighted as a prime topic.

Bill Gates is not just brilliant and exceedingly intelligent, he's a walking encyclopedia of technology—his own and everybody else's. His understanding and retention of detailed facts at every level of a subject is as impressive as his personal involvement with decisions being made in every corner of his vast company. He spews facts, figures, and company-wide specifics with a thoroughness and ease that escapes most CEOs.

If Bill has a sense of humor, it doesn't show in typically responsive smiles. Talking business is serious stuff to him and thoroughly absorbs his mind. If you try to crack a joke or put a jocular twist on an idea, Bill either lets it whiz by or really just doesn't get it. I was finding it difficult to add levity to the dealings; so far, I had not found a way to reach out for a friendly connection to this man.

Although top-level meetings, often pompously referred to as summit meetings, tend to be formal, I've always believed the adage that companies don't do business with other companies, people do business with people. I prefer that CEOs know each other as people, build a relationship, and seal agreements with trust. Bill and I could begin building that trust if our friendship could somehow get started.

It's a standard practice of mine in a meeting of this kind to arrange for some one-on-one time. Two o'clock came, and I suggested to Bill that he and I do a recap together. He readily agreed, and we moved across the hall. His ground floor office, because of a long glass wall, permits anyone walking down the corridor to get a glimpse of Microsoft's chairman at work. I wondered if he had some specific reason for that showcase style; it would be interesting to get his thinking on that. I never did.

The office where Bill Gates spends long working days surprised me on a number of scores. It's reasonably large—perhaps twice the size of mine. I thought, *What did you expect to find as the office of the richest man in America?* The all-green garden just outside filtered shimmering light into his space and helped to reflect the luster of quality to the fairly unremarkable dark wood office pieces, so different from the blond wood finishes that are de rigueur for office furniture today. Altogether, a mixture of modesty with brave new world.

Once he's explained his position, Bill sincerely can't understand why you don't want to do what he wants you to. On the other hand, when you make the point that the best deals are "I'll scratch your back, you scratch mine," he's ready with a list of reasons and excuses why that isn't possible in this case. I rapidly came to realize that Bill found it difficult to meet another person halfway.

He wanted me to embrace his Internet Explorer, the Microsoft Internet browser that competes with the Netscape product. And, of course, he wanted one or two other things, as well. Making a commitment on the Internet Explorer was, I thought, not the best choice for Apple. Nonetheless, I was willing, if he would make a commitment in return to produce Mac versions of Microsoft Office contemporaneously with the Windows releases. He refused to even consider it.

I said, "Bill, you're asking me to do this, this, and this, and I'm agreeing to do it all, but I ask you only one thing, to release Office applications for the Mac at the same time as for Windows."

"I can't make that commitment," he said.

He wasn't bending. I told him, "There's only one answer that's acceptable to me and that's yes. And I want to know what I have to do to get it."

I wouldn't make the commitments that Bill wanted because he was unwilling to give anything significant in return; I was prepared to wait him out. In the end, Gates would win by waiting *me* out.

At the end of the day, summing up, Bill and I agreed on action items. My action item for Apple would be to try to help him increase sales of his Mac applications.

His action item would be to find a way to improve the user experience of Microsoft Office on the Mac.

And this would turn out to be one of the warmest conversations I would have with Bill Gates until my phone conversation with him the day after I was fired from Apple.

8

Done Well If Done Quickly—
SHAPING MY OWN
EXECUTIVE TEAM

The 100-day report card, inadvertently initiated by me in that offhand remark at the first press conference back in February, had taken on a life of its own, becoming almost a feeding frenzy among reporters. Articles began appearing about "What is Gil going to say?" Even some editorial writers speculated in print on how Apple was faring and what plans I might announce. I was bedazzled by the fact that so many people were interested.

Even people who use Windows machines, people who have never owned any shares of Apple stock, who never use the term "high tech," seem to follow the ups and downs of Apple Computer with fascination. Steve Jobs had, like Walt Disney, created an institution. What is it about some companies that elevate them to a stratum above and beyond the average business? Disney, Levi Strauss, and Apple are more than companies—they have become American *icons*. Their brand logos are treasured by some with the zeal of loyalty to the American flag, and their company cultures are looked on with the righteousness of the national Constitution.

All of which may go some little way to explain the fervor. The advance hype drew an audience to make any politician green with envy—a standing-room-only crowd of 4,000 in the auditorium, augmented by what I believe was the first "Webcast," putting my words out over the Internet moment by moment as I spoke, to a worldwide audience of 600,000. One photographer captured the tone of the live audience in a single frame showing a bearded, ponytailed young man in a T-shirt sitting on the floor in lotus position, gazing expectantly up at me on stage.

On day 100, May 13, I fervently disagreed with whoever it was who said the only thing worse than being talked about is not being talked about. My fear was that, no matter what I said or how well I said it, the excessive buildup had raised expectations that I could not possibly satisfy. And there were additional knots in my stomach over the still unclear futures for Copland, Pippin, and the Newton; my uncertainties about all three would soon be resolved, but on that auspicious day, I would be perceived as indecisive.

The speech went better than I had a right to expect, and the media coverage was comfortably balanced—leaning toward factual reporting of what I said rather than emotionally charged reporting on how the crowd responded, how confident I seemed, and the rest. About the strongest criticism was disdain at my wearing a suit and tie to address an informally attired group. As a matter of fact, I was, as never before in my life, making statements by what I chose to wear. The suit had been a conscious decision intended to show that Apple, for all its maverick reputation and style, was absolutely serious about business.

The superficial values of modern life afflict us whether we choose to conform or reject. I've come to realize the extent to which we're caught up in a world of images: clothes, cars, and the rest, rather than anything more substantive, are the symbols by which we're often judged. A few months later at MacWorld, I would be ridiculed for wearing a casual, high-fashion collarless shirt.

At the end of the 100-day speech, I closed with the words, "This is Apple. Expect the impossible," and then, in the space of a heartbeat, the stunning new TV commercial based on the about-to-be released hit movie starring Tom Cruise, *Mission: Impossible,* rolled on the two huge screens.

Reporter Jim Carlton was not always gentle with me in the pages of the *Wall Street Journal,* but in his book *Apple,* he described the event in generous terms: "For a speech that had had one of the biggest media buildups in corporate history, the consensus among developers was that Amelio had performed as best he could, given Apple's dire circumstances."

I had arranged to do a cover story in *USA Today*, to be certain my 100-day messages were clearly conveyed, without filtering, in at least one place. Much to the chagrin of Apple's PR staff, I did not permit them to get involved—this was my own message, with no PR spin. The heart of the story was my view that I "would have liked to find quick-fix solutions . . . but management by impulse is a temptation we need to resist."

At the end of this milestone day, driving home, I reminded myself of what Winston Churchill had said during very difficult times: "Success is never final."

o   o   o

Although I had adopted the mantra of patience in regard to the members of my executive team, I was to experience a painful turnover in the ranks. At an off-site in April, Dave Nagel pulled me aside and said, "Gil, I've got bad news for you. I've accepted a job running AT&T Labs." I admired and liked Dave, and although I wished he had attacked our problems more aggressively, I was genuinely sorry he had chosen to leave; I had hoped to infuse his knowledge and style with my emphasis on productivity, focus, and process.

Dave was already managing Apple's R&D when I was at National Semiconductor. We had worked together in my effort to get National chips designed into new Apple products. As my guest at a 49ers football game, we had a chance to chat in a relaxed setting and I came away that day realizing what a perceptive and discerning man Dave is. At Apple, I reached out to him in hopes we could work closely together. Unlike some of the other people on the executive team, Dave's behavior toward me was always respectful, patient, and thoughtful. Eventually I came to be disappointed in his follow-through, but had been sure we could, over time, develop a tightly-knit, focused working style. I'm regretful now that I didn't move more rapidly toward convincing Dave to participate more fully.

Another executive would take Dave's position, but there are few who could take Dave's place. Others would soon leave and I would accept their departure in a resigned way, but I considered Dave's departure a significant loss to Apple.

o   o   o

Walking around R&D, I had been shown some impressive technology and products. But in a long-standing Apple tradition, many of the engineers were simply following their own dreams, working on what they felt was "cool." Nice work if you can get it, but not what the company needed.

Then some e-mail messages from employees alerted me to an undeclared war: Sales people would only agree to introduce technologies or products they had independently decided they could sell. The disconnect between sales and engineering had become an accepted fact of life around the company.

In time, I would come to see this disconnect as more the rule than the exception—a technology the R&D guys were enthusiastically working on would turn out to be a product the salespeople had absolutely no intention of selling.

Apple had no process in place to cross this chasm. And I was told there had never been one. Where was the voice to say, "Hey, you R&D folks, you've got to quit work on this because it's not a supported product." Nor could I identify the voice within sales that would say, "Okay, you sales folks, you've got to sell this because it represents a strategic position for the company."

In my experience, problems like this can't come to light when managers protect their own domains. Overlaps and conflicts cause progress delays and become expense holes, and must be ferreted out. It would be months before I fully recognized the breakdown between R&D and sales, but once recognized, it wasn't hard to fix. In the reorganization just ahead, I would create separate product divisions, each with its own divisional general manager. These GMs, committed to the success of their own products, would guarantee they had buy-in from sales.

o   o   o

The head of a large organization, like the captain of a large ship, bears a lion's share of the responsibility for everything that happens. Given the impossibility of knowing everything that's going on, it's a responsibility not easy to live up to. But with experience, you gain a sense of telltale clues. I was becoming aware that something was amiss in the sales channels, and began to focus on the events of the previous Christmas.

At home, Christmastime brings the cheery tradition of stocking-stuffing for the children. At Apple during the Christmas season, there turned out to be an unscrupulous tradition called "stuffing the channel." It's a practice by no means unique to Apple but familiar to many people in sales. Curiously, sales people are victims as well as benefactors.

It became all too painfully clear that at Apple the business of channel stuffing happened often, but was played out at Christmas with a vengeance.

The trouble begins innocently enough when executive management, based in part on forecasts from lower-level managers, decides on a revenue number and communicates it as the plan for the next quarter—"We need to do $2.4 billion," or whatever. Everyone down the line is expected to say, "We'll do it!" even if they don't as yet know how. The $2.4 billion target is parceled out to geographies, regions, districts, or however the sales organization is grouped, ending with each salesperson being handed a quota.

For sales reps, the quota is everything. Their bonuses and future successes, all the measures that count to the upwardly mobile, are hinged on making or exceeding the assigned quota. But at Apple, there was a time-honored third alternative: If you couldn't make or exceed, you could try to get the playing rules changed. Time after time, as the end of the quarter neared, the salespeople would begin to panic and offer up the complaint, "There isn't a prayer I'll make my number." The sales VP, captain of their team, would respond by leaning on the CEO: "The competition has lowered their prices, we're no longer price competitive, we can't make our revenue goal for the company unless we lower prices."

In my opinion, this is the ultimate cop-out; I've heard it too often in my career. "It's not our fault, it's your fault—you priced the stuff too high." In other companies, I just held a hard line. Apple had its own traditions. The company would drop its prices, causing gross margins to shrivel. This had become a behavior pattern repeated so many times that the channel partners—the big retail chains—knew exactly what was going to happen. Neither dull nor stupid, they had learned the pattern and counted on its being repeated. Early in the quarter, they did little in the way of display, promotion, or advertising. They just waited and smiled knowingly to themselves, until, voilà—the phone call would come from their sales rep announcing the expected price reduction.

In his book *Talking Straight*, Lee Iacocca describes uncovering just the same practice at Chrysler, which left that company the constant legacy of a vast lot filled with many thousands of unsold new cars rusting in the Detroit snowy winters and rainy, windy summers.

But Apple's make-your-numbers story doesn't end there. Even price reductions weren't enough. The step beyond price cutting is to stuff the channel. A customer is told, "Look, they signed the region up for $300 million for the quarter; we've only done $120 million. I'm going to be in deep trouble with my boss. You guys have got to do your share and take another $50 million worth of product." In some cases, an Apple sales executive would call a major wholesaler himself to make this demand. There was an implied threat hanging in the air during a call like this: If we can't count on you to help meet our quotas, we may have to look for some other chain to sell to instead of you. (Later, of course, declining Mac sales would weaken this leverage. By February 1998, retail sales had fallen so far that Apple pulled the plug and stopped selling hardware to all major retail channel partners except CompUSA.)

It's not widely known that retail stores made 30, 40 even 50 percent more per box selling a Macintosh than selling a Windows machine. Even though the volumes are smaller, Apple had provided a lucrative profit no authorized retailer wanted to lose.

So the chains buy product they don't need that's going to sit on the shelf for weeks, and Apple starts the next quarter with essentially zero orders coming in because of all that unsold product already in the stores. And when the company gets to the middle of *that* quarter, the same panic sets in, and the cycle repeats itself.

But there's an even more reprehensible variation of channel stuffing, saved for emergencies when everybody is saying, "No, I just can't handle any more product from you." In the crisis scenario, the message to the retailer escalates to "Take the product, and after the beginning of next quarter, *you can send it back*"!

It's understandable that sales reps are willing participants in this ugly game, because the richest part of their income is from the bonus for achieving or exceeding quota—an amount that can be larger than their base salary.

One executive formerly on Jim Buckley's immediate team and now at another computer company remembers being "dumbfounded" by the staff meetings. "Seventy-five to ninety percent of the time was spent discussing what could be done to maximize the managers' year-end bonuses. And Jim would lead the discussion into details of how the channels could be stuffed—right out in the open. At one time I thought Buckley and his sales squads really cared about the company. I had a rude awakening when I realized how much of it was about stuffing their own pockets."

Buckley's strategy showed loyalty to his sales team, but stuffing the channel, although a common practice, is selling out your company instead of selling products. When I told Jim that the channel stuffing days were at an end, I probably turned our relationship over to the undertaker.

o   o   o

Another facet of this whole unfortunate setup hurt us in a different way: In our forecasts of what products to build and in what quantity, we were relying heavily on our salespeople, who are the front lines of any company, in closest contact with the customer. But the salespeople weren't talking to the consumers, the actual buyers of the product. They were talking only to *their* customers, the channel folks.

The reality is that the retailers don't spend a nanosecond doing real, honest-to-God primary market research. Their forecasts for the future are based on what they've been experiencing in the immediate past. If the last two or three quarters have been successful, they will forecast a successful future. It's all based on emotion and seat of the pants, so when the market is changing, the channel never sees it coming. In my experience, they've never correctly called a turn.

Yet Apple not only asked the channel partners what we should expect for the upcoming quarters, the company actually used their information as the basis of forecasting sales and planning production. No wonder we had been doing such a rotten job.

o   o   o

I perceived that Apple's problems with the channel partners had another thorn, because it created a situation that invited kickbacks. With these huge amounts of money involved, there were just too many opportunities for people to be tempted.

Suppose Apple drops prices by $100 per computer. The channel partners might pass only a portion of this reduction through to the customer, knowing that with this particular type of product, a price drop doesn't result in much of a sales boost. Most of the $100 would then go into their own company's pocket. When Apple was selling about 1 million machines a quarter, a $100 price drop meant some $100 million in discounts—a *lot* of money. Nobody would be very surprised if the partners were interested in showing their appreciation to the tune of a few hundred thousand dollars or so in gifts, paid vacation trips, or cash to the salespeople who had helped make their improved profits happen.

I gave direct orders to the senior sales executives that the price cutting and channel stuffing were never to be repeated, and assigned Fred Anderson to monitor for me and insure those orders were obeyed. Nonetheless, Apple executives continued in their attempts to change my mind, and looked for new ways to get around me. I was forced to insist, "No, we're not going to cut the price; no, we're not going to cut the price." Despite the continuing pressure, I remained determined to break this self-defeating pattern and call a halt to the dysfunctional relationships with our channel partners. It's an understandably human temptation to return to the "just one more time" rationalization of the dieter, the drinker, the gambler; I was determined to hold fast to my unpopular resolve for the sake of the company's survival, and caved in only once, the following Christmas, and then only because we had no attractive consumer products and were desperate for a boost in sales.

o   o   o

Many highly innovative companies are like artists whose greatness seems an integral part of their wildness. In trying to bring the people of Apple to a heightened sense of reality, would I destroy the very qualities that made the company great? I would continue to struggle over the issue of what to do with this dynamic but dysfunctional company.

Instead of being recognized as problems, a lot of the dysfunctions at Apple were called traditions and held up as virtues.

For example, throughout the years a manager who had a bright idea just created a new department and did it without bothering to find out, or maybe without even caring, that there already was another department elsewhere in the company that was chartered to do the same thing. This ebullient spirit reflected no care about supporting company goals, no sense of financial responsibility or wasted effort. One admires the intent while wondering at the innocence.

Sure, there's probably not a company of any size in existence without a certain degree of overlapping functions and responsibilities . . . but in my book, Apple took the prize for groups with conflicting and overlapping functions, doing essentially the same damn thing.

A very visible example was the one I had pointed out at the employee communications meeting, that a Macintosh user had to go through at least three control panels to set up a connection to another computer for exchanging messages or files—all because three different organizations had each created one of those panels, and none of the three had bothered to coordinate with the others.

And then there was the marketing—or rather the lack of it. Sometime in the past, Apple product managers had convinced the leadership that a centralized marketing operation couldn't understand their separate, individual needs or represent the products properly. So for years, each product group in Apple had its own marketing organization, as did engineering, the geographies, and so on. On the day I first drove into the parking garage as CEO, the company had twenty-two separate marketing organizations. (Maybe more. The organization was so chaotic that no one was ever sure of the exact number.) As this information unfolded I kept hearing a little voice in my head that said, "Surprise!"

A group called the Marketing Council, made up of representatives from each of the twenty-two official marketing groups, met regularly with the goal of providing coordination. A noble motive, but I knew the difficulty of getting twenty-two different representatives to agree on anything, and wondered how long it must take the group to share even the basic information.

I found it fascinating but frustrating that the people of Apple genuinely wanted to move ahead. Yet the culture of collaboration just wasn't there; it didn't exist. With what seemed to me few exceptions, the people lacked a tradition—perhaps even a respect—for accomplishing work with others and simply didn't know how to go about working together, relying on each other, or being part of a team.

All this stumbling over each other described not just the working levels, but all the way up the corporate structure. I told one friend, "Apple is more balkanized than any company I have ever seen—it's divided into principalities each ruled over by a top executive who, like the prince of a city-state, could do damn well what they wanted without anyone else's by-your-leave."

Manager John Osborne said he heard this ownership attitude even in the language Apple people used. "It's very ownership oriented. They'll say, 'Oh, that's Satjiv's group,' or 'That's Bob Calderoni's group.'" Expanding on what he'd been hearing from me, John said that Apple people needed to talk not about "This function will reside in his group," but rather "This function will be *led* out of his group."

Perhaps one of the best ways to lose friends is to give them advice for their own good. The same can be said of trying to change people. Over the years, I've given enough speeches on the subject of change to write a book on that alone, but the bottom line in my thinking has evolved to the single fact that any effort to induce people to *change* is largely futile and painful for all involved. People can accept new ideas, but imposing new behaviors brings out the worst in us all. (The idea that progress in an organization comes out through changing the organization, not through attempting to change the people, is a theme that runs through *Lasting Change,* coauthor Bill Simon's book with Rob Lebow on how values can be brought into the corporate workplace.)

In the early months, I had tried to simplify and root out the redundancies, and convince the executive team that collaboration was the new order of the day. I was also hoping we would achieve some of this through a reorganization, which would be necessary as we went to a thinner and more economical company. The idea of a reorg had been one of the foundation concepts built into the strategic White Paper in April.

The restructuring we announced on May 31 would involve the painful business of telling a lot of talented and worthy employees that we couldn't afford them anymore—an action that always gnaws at the conscience. Three thousand people, out of a workforce of sixteen thousand, would be laid off.

For the new organization, I created a product-oriented structure, a different division for each product family—high-end desktop Macs, low-end desktop Macs, PowerBooks. And there were also to be geographical divisions for North America, Asia, and so on. Each organization would be given a very clear charter, so that the ridiculous and wasteful duplication would finally be stopped.

As could be predicted, the employees were fearful of the coming organizational changes. Giving people cause to feel uncertain about their futures needed to be balanced against the reality that the company had become unworkable, and changes had to be made. Although I think most of the Apple people were willing to give the new structure a try, I hadn't yet been able to change the atmosphere around the company enough to spread a lasting feeling of reassurance and hope. I was too busy with the *crucial* matters and letting some of the merely *urgent* issues take second billing.

○   ○   ○

I believed Apple people would quickly perceive how effectively the new organization plan would be in eliminating the dysfunctional empires within the company. By giving the divisions a narrower focus and restricting their autonomy, we would create a company where employees could work together instead of conspiring against each other. It was a radical change for some people and I knew it would cause fiery reactions from the few who had enjoyed freewheeling and unbridled power for too long, to the detriment of the company.

Jim Buckley's role would be downsized; he would retain his title as president of Apple Americas and would retain most of his authority, but would report to me through a new chief operating officer, a position I was creating to handle the day-to-day operations.

The sales organization needed major restructuring and reorganizing. Would Jim be willing to move it forward?

This wasn't a time to beat around the bush, it was a time to speak directly. Shortly before the reorganization was announced, Jim Buckley heard the plans from me personally. "I need some help managing this company. I've decided to create a new position of chief operating officer, and one of his responsibilities will include authority over the worldwide sales organization. You will be reporting to him rather than to me, and I want your support on this."

Jim was so offended by this change in structure that he responded, "It's not going to work."

"What's not going to work, Jim?"

"I need to report directly to the CEO."

I asked, "What is it about this change that's not going to work?"

Buckley is an uncommonly smooth communicator, but seemed unable to formulate an appropriate answer. I can only assume that he was upset by what he was hearing, unhappy with what would be perceived by others as a demotion, and it had rendered him unable to make a meaningful reply. This highly capable, articulate man never gave me any valid reason. He merely kept repeating, "I just don't think it's going to work."

The conversation was going nowhere, and Jim was intractable. It was clear he was not willing to accept the role I had described.

So I brought our nonconversation to a close: "Jim, you won't sign up for this. I think it's best we part company."

He got up and walked out, looking stunned and frustrated, without another word.

Reports appeared in the papers not long after announcing that Jim Buckley had decided to resign.

o   o   o

Faced with an important decision to make, I ask for advice from a lot of people. I immediately began asking for recommendations of who could best replace Jim Buckley. One name kept coming up, and it seemed at first an unlikely and improbable choice—someone who had been with Apple only a few years, a sales manager with a background in, of all things, the banking industry, currently head of all Apple Asian operations out of our offices in Hong Kong. Her name was Robin Abrams, and I had had the chance of observing her work close up.

In order to get firsthand input about what was going on in our markets around the world and at the same time get a "read" on some of Apple's managers assigned to outposts on other continents, I had held a review session in Cupertino when I first took over.

Robin came across as very self-assured, no-nonsense, a clear thinker. She struck me as a "say it like it is" kind of manager, a style I much prefer. And she was both well prepared and knowledgeable. I was impressed at the time and that image held fast in my memory.

Of all the people I had talked to, Abrams had made the greatest impression. I then inquired about her from others and the only reservation I heard was that she seemed to like living in Hong Kong so much, she might be reluctant to leave.

In fact, she was delighted to be offered the job and accepted enthusiastically. Robin proved to be an excellent choice and served the company well, though the episode ended badly. But that's a story for much later.

o   o   o

The first new management-team member I had installed on arriving at Apple was the man for whom I created the post of chief administrative officer and who I counted on for handling many of the day-to-day activities. Educated as an engineer, George Scalise worked for a number of high-tech companies and had done a stint as CEO of Maxtor Corporation, a computer storage-devices company that is now part of the South Korean firm Hyundai Group.

Following his departure from Maxtor, George became part of my corporate team at National Semiconductor, using a firm disciplined style to keep people on track and projects moving forward. I brought him into Apple to do the same, with the responsibility of handling routine issues that might distract me from more urgent matters. Reporting to George were Personnel, Legal, External Relations (which in this case meant licensing), Developer Relations, Facilities, and Communications. But beyond these, George was very protective of my time and often assumed the responsibility of deciding which people would be granted access to the CEO. Because of his firm hand, he was frequently referred to as "Gil's hatchet man," a description he didn't entirely deserve. The position that George accepted was not an easy one; it's the nature of that position. Both George and I knew in advance what the risks would be.

o   o   o

When a CEO gets trapped into solving short-term problems and dealing with emergencies, no one is steering, no one is looking toward the horizon to warn of icebergs or clear-water opportunities. As never before in my career, I had come to feel a victim of the everyday. I needed a chief operating officer who would be assigned responsibilities for overseeing routine operations, freeing me to focus on the vital issues dealing with the company's survival and eventual success.

Heading Apple's European office was the formidably capable executive Marco Landi, who held the title of president, Apple Europe, Middle East and Africa. Michael Spindler had identified his talents while Landi was still at Texas Instruments and convinced him to add structure and direction to Apple's European operations, which were in a sorry state of disorder. The report I got was that Landi had done an impressive job at centralizing operations, bringing discipline and cutting costs. And sales were reasonably strong under Marco's leadership. The company could take some pride in our European stature, and the three-year projection at the time was that revenues would increase from under $2 billion to the $5 billion level.

Shakespeare could have been referring to Silicon Valley when he wrote "So are they all, all ambitious men." And Landi is an ambitious man, which is not meant as a criticism but rather as a quality to be admired. I especially liked the fact that he was never ashamed of his ambition, but let it show for anyone to see.

When he had first heard rumors that Spindler would soon leave, Marco, I was informed, had begun a campaign to be considered for the position of CEO. The board discussed the possibility, but judged him basically a salesman and manager—doing a fine job for Apple in Europe, but the CEO job certainly required more all-around experience.

Once I was named CEO, Landi, without breaking stride, began to lobby for the as yet nonexistent position of chief operating officer—COO. He worked to insure his selection by presenting his qualifications to George Scalise in a convincing way. With his background as a salesman, Marco could be very persuasive. He reiterated his history at Texas Instruments, his experiences in Asia where he had managed the TI factories, and underscored his diverse experience and success for Apple. George eventually became convinced that Marco would be the best COO I could find.

My first reaction was, "No." But I did see him as a possibility for being appointed to a new position as head of worldwide sales, as a way of lassoing the out-of-control behaviors of the sales force that had been allowed under Buckley.

George became an intense campaigner on behalf of Marco. This put me in a situation that Bill Simon and I had written about in *Profit from Experience*, when your ears are telling you one thing and your gut is telling you another. Everything George was telling me sounded right . . . yet I had a gnawing feeling in the pit of my stomach that there was something about this fellow that spelled trouble ahead.

George tried to convince me to let him make the decision, but I insisted we bring Landi in from Europe. I wanted to size him up myself and decided to be exceedingly frank and up front.

"I'm still very skeptical about choosing you for this job. I don't know you that well, but I've heard you have a reputation for emotional flare-ups that hurt people." Even that was putting it politely, because what I had heard described his behaviors as out of control. Was Landi really someone who demeans people in extreme ways that would cause lasting pain?

My questions didn't phase him. "I know I have that reputation. It came up when I was at TI, and now I really understand the issues." He insisted that he had changed and with grace blamed his volatility on his Mediterranean heritage. "I just get excited sometimes, but I can rise above this and it won't be a problem."

"I'd be putting a lot of trust in you," I said. "As COO, you'd have to be able to carry my message forward. You'd have to be extremely loyal to me from day one. I can't be sitting here looking over your shoulder all the time to check up on your behavior. The whole purpose of a COO is to relieve some of the pressures that are channeled to the CEO."

He said, "Give me six months on the job. If that time rolls around and you think you've made a mistake, just tell me and I will politely step aside and leave."

A very effective sales technique, the equivalent of "Try this used car for two weeks, and if you don't like it, you can bring it back."

Only the foolish can be won over by a charming smile and a personable manner; I had one of my foolish days when Marco came to town. But in addition, time was on Landi's side: I was feeling highly pressured to get someone into the COO position. I had seriously thought about two candidates from outside the company, but was warned that giving the job to a non-Apple person would require much longer for them to get up to speed. I remembered the months without a CFO and worried that by hesitating I would waste too much time, spend too much effort, and let precious hours slide by. George talked me through my misgivings and so Marco Landi was chosen. . . .

And I regretted the decision almost from the first day. I had made a serious mistake, one that became increasingly obvious as time went by. I would have reason to regret not listening to my own instincts.

9

Nerd's Labors
Lost and Found—
SOLID GUIDELINES FOR
NEW PRODUCTS

Expecting explosions between people is facing the hard truth of reality. Exploding products is an altogether different magnitude of challenge. Our experience in this area was a disconcerting episode, and a dark secret within the company.

A Macintosh user in Japan reported a problem that he handled in an elegantly quiet way, a style unknown to most American consumers. We received word from the Apple office in Japan that the customer had reported "a little difficulty" with the desktop computer he had bought from us, and was requesting help with the cost of repair.

Not repair of his computer, repair of his *home*.

A team from Apple Japan had gone to take a look and found that, for reasons nobody would ever be able to explain, the monitor on this man's Power Macintosh had exploded, demolishing half the room— walls, ceiling, furniture. Fortunately he wasn't at the keyboard at the time of the explosion. Apple Japan wisely decided to protect the company's image: They paid for the repairs, replaced the computer, and expressed sincere appreciation to this considerate customer for coming to us instead of running to the media. One can only shudder at the legal battles that would have been fought over this situation had it happened in the United States. And the field day the media would have had.

While thankfully no other customer ever had a similar problem, this was just one more piece of evidence that there were major problems in much of our product line. Warranty complaints ran as high as 10 percent during one period and that, of course, delivers the clearest possible message about product quality.

o   o   o

There were, blessedly, no other monitor explosions, but product quality headaches throughout the line reached such an intense level that we finally had to contemplate a massive recall.

The PowerBook 5300 laptop was plagued with a series of difficulties, each a very small issue from an engineering standpoint, but enough from a customer's perspective to make the units virtually unusable.

On the power cord, the pin that plugs into the back of the computer was too thin, and unprotected, so that it snapped off easily, leaving the owner unable to recharge the battery or run from AC power. And the bezel—the piece of plastic that holds the screen in place in the cover of the laptop—easily came loose, exposing the fragile edge of the screen. Apple products, long respected for quality, were letting customers down and seriously damaging the company image.

By spring, when the full magnitude of the quality problems in the PowerBook finally came into focus, we realized we had an absolute bloody disaster on our hands. But when does bad become bad enough? When do you decide a problem has grown so serious that you need to initiate a recall? I don't know what guideline others follow, but my measure is "the rule of two": If the situation is twice as bad as the industry experience, then it's time to take action. Probably 20 to 25 percent of the new products we were selling were being reported as defective in one way or another, well above the industry standard.

On May 10 I ordered production of the 5300 to stop, and set into action a process for massive recall. My view of the best approach was to commit enough resources to conquer the problem thoroughly and quickly; I wanted it behind us in short order. This was a fire I insisted be put out in record time. Teams of engineers were organized to come up with solutions, vendors were pressured to produce the materials we needed almost overnight, and we set up a special line at the plant, staffed by teams of people who had been put through a crash course in correcting the faults.

The attitude of our dealers presented a serious problem—understandable but difficult. If they returned for repair the inventory in their stock, they wouldn't have product to sell. Many of them simply ignored the recall, preferring to sell the faulty units even though each sale might produce a disgruntled customer. Short-range thinking to say the least, but, in my view, also an inconsiderate practice.

Although my target was to have the entire situation cleared up in a month, it would take four ... with frustration and embarrassment as constant companions. The PowerBook 5300 was probably the worst product Apple ever produced, but, because production had been shut down, the 5300s completely sold out a month before the new Power-Book 1400 was ready to ship. The business proposition took a heavy hit because Apple would have to function for an entire month without laptop computers to sell.

o   o   o

Amidst all the gloom and bad news bearing down in June, *Mission: Impossible* reached the screens and gave Apple people something to be proud of. The Tom Cruise film was a big box-office winner and told the world that the good guys use Macintosh, presumably leaving the baddies to use Windows. The Apple tie-ins gave reason to smile in all the gloom and bad news.

An overnight blockbuster movie, Apple received more positive feedback from this marketing effort than from almost any other promotion or advertising. It didn't give people the reason they needed to buy a Mac, but for Macintosh owners, it let them justify their Mac decision to others.

Did it boost our PowerBook sales? It probably did, in the following quarter. But for helping us sell product, the film couldn't have opened at a worse time: It was during the period when the laptop line was shut down, before the new product began to ship, and after available supplies had already sold out. Buyers motivated by the movie arrived at their local store to find the shelves empty.

o   o   o

While we were in this terrible limbo state of having no laptops to sell, actress Whoopi Goldberg came calling.

"I promised my nephew I'd buy him a laptop," Whoopi said over the phone. "He says it has to be an Apple PowerBook."

"And you can't find one."

"Right. I had people out checking every store and nobody had any."

I said, "No problem, I'll send you one."

"No way," Whoopi said, "I'm not asking for a gift. I want to pay for it—just help me get one."

I pictured Whoopi telling the story at Hollywood dinner parties of how she had called the CEO of Apple, who had personally arranged to get her a PowerBook—great PR, the kind you can't even buy.

I had a unit specially checked to make sure it was perfect and shipped out to be sold to her through her local dealer, so we could keep good faith with the dealer community. Her nephew had his new Power-Book within forty-eight hours.

The morning after, my modest office was transformed into a hot-house with the largest bouquet of flowers I had ever seen, a display of blooms that seemed six feet high and were surely wider than the door-way to my office, leaving little room for me to squeeze by to my desk. A tiny card dangled from a sunflower. In her own hand she had written, "Thank you, thank you, thank you. Whoopi Goldberg." I never did fig-ure out how the delivery service got that many flowers up the elevator, through the corridors, and into my office.

o   o   o

Why were we doing such a rotten job in product quality? I may not have followed up on how flowers were brought into my office, but I sure wanted to know what had caused the sorry state in the quality level of Apple products. We had approximately 650 people throughout the company working on quality, we were budgeting vast amounts of money to be the quality leader, and it felt like we couldn't ship a single product that wasn't plagued by either design or quality difficulties.

Companies normally expect to spend about 1 or 2 percent on quality. Not even counting warranty costs, we were spending on aver-age 5 or 6 percent.

The reason, I eventually discovered, was another long-time flaw in company behavior. Some Apple engineers, instead of finishing a product and turning it over to the quality people to get their blessings on it, were operating with the attitude, "Why put in all that effort? We'll just get it pretty far along, and then let the Quality guys find the problems." So they were in the habit of turning their projects over to Quality prematurely. Quality would find flaws and send the product back. The engineers would do some more work, and send it over to Quality again. And it would continue bouncing back and forth until it appeared to be ready. Meanwhile the product launch date had probably been missed, and the release version likely had some lingering problems that slipped by undetected in the under-the-gun pressure to get the product to market.

Quality is supposed to be designed in by the engineers to begin with, not painfully arrived by the expedient of fixing whatever problems you manage to discover. And the proper task of the quality organization is to confirm the fact that the engineers have successfully created a trouble-free product. The Quality troops had become a kind of secondary engineering organization, and had bloomed in size because of it. At budget time, everyone would complain that the quality organization was getting too much money. As bizarre as this sounds, the biggest complainers would be the engineering people, sounding off that there were too many folks assigned to quality.

I would soon lean on the engineers, trying to implant a new perspective on all quality issues. "You should be *embarrassed* when the quality organization rejects a product you've submitted. Your goal should be to use them so that they help you build a bullet-proof product. When it's completed, all they should need to do is put their stamp of approval on it." Eventually there would be signs of headway, but this better system took hold only very gradually.

o   o   o

I soon came to realize that another major part of the existing quality problem could be laid at the feet of operations. Fred Forsyth, the man in charge who held the title of senior VP, worldwide operations, was responsible for the manufacturing plant, for production control, and for all system-level engineering work in creating the products once the design decisions had been made. So from the time a design was approved, it was up to him to manage every step from creating the products to building them to getting them out the door. This even included the purchasing of about $7.5 billion dollars worth of goods a year for the company and the factories. No wonder most of the people in Apple worked for Fred Forsyth!

I found Fred a very loyal, hard worker, imbued with an unusual intensity about doing the best he could for the company. And he had some very strong people working for him, like Jim McCluney, who ran the manufacturing plants, and Mike Campi, running procurement. But although Fred had the right attitudes, he lacked the management skills to follow through on his ideas. He understood what needed to be done, he even articulated what needed to be done, yet when it came to seeing it actually happen in the trenches, he was simply not effective enough. For example, I had visited the Apple plant in Singapore and found the place dirty, badly organized, and with too much manual handling to permit turning out quality boards. I had told Forsyth, "You've got a disaster waiting to happen." He agreed that changes were needed, but nothing ever happened.

Shifting responsibilities in the reorg, I tapped Jim McCluney to step up as the head of worldwide manufacturing, including procurement, as a way of getting some fresh thinking about how we built our products.

But quality needed a much better focus. I decided we would pull together quality people from every part of the company and group them into a single quality organization that could bring to bear a unified, coordinated effort. And to fill the newly-created position of quality czar, I jump-promoted a man who didn't fit the typical Apple mold, but could offer talents I believed were sorely needed. Mike Connor is a disciplined, precise, and proud West Point graduate who would not cut corners. Mike would not report directly to me, but I told him, "My door is open to you. Come see me whenever you're having a problem. You are handling a matter of highest priority and we need to do it right."

Then I announced to everyone, "This company will not ship a product until it has Mike's approval."

Mike had his detractors, but he was a strong choice for the job. By serving as a bridge between engineering and manufacturing through his effective team-building skills, he was able to get the efforts of these organizations aligned. Before Apple and I parted company, the product quality had bounced back and surpassed its former high level. In a mere eight months, Apple led the industry in every quality category.

o   o   o

Quality problems weren't the only reason for declining sales and revenues. A finger could be pointed at the sodden procedures we were following for product planning. I was startled to find that at Apple, new products were decided on not through a careful planning process but in a verbal boxing ring where contestants threw heated arguments instead of uppercuts and jabs.

The marketing people produced a familiar kind of planning paper called an MRD, or marketing requirements document, which describes the features they want in a particular new product. They hand this over to the hardware people. But it seems that at Apple, the ingrained culture allowed the hardware people to ignore any features and requirements they didn't like. The marketing folks would get heated up over having their input demeaned, and the two sides would have at each other.

One might naturally expect that John Sculley or Michael Spindler would have been the ones to buy off on every proposed new project. After all, each product decision means gearing up to spend a few hundred million dollars. But at Apple, the CEO was never included in the basic product decision-making process, with an occasional exception like the Newton, which was a Sculley pet project. When it came to day-to-day product decisions, Apple had its own way of deciding without the CEO.

A lot of consumers looking for their first computer, we had learned, didn't like the flat, pizza-box style design of what we called our "entry-level" machines. People seemed to think that *real* computers came in the "tower" design—the box that stands upright. That had led to the machine we called the Performa 6400.

The 6400 was supposed to be available for the back-to-school season, which would have meant ready by the end of June, but wasn't ready until September. On top of that, it was missing some important features. And where the overall trend in the industry had been for prices to keep inching lower, Apple ignored that and the plan was to release a product that would be substantially higher priced than the comparable products in the Windows world.

Overall the desktop product line was lackluster, and something of a yawn. Clearly, the hardware product development teams just weren't getting the job done. I decided we needed to go do some stellar machines on the high end, machines that would make people sit up and take notice, computers that would serve to polish the reputation of the whole Macintosh product line.

The R&D people working on high-end computers were told, "Go create some truly high performance machines." They set their sights on models that would run at 250 and 300 megahertz. If we got it right, we would have the fastest desktop computers on the market. Could they do it, and on time?

∘　∘　∘

The creation of a "Customer Value Council," comprised of about sixteen or seventeen people representing all aspects of the company, and chaired by me, would put some order into product planning. The council's charter was to look at new product ideas, represent the point of view of the customer, and decide which projects would be funded and which wouldn't. They were to be the conscience of the customer, guiding decisions that would be more responsive to customer input.

The first time we got this group together, they all looked around the room and wondered, "What are we doing here?" It took several months of meetings before they finally got the hang of it, before the light bulb went on. But once we got it cranking, it became an effective body, and the results began to show in a new line of PowerBooks and new desktop machines delivering what customers wanted.

It still amazes me to this day that Apple people were astonished the CEO would want to "get his hands dirty" by being involved in decisions on new product strategy. There are very few issues more important to a company than its product decisions. I can't figure out why any CEO would leave these essential product decisions entirely to other people.

∘　∘　∘

I had included the term "DSUV"—Distinctly Superior User Value—in the original strategy White Paper, adapting it from a similar term I had used at National Semiconductor and hoping it would become a catch-phrase to express the product values that the company needed to embrace.

I explained DSUV by saying, "There are five things we have to do as well or better than anyone else." Those five were: User experience—which had to do with stability of the system, product quality, and quality of the service and support. Performance—which would have to be equal to or better than our competitors. Connectivity—meaning how easily the machines could be hooked up into networks, which are becoming the dominant feature of the way people use computers. Industrial design—keeping alive the Steve Jobs ideal of producing great-looking machines. And compatibility—which meant accepting that we lived in a world dominated by another standard, and doing whatever we had to do so that our customers wouldn't be frozen out when they chose a Mac.

If the company could intensely focus on these five areas, with the goal of being best-in-class in each area, I was sure a comeback and transformation of Apple would be achieved. At the end of my tenure we were only partway there, but the people of Apple had made enormous strides in each of these areas.

With some trepidation, I tapped Cynthia Cannady to run the task force on DSUV—trepidation because this was a highly unusual choice: Cynthia is an attorney, and in the business world, attorneys are not typically asked to do this sort of business assignment. But I had sized her up early on as a high-energy person. Cynthia became convinced that the DSUV concept would be the salvation of the company, and she turned into a single-minded evangelist. That plus her articulate skill as a seasoned lawyer made her very effective as the task force leader.

o   o   o

On connectivity, I didn't succeed in doing all of what I wanted.

For people working in publishing, it's not uncommon to have a 200 megabyte image file. When they want to transfer a file like that to someone else's computer, they need a fast transfer technology. Apple was supplying an outmoded, ten-year-old network technology operating at 10 megahertz, while the rest of the computer world was moving on to 100 megahertz speeds. An Apple user could start a file transfer, go to lunch, and come back to find the computer still struggling to complete the job. Too damn slow.

So a lot of people in publishing had come up with a work-around that might be called the "traveling hard-drive method." They would have a cart with an external hard disk. To do a transfer, the designer would locate the cart and roll it in. He'd shut down his computer, connect the hard drive on the cart to the desktop machine, and power everything back up. Then do the transfer. Shut everything down. Wheel the cart to the computer that the file needed to go to. Shut that computer down and connect the drive. Turn everything back on and do the transfer.

In the year and half I was with the company, Apple never managed to move up to the faster 100 megahertz technology despite my best efforts. Whenever I would bring it up, the answer was always, "Well, we can't do it now, but we'll do it in the next model." I tried to coerce our people into it—I'd stand in front of them, tell this hard-drive-on-a-cart story, and tell them that what we were giving customers was an embarrassment to Apple. I emphasized that the whole rest of the world was already migrating to the faster standard. The heads would nod, they would agree in principle, and then go back to the problems they were working on that day and forget all about connectivity.

o o o

I also had an issue with the fact that computers are downright ugly. My gut told me that a more attractive machine would sell better. I was and still am convinced that if companies made computers more attractive, more people would want them, and the manufacturers could also get a slightly better price. That still remains my unproven hypothesis.

I found it highly frustrating that I could not get the Apple engineers to appreciate design. They were so tuned in to performance, features, operating systems, and speed that I had more pushback on industrial design than any of the other DSUVs, which frankly surprises me to this day, since Apple R&D is filled with engineers and engineering managers like Jonathon Ive—among the most visual and creative people I've ever met.

o o o

But we did manage to achieve a few design successes. One triumph of industrial design made me face once again that no matter how well intentioned the individuals, still the culture of Apple was certain to get in the way. In this case the issue was over a project code-named Spartacus.

Spartacus was a ground-breaking concept, a desktop computer conceived as a flat screen on a handsome curved-metal stand, with all the works built into an extremely narrow space behind the screen. No tower, no pizza box—from all external appearances, no processing box at all. Just a flat screen. This was industrial design fit to be displayed at the Museum of Modern Art along with the Eames chair, the Wagenfeld glass teapot, and the handsome Richard Sapper "Tizio" desk lamp.

I discovered that Spartacus had been languishing in the R&D lab for three years. There were people within Apple who saw it as a prestige computer that could bring the company much attention and acclaim, and others who considered it a waste of resources. Those opposed had attempted to do whatever was necessary to smother it. At the forefront of that negative force were the people in sales, who maintained, "We don't think the customers want it, there's no demand for it, so we won't sell it." And they were committed to making sure Spartacus wouldn't happen.

They weren't the only ones. Several times during the course of that program, various organizations with their own agendas tried to sabotage it, even knowing that the CEO had given orders to bring it to market.

A senior engineering executive fought with me over the product on the grounds that it would never succeed because there was only room for a comparatively slow CD-ROM drive—4X instead of 12X. In my view, most customers would never notice the difference. Yet as far as this executive was concerned, it couldn't support the fastest CD-ROM, therefore the product wouldn't pass muster and had to be killed. That narrow focus again—I couldn't seem to get most of the execs to see a bigger picture, to consider the image impact that this stunning design could bring to Apple.

Even after Spartacus finally cracked its way out of the shell, manufacturing tried to kill it. Once again, the culture of principalities was at work, doing pretty much what they wanted without any real recognition that there was a leader, a company, a plan, all pointing in one direction.

In the end, Spartacus would reach the market—somewhat late, but intact—despite the roadblocks. By then, other companies were ready to introduce similar machines; once again Apple had given away its marketing lead.

º   º   º

A June executive off-site was coming up. I called Bill Gates and said, "I'm getting my people together. You've talked about the fact that we don't have the kind of connection between the two companies that you'd like. Why don't you be my guest speaker for the evening. And," I added, "you can say whatever you like—no restrictions."

He agreed without hesitation, even though he would have to fly down, spend the time with us, and fly back that same night.

Sometimes a way to build a connection with someone is to ask them to do something for you. This was one of two occasions when I asked Bill Gates if he would give a presentation for me, and I also extended or relayed invitations to give speeches. He accepted all four times—even though I think he does not take well to standing at a podium.

The appointed day for the off-site was June 18. I held one of my regular strategy retreats with about twenty-five of the top Apple people at the Fairmont Hotel in San Jose, talking about the issues facing the company as a way of trying to build a consensus and get an informed view on where we were going. Bill arrived late in the afternoon, joined us for dinner at the hotel, and gave a straight-from-the-shoulder talk. Then it was time for questions.

Larry Tessler is one of the most brilliant computer scientists on the planet. Slight of build, with gray hair and an easy smile, he's a born teacher. At the company, he was one of a very small, select number of people holding the title of "Apple Fellow," which is akin to being a University Professor at Harvard: The Fellows are not limited to working in a particular department or area and have no specific assignment beyond thinking about the future and helping to shape the future technology of the company. Their value to Apple is measured in their ability to help define and develop the basis for the company's next-generation products. But Larry's long-term, absolute loyalty and devotion to Apple had built within him an enormous animosity for Microsoft; I wouldn't be surprised if Tessler was the one who first applied the "Darth Vader" and "evil empire" metaphors to Bill and his company.

In his penetrating style, Larry targeted Bill Gates with a series of questions designed to put Bill on the spot; Bill would visibly tense every time Larry got started. A typical Tessler question went something like, "How can you stand there and say you want to see us build together when we want your support on OpenDoc and you're refusing to make it happen!" More an accusation than a question, but Bill adeptly heard the request at the heart of the attack.

That session was emotionally charged, but I was disappointed at the lack of lasting carryover by the Apple executives. Bill had come bearing an olive branch. I had hoped our people would respond positively and see an opportunity to build a better relationship with his company. Instead, most of the executives snapped back to their original positions and that was that.

I later told the Apple people, "The only way Apple can survive is by developing a positive relationship with Microsoft. The truth of the matter is that Microsoft has won the war. If tomorrow morning Gates announced that he was no longer supporting Microsoft Office on the Mac, we'd lose customers in droves. It would be a crippling blow to us."

What we needed to do, I said, was to figure out where we wanted to align our interests and where we want to consciously choose to be different. "Just to be different for the hell of it is not good business sense."

I didn't know it at the time, but somewhere out there in Silicon Valley, Steve Jobs was saying the same thing.

o　o　o

The pressures in a CEO's office extend to everyone on the immediate staff. My executive assistant Cindy Simms was living in San Francisco, commuting the hour-plus each way, and working until 8:00 or 9:00 every night. She had somehow managed to do this same job for Michael Spindler, who had earned his nickname "The Diesel" for his nonstop, nearly round-the-clock working habits.

But the long hours and constant pressure had taken their toll. Despite Cindy's professionalism and always pleasant manner, underneath she was near the breaking point. Her cat fell ill; Cindy couldn't find the time nor muster the energy to get the cat to the vet.

The cat died. Cindy quit, and I couldn't blame her.

10

A Piece of Work—
LAUNCHING THE QUEST FOR A NEW OPERATING SYSTEM

In June I finally managed to resolve one of the issues that had been on my original urgent list, a problem that had begun building a long time earlier: cash.

Back in 1995, while still a "Johnny come lately" to Apple's board, I had been fascinated by the contrasts in behavior and style between CEO Michael Spindler and Joe Graziano, who was the company's chief financial officer and also a board member.

Graziano showed up at board sessions dressed in the very high style of a *GQ* ad; Michael's persona was in sharp contrast and carried the Apple nonconformist attitude of "to hell with how I look." Joe sported the image of a prosperous clotheshorse, while Michael gave the impression he'd forgotten a barber's appointment and had tossed on a shirt that had just come out of a suitcase. The images conveyed that Michael was preoccupied with important business concerns while Joe didn't have a care in the world. At the time, I simply noted the differences as superficial observations and drew no conclusion. Shirts and shoes would turn into important clues to a series of misbehaviors the board was soon to witness.

Why was it that when it came time for financial reports, Joe, the

CFO, didn't do them? He'd have Jeanne Seeley present the controller perspective, and Mary Ann Cusenza would be asked to handle the treasury aspects. Joe would calmly listen with the detachment of a board member as though the reports weren't a personal reflection on him. At first I chalked up this laid back behavior to an individual management style, but gradually came to conclude that Joe was in fact not on top of the financial details and wasn't fulfilling his CFO responsibilities. He had, I decided, virtually retired, leaving Apple's financial duties to his direct reports.

It became all too obvious to me that Graziano's preferred function for Apple was as a board member and that his primary interest was the money he'd make from stock options when the company was sold. He was pushing for a sale to IBM, I now believe, because he expected they would pay the heftiest price. I thought, *No wonder he's holding on to the CFO title. No wonder he keeps pushing so hard to get the company acquired by IBM.*

A confrontation between Joe and Michael had been slowly building ever since IBM had said no to buying Apple, a response that Joe was sure Michael had engineered.

The fireworks went off at our October 1995 board session. We were to meet in Austin, Texas, giving the board a chance to visit a critical facility for Apple, where the finance operations and the customer support call center are located, along with a number of other key functions. Holding the meeting there would give Austin employees a sense of visibility. Once again I arranged to hitch a ride with Mike Markkula in his aircraft.

The meeting in Austin had only just begun when Graziano thought it an opportune time to set off his personal eruption. Basically Joe's message to the board was along the lines of, "It's me or Michael, this place isn't big enough for both of us."

An ultimatum like this is almost unheard of—it's simply not done, especially not by a CFO whose recent performance left so much to be desired. I looked around the room, and the expressions told me that the others saw Joe's ultimatum the same way I did: insubordination.

Mike Markkula asked Joe and Michael to step out of the room. For such a dramatic moment, it all happened very quickly. After little discussion, with virtually nothing offered in support of Joe despite his years of service to the company, the group was ready to vote in about five minutes, and the vote was unanimous: Joseph Graziano would no longer be the CFO of Apple Computer.

Graziano had bet it all on one roll of the dice and they came up craps. He looked devastated.

The episode revealed to me a truth I had never before recognized. Any company executive who is also a board member is essentially reporting to two bosses at the same time—holding divided loyalties between the board and the CEO. Michael Spindler the CEO was Joe Graziano's boss, but Michael Spindler the board member was just one more equal when it came time for a vote. In a real sense, since he could vote with the other board members against Michael, Joe had, I realized, begun to picture himself as Michael's boss, and essentially stopped reporting to him. It didn't require a soothsayer to predict the explosion we had just witnessed.

In the late afternoon, when the meeting finished, Joe had still another surprise: He asked Mike Markkula for a ride back to the Bay Area. Mike graciously invited him to join us.

So there we were at 39,000 feet in the night sky—the company's chairman; me, a director at the time; and the just-ousted CFO whose impeccable packaging was sadly frayed at the edges. A stilted conversation limped along between us, and unfortunately, but I suppose inevitably, landed onto the subject of what had just happened. Joe needed to talk about it, so we let him. But the more he talked, the more upset he became, and the more upset he became, the more irrational were his words. And then the enormous pent-up frustration spilled over into a flood of tears.

I was sure that Joe had carefully prepared what he was going to do at the Austin meeting. He must have convinced himself of being right and figured at least a fifty-fifty chance of succeeding. But he had failed miserably, to a degree he must not even have foreseen as a possibility. Though he didn't lack for money, he was flying home to no job, no income, and, it must have seemed, a clouded future. He was leaving Apple, the company he loved, and leaving it in disgrace. This must have felt like a major tragedy—hence the unexpected tears.

Mike and I knew that we shouldn't be seeing this. I thought, *There goes any chance of our saving any piece of a friendship. He won't want to be around the people who witnessed this display of emotion.*

In hopes of engaging his mind and calming him, I tried to redirect the conversation away from what was tearing him apart. "Joe, I've been thinking about buying a sports car. What do you think, can you give me a recommendation?"

Ever the sports car aficionado, he began to pull himself together. "How much do you have in mind to spend? What sort of car would you want?" He began to contrast two Ferraris, the Testerosa and the 355 Spider. Markkula joined in, and we managed to fill the rest of the flight talking about cars and other innocuous subjects.

By the time we landed in San Jose, Mike and I were pleased to see Joe emotionally stabilized. He generously offered to follow up by sending me some sports car literature, and warmly expressed regret: "I'm really going to miss seeing you at the board meetings." Then he added, "I really enjoyed our relationship." I wished him well, meant it, and felt some sadness over the fact that our burgeoning friendship would not continue to evolve.

As soon as I became CEO, Joe began to take verbal potshots at me, using any reporter looking for a negative quote as a conduit for revenge. He had a way of sounding as if he were an authority on company happenings when the blunt truth was that Joe Graziano didn't know what he was talking about. He hadn't been in touch with the facts even when he was CFO, and he surely didn't know what had been going on inside the company during my tenure.

o   o   o

Banker Lew Coleman had rendered enormous service in my first weeks on the job by evaluating our financial situation ("desperate") and suggesting the best way to raise sorely needed cash ("convertible debentures"). He had then gone back to his new position as a top banking executive at Montgomery Securities.

A convertible debenture is a financial instrument whereby the company borrows money on which it pays interest for a given period of time, typically three years. At the end of the period, the company has a choice of actions, but usually pays off the investors with shares of stock, *converting* their money from one form of investment—interest-bearing loan—into another—shares of stock. If the company's stock has appreciated significantly in the interim, the debentures can turn out to be highly profitable for investors.

After Lew, I had turned to Larry Howell, who I had first met when he was at Goldman Sachs. A tall, well-composed man with the steady gaze of the self-assured, and as classy as they come, Larry had been an enormous help with my first convertible debt instruments for National Semiconductor. Since that time, although he claimed to have retired, those of us who really knew him interpreted that to mean that he preferred to act as a consultant.

It's highly unorthodox for a major company to use an outside consultant on internal financial matters, but the situation I was facing required immediate concentrated and expert attention. Larry responded to my request for help by offering to take a risk: "If we have any success, you can pay me whatever you think it's worth—$1,000, $100,000, it will be up to you." We moved forward on a handshake. (He would in the end not receive any pay for his efforts; despite that, we still remain friends.)

I needed Larry's guidance on how to proceed and details on what we could expect the cost to be, and I needed him to guide us through the steps of the highly complex transaction. Within a month, Larry had readied the needed documents to submit to the investment banking houses for bids. His patient answers to my never-ending list of questions tested even Larry's heroic spirit.

When I went to the board for an okay, audit committee chairman Bernie Goldstein flew into orbit. He insisted we not move forward until Fred Anderson, our already hired but not yet reported CFO, would arrive and lend his support to the plan.

The essence of taking risks is based on the courage to face disappointment and even despair. I felt both, plus a heavy sprinkling of pure frustration thrown in.

"Bernie," I said, "just thirty days ago we were talking about how desperate we are for money. I've now come up with a plan to raise the money and you want to slow me down."

I verbally drew an image of the situation and included all the panic of an Edvard Munch scene. They needed to be reminded that the company could be out of money in three months. And here was Bernie telling me to wait for a month until Fred showed up before taking any action. I tried to convince the board we couldn't afford to wait, because it would take weeks to put together a transaction like the one we needed.

The board squared off to do battle. I support the old nugget, "If you want to kill a worthy idea, refer it to a committee." It was a useless battle; I finally gave in and said, "Okay, if that's what the board wants, I'll wait till Fred shows up."

When I finally got the green light, in April, it was to proceed with exactly the terms I had proposed to the board weeks earlier—seeking to sell convertible debentures, to be handled by the firm that had been my first choice all along, Goldman Sachs.

We had calculated that a cash infusion of $575 million would keep Apple afloat until the bloated inventory from Christmas past could be unloaded and fresh revenues would start flowing in.

The procedure for an offering like this is for the CEO and some other key members of management to go out on a road show in hopes of drumming up bidders. You go from city to city and hotel to hotel giving presentations on the company, and then people from your investment banking firm stand up and say, "You just heard the story of the company, here are the terms and conditions of the convertible instrument they are offering. If you're interested, we'll give you a prospectus. Bids are due by such and such a date."

A typical road show can take up to three weeks of travel around the country and might also include Canada and sometimes Europe, as well. The process of selling to audiences of retirement-fund and investment-fund managers, plus a scattering of wealthy individuals who like to play in this game, can be as grueling as a music group's tour around the world or a major political campaign.

On the assigned date, you take a deep breath and open the bids. If there isn't enough demand, the date can be extended and the executive team, if they aren't thoroughly worn out, can try again.

I had been concerned about Fred Anderson and me being away from the day-to-day operations of a very needy Apple. When the time came to start talking about the road show, I said, "I don't see any way that Fred and I, or any other member of the management team, can afford to be out on the road for three weeks, or even two."

The Goldman people were shocked. "Gil, a road show is how it's done. Surely you knew that."

I asked, "Is there another way—a way that won't take us out of the office during this critical period?"

Leading the Goldman Sachs team was the enormously capable Eff Martin, head of their West Coast branch, based in San Francisco. Eff didn't flinch at my request and came back soon after with an idea: "There may be one possibility. When the markets close for the day, you get on the phone and do a giant conference call. We tell everyone before the call it has to do with a financial offering that Apple is coming out with."

He explained how it would work: "Gil, you'll make your speech on the telephone, and they ask their questions. When you get through, they place their orders—same as on the road show, but . . . "

At this point, he dropped the capper: ". . . the difference is that the whole deal has to be wrapped up before the market opens the next morning."

He was a bold man who ate the first oyster.

I said, "Play me the downside."

Eff said, "We've never before done an offering with a Fortune 500 company this way." And his eyebrows arched up as he added, "Nobody has—it's simply never been done. And it will probably be a one-shot."

If it didn't work—if there weren't many offers—the financial community would know that Apple had made the offering and failed. Eff warned it was unlikely the same package could then be taken on a road show. My brain translated his words into *Apple will face insolvency before we could have another chance to try again.*

The conference-call approach was a very long shot. Once again, I would hear from perennial pessimist Bernie Goldstein, who said, "Forget it. I've been on Wall Street for thirty years and there's no way you'll be able to make this deal happen." The pessimist may be right in the long haul, but the optimist has a better time during the run. Still, I give Bernie credit: He was willing to let us try.

Even the Goldman people, who are paid to be optimistic, were highly nervous about whether we could really pull this off. But they did some careful exploring of the transaction and reported that there might be enough customers to support doing the offering this offbeat way.

And so, with Eff supplying the fuel, we powered up. He practically moved in to insure that we would work on the preparations—around the clock if that's was what it would take. Fred Anderson and Eff crafted the financial aspects of the presentation while I designed the strategic messages. It was fundamental that I open the kimono to a full accounting of what I had discovered at Apple before describing what I would do to make the company healthy again and why I was optimistic about the shape Apple would be in three years from then, when the debentures could be called.

Talk about grueling reviews and rehearsals: "No, you can't say it that way, it's stronger this way." Eff and his team coached us until we emphasized only the cogent points, in the right tone and with a style that would project positively across telephone connections.

What Goldman had set up was very different from other financial auctions, where one fund says, "I'll take 40 million," and another says, "I'll take 25 million." We were warned to expect responses like: "I'll take so much, but only if you'll give me *these* terms." Some bidders could be expected to ask for special interest rates, or greater equity, or some custom-designed settlement condition. It would then be up to us to decide which orders would be best for Apple to accept. The investment bankers advise, but Fred Anderson would have to make the final decisions on behalf of Apple.

And that's why, on Monday, June 3, Fred and I flew to Washington, D.C., and checked into the Willard Hotel, near the White House, where I had a suite with an adjoining office, all done in the style of traditional elegance that makes the Willard a favorite. The decision to stage the conference call from the East Coast had been made for many practical reasons, in particular because Fred would have to work through the night and into the following morning to evaluate bids with the Goldman team.

The situation called for a pep talk to override the palpable anxiety in the room, but all I could conjure up were a few casual and rather inane remarks. I couldn't coax my eyes away from the hands of my watch as they ticked toward four o'clock. During the period when the audience was being "seated" via telephone connection, I experienced a greater adrenaline rush than I had ever suffered on any platform or at any podium. A great deal was at stake, yet I felt highly confident, even exhilarated, and not the least bit fatigued at having just flown in from California.

How well the session got started is left in my mind as a blank, black screen. I know I spoke first about the situation I had found and the strategies we had designed for future success, and then introduced Fred.

After that, Fred and I answered questions for another half hour or so.

I thought we put on a powerful presentation. But powerful enough? It might be several hours before we would begin to have an answer. The wait promised to be excruciating.

A good sign: The first responses began coming in about an hour after the call was over, and continued coming. But I knew that letting that raise my spirits would risk the potential of an even greater disappointment. Fred, Eff, and the Goldman people worked frantically against the 10:00 A.M. deadline. I escaped for a few hours of troubled sleep, with Bernie Goldstein's words of warning hanging over me.

I woke in the morning to learn the offering had been oversubscribed.

It felt as though I had lost twenty pounds. Though eager to break the welcome news to the board, I first had to concentrate on what the oversubscription had triggered: a standard provision, curiously called a "green shoe," which says that you agree to sell as much as 15 percent more of the debentures than you had offered. We had sold not only the $575 million we had put on the table, but an additional $86 million, as well. What's more, we didn't have to give any ground on the terms and the bidders agreed on the interest rate we were offering—6.5 percent, which was, incredibly, almost two full points below prime.

Goldman Sachs had done a sensational job. They deserved a full measure of our appreciation. Eff Martin, whose wisdom and experience served as both inspiration and anchor, won the admiration of everyone who worked with him; here is a man who represents a rare combination of strong judgment and professional know-how.

Much later, I would meet and discuss the telephone road show with a Wall Street guru and learn that in his view our success was primarily due to the fact that the investment community still remembered the first convertible debenture deal I had offered at National, which had not only paid a very respectable interest but had also returned roughly triple the investment because the company had done so well in the interim.

When Bernie and I met at our next board meeting, I didn't have a chance to get a word out. He rushed over to me and said, "I'm really sorry I caused all that hullabaloo. Was I ever wrong! You guys amaze me. My hat is off to you." And he admitted, "I thought I really knew Wall Street after all those years, but you read it better than I did."

Responding positively to his sportsmanlike remark, I said, "It worked out fine. The money came through before the situation got desperate. We should be rejoicing that we got it in time." And, I couldn't help adding, "Bernie, we've all got to understand this unusual industry we're in. If we don't respond to changes and stay ready to move forward at lightning speeds, we'll put ourselves out of business."

So Apple made Wall Street history. Fred and I and the entire team had done something that had never been done before—in one night, we raised a ton of money, money that represented Apple's survival . . . at least for the time being.

Steve Jobs is not one to give credit to other people. But much later, he was to pay me a singular compliment. Referring to selling the debentures that had brought the company enough money to survive, he told me, "I certainly couldn't have done that and I don't know of anyone who could have, other than you. It was one of the more brilliant business maneuvers I've ever seen." That compliment coming from Steve, who doesn't give many, made me feel very good.

But it was, I think, the only compliment I ever got from him.

∘ ∘ ∘

In July, Dave Nagel's replacement joined the company. Ellen Hancock was my first choice for the job, which now carried the title "executive vice president of engineering and chief technology officer."

Ellen was something of a legend in high technology, having reached a higher level in the IBM bureaucracy than any other woman, and her willingness to join Apple was considered a definite win in the industry.

I had originally met Ellen in 1984, in the aftermath of an episode with IBM while I was at Rockwell. A group within IBM—one that did not include Ellen—wanted Rockwell to build a modem for them to sell under their own label. Although this is a standard industry practice, the problem was that IBM had specified a 1,200 bit-per-second design. We knew the industry was about to transition to 2,400 bit-per-second units. Besides, the case they showed us was too boxy and bulky—a rotten example of industrial design. For their own good and ours, we tried to get them to understand. "We've done a lot of work in the modem business, we think we're knowledgeable about this market, and what you're proposing here doesn't add up." We said, respectfully, "This unit won't sell."

The IBM managers on the project said, "We don't need your advice. Are you going to make this product or should we go somewhere else?"

"You're the customer," I said. "We'll make what you want, but we need a guarantee." It seemed highly likely to us they weren't going to sell more than a fraction of the number they ordered, so we put a cancellation penalty of $5 million in the deal if they didn't wind up buying the full quantity.

Unfortunately, we were right; they ordered 53,000 units, sold about 5,000, and tried to cancel the contract. Then suddenly the three managers vanished into the night, and Ellen Hancock was brought in to pick up the pieces. She called, we got together, and I said, "There's a penalty involved if the order is canceled, and I'm going to have to ask you for it because we've got that much money in the project."

Being the honorable person Ellen is, she fought for us and arranged for all invoices to be paid. Based on her ability to restore our confidence, we went on to produce some other successful products for IBM with Ellen's input. She wasn't just smart; unlike some other IBM managers I had met, Ellen really knew what she was talking about and could get down into the nitty-gritty technical level. She was proud of that capability and only later would that pride of technical detail get her into some hot water with Steve Jobs. I was neither intimidated nor put off by her strength. Typically at IBM you meet a spokesperson from the business side rather than a technical manager. Ellen was the first IBM senior manager I had met who was also a brilliant engineer. And blessed with business know-how, as well.

Eventually I hired her into National Semiconductor as the executive running the technical side of the business. Eight months later, my departure for Apple left her to deal with a new boss who apparently did not share my acceptance of women managers. That made her available again, I had the opening that Dave Nagel had left, and it looked like a perfect fit. Ellen was the second executive I brought over from National Semiconductor. There were others I would have liked to hire but had chosen not to take the predator's route.

o   o   o

The leader who expects to know where the next challenge will come from is not tuned into reality. I had always been sure my feet were solidly planted until all at once some strange items began to appear on my Worry List—a kind of list I had never before needed. My experience with the people and problems of this singular company turned into a complicated series of wrestling matches with some of the most prominent, well-muscled title holders of the high-tech ring.

I had told close associates soon after I arrived that it looked like new problems would continue turning up to bite me in the backside for at least six months. On Ellen Hancock's very first day, she heard the message from me that "We need to focus on doing something about the operating system." She understood the importance to Apple of updating this vital software that tells the computer what to do when the mouse is moved, a keyboard key is pressed, or a "quit" command is given.

All high-tech groupies know that the biggest operating-system evolution of recent years was the introduction of Windows 95 by Microsoft. It enabled millions of IBM-clone users to take a giant leap toward a more intuitive, Mac-like environment. Apple loyalists defensively pasted stickers onto their car bumpers that boasted "Windows 95 = Macintosh 89."

But for all the bragging, Apple's operating system suffered from problems tracing back to the company's transition to the newer generation PowerPC machines. The Mac OS had been modified to accommodate the changeover, but so that it would run on older machines as well, the new software version depended heavily on "emulation"—which works by making hot new software behave like its clunky predecessor—and was so unstable that users worldwide were suffering the frustration of frequent crashes and lockups. A series of quick fixes would have overcome the problems, which would have been chalked up to the customary new software bugs and soon forgotten. Instead, Apple engineering managers shifted most of their programmers to work on the next-generation operating system, Copland, figuring that its release would erase the need to fix the problems in the earlier version. The System 7 problems had never been fixed and weren't being addressed as a top priority.

∘   ∘   ∘

From day one, I had asked for reports on the status and promise of all the leading development projects and perceived the need to personally get involved with Copland from very early on. I was impressed by the engineers who were infusing great features and capabilities into the software, but I intuitively sensed a thunderstorm building just over the horizon. The project was already a full year behind schedule and racing backwards toward being *two* years behind. Wasn't there a tune, "Promises, Promises"? I had the urge to make it the new Apple R&D theme song.

Copland was still just a collection of separate pieces, each being worked on by a different team, with what appeared to be an innocent expectation that it would all somehow miraculously come together. But it wasn't and it wouldn't, and it didn't take a genius to see that reality.

Because the software group had almost stopped work on upgrades to the current operating system, the company was dead in its tracks, without a single OS upgrade in the pipeline that could be counted on.

Beyond Copland was to be a still more advanced OS, code-named Gershwin. It was to include the powerful memory protection we needed so badly, insuring that if one program misbehaved, the rest would still keep running—users wouldn't have to restart the computer.

But no engineering had been done on Gershwin, nobody had done even one damn thing to define it. At that point Gershwin was little more than a name and a dream out there somewhere in Tomorrowland.

I had Ellen put a team back to work on upgrades to System 7, building in some of the features that had been designed for Copland—improving its stability while also trying to breathe more life into it. At least we could let customers and critics see some signs of progress.

But I was unconvinced that our R&D organization could create a valid next-generation operating system.

The OS problem seemed glued near the top of my Worry List and possible solutions became the storyline of my nightmares. Every train of thought kept leading me back to the same conclusion: The answer would have to come from outside.

So we started looking around for an existing OS that might transform nightmares into dreams. It was like a teenager who wants a car—we needed an outstanding OS for Apple and we needed it *now*. My search team proposed four outside possibilities; despite my skepticism, I let them put an Apple internal solution on the list for practical, political, and people reasons—even though I was convinced it would not fly.

o　o　o

"Bill, how about Microsoft helping to create a Mac operating system based on NT?" On the other end of the phone line, Bill Gates erupted with enthusiasm. Clearly he wanted this. Judging by his response, he wanted it badly.

An OS deal with Microsoft would undoubtedly be among the least popular decisions an Apple CEO could make. But ask the question, "How do we create the greatest opportunity to have the Mac platform accepted by the broad base of users?" and the leading answer had to be, "By giving it an operating system that would be a variation of Windows NT."

Unpopular or not, it was a course that had to be explored.

In that August phone call, Gates bubbled, "I'll put hundreds of people on the project."

As usual, Bill Gates the ultimate negotiator wanted some advantages in return. Even though Windows 95 had been a dramatic improvement over Windows 3.1, the user experience was still sorely inferior to the intuitive interface of the Macintosh. He candidly admitted it: "Apple is really good at the human interface, much better than we are."

And he effectively argued, "We're really good at a lot of other things. An Apple OS based on Windows NT will let Apple stay focused on the interface and not have to worry about the core technology."

As part of a package, Bill wanted to move ahead on the intellectual property deal that the two of us had been negotiating.

I still had three more OS options to consider, but about Microsoft, I concluded that if they created a new Mac operating system based on Windows, Bill Gates would be canonizing us. He'd be saying to computer users worldwide, "It's acceptable to Microsoft if you use the Mac operating system." That clearly would have made a huge difference to the 90-odd percent of people who work on Windows computers. It would have *legitimized* the Macintosh. So the Microsoft option carried a compelling reason to decide in their favor.

But what Bill Gates didn't say was, "This will make my ownership of the PC world complete. It will anoint me King of the Universe."

Yes, in many ways this would be selling out Apple and lots of other Microsoft competitors. I would be vilified by scores of people, alienating the Mac community, which is so anti-Microsoft. The press would label it "doing a deal with the devil." Yet if it turned out to be the best option . . . I was prepared to go for it and bear the brunt.

Bill Gates was on the phone every day trying to sell me on the idea of our adopting the Windows foundation. From my perspective, the primary roadblock was not political but technological. Converting Windows NT into a Macintosh operating system would require scaling some very tall mountains, with pinnacles where no one had ever gone before.

A group of Microsoft engineers and business people flew down to meet with Apple counterparts. The e-mail report sent to me by one Apple senior software engineer typified what I so admired about Apple people. With long blond hair to his shoulders, Wayne Meretsky looked the part of a Steve Jobs's "pirate" from the early days, but was able to provide an analysis not only of the technical hurdles that had been discussed, but the business aspects of the Microsoft offering, as well.

The Microsoft people were extremely cordial, he wrote, and seemed willing to bend over backwards to do a deal. But they had come empty-handed with regard to the major technical objection, a problem over an obscure but crucial concept called "endian-ness." Meretsky found the solutions they proposed to be sophomoric at best.

Yet Bill kept insisting, "These are no big deal, we solve problems like this every day." He sounded as if he had personally dug into the technical intricacies and was convinced it could really be done. He said, "Your engineers are telling you it's impossible because they don't want to accept a Microsoft option." This is another instance where I asked Ellen Hancock to sort out the truth for me, and she reported the problem was real—it was Bill Gates who was glossing over the reality.

And in time I came to believe that even if it were possible, it would mean a sacrifice of performance. We already had some performance disadvantages to Windows, and I didn't want to aggravate that. Still, his confidence was infectious.

Bill Gates is not an easy man to say no to. But it was becoming clear during our discussions that a Microsoft OS shouldn't be considered a slam dunk for Apple. I needed to keep Bill on the hook while we looked elsewhere and investigated other options.

◦   ◦   ◦

Jean-Louis Gassée grew up in France, drifted into the computer industry as a terrific engineer, and scrambled to the top of the Apple organization in France, turning it into the most successful of any Apple overseas operations. John Sculley, recognizing the talent, imported Jean-Louis to lead Apple's product development efforts in Cupertino.

Theirs was a tempestuous working relationship. Though they didn't descend to the shouting matches that some writers have reported, things weren't exactly smooth between Sculley and the hot-tempered Frenchman, who considered his research organization sacrosanct and didn't appreciate a technology neophyte like John Sculley trying to tell him what to do.

Sculley believed that in an industry with product cycles already down to a year and plummeting, no high-tech company could survive without a steady stream of new products that customers would perceive as dazzling if not groundbreaking. But getting new products out of the lab was not Jean-Louis's greatest strength. Their conflict became part of Silicon Valley legend.

In the end, Sculley fired Jean-Louis. Unfortunately for Apple, Gassée took with him some of the company's best software engineers, and used some of his Apple-acquired wealth to start Be, Inc. (Sculley's respect and admiration for Gassée was later enhanced when, it's said, Jean-Louis secretly warned him that Steve Jobs was trying to talk the board into ousting him as CEO, allowing Sculley to prepare for the showdown that ended in the board firing Jobs.)

Jean-Louis continued pouring his own money into Be, spent an inordinate amount of time courting and winning other investors, impressed the media with product announcements, but by late 1997, after being in business for six years, had still never moved the first unit of product out his door or taken in any sales revenue. The joke went around in Silicon Valley that "Be had never been."

Along the way, though, Jean-Louis's very capable programming team, including engineers like the brilliant Bob Herold, who had followed him from Apple, had developed a respectable backbone in their operating system, BeOS.

Jean-Louis maintained strong contacts within Apple and became aware of a possibility for Be when he got wind of Apple's OS predicament. He came on strong about the virtues of the BeOS as a solution for us, proclaiming it to be "up and running," "ready now," with a new, complete version "just weeks away."

At the same time, I was getting warnings about dealing with Be, advice once again based on personality rather than technology. Given the players, if I struck off the list everybody with a powerful, dominating personality, I would have had no one left to deal with. Jean-Louis had technology worth considering, and I was determined that we should move forward on considering the BeOS option.

11

Crack of Doom—
DYSFUNCTIONAL
RELATIONSHIPS

Some people relax over a newspaper or magazine. I could no longer find much pleasure that way—Apple and its CEO were featured too often, and even the computer magazines for Macintosh fanatics were frequently critical, while other periodicals seemed to be having a field day sharpening their sticks.

Business Week's Peter Burrows ran a snide little story acknowledging Apple's "notorious over devotion [sic] to consensus," but then had to tear at my hide by including a joke he claimed was going around the company: "A vote can be 14,000 to 1 and it's still a tie."

The media blitz about Apple should have been a delightful experience; as hoped for in Barnum's famous phrase, they were spelling my name right. I once asked for a count of how many articles on Apple appeared in a typical month. The answer our PR department came up with: over 1,000 stories, articles, profiles, and interviews. And this was in a *quiet* month, when we didn't have any headline activities going on.

I could well understand an extensive interest about Apple in the Bay Area and the trade press covering high tech. But why this excessive level of coverage in other locations? So I posed the question to a *New York Times* staffer: "You're a New York newspaper and we're a California company, why do you include so much coverage of Apple?"

"Because we sell more papers."

I asked him to be more specific.

He said, "I can give you the exact statistics. When we run a strong story on Apple, we sell three percent more papers. So we run stories on Apple. That's the bottom line."

Glamour magazines put supermodels on their covers to sell more copies, the supermarket tabloids use movie stars and serial murderers, but you don't think of a reporter being sent out to do a story on a company or a CEO based on how many more copies it will sell. I was stunned to learn that the media considered an Apple story as a way to build readership, even more stunned that they knew the exact figure of readership increase. Even if these numbers are inaccurate, at least some of the press people believed it to be true. And so I finally came to understand why I was the focus of an inordinate amount of media attention—even if the knowledge didn't make my life any easier. More proof that Apple had gone beyond being a company, to becoming a national icon.

I would, though, continue to squirm over the stories about me personally. Those Amelio-as-celebrity articles had begun with speculation over who would succeed Michael Spindler; the coverage intensified the night I was hired at the board meeting and had been increasing ever since.

When the board voted to replace Michael, he left the meeting and, for the first time in three years with the heavy load of Apple off his shoulders, headed down the block with his wife Maryse to Il Tinello restaurant for a private, relaxing dinner. Jim Carlton of the *Wall Street Journal* must have been skulking around the lobby and hiding behind pillars, or else had a hotel employee in his pay, because Michael's dinner was interrupted by a phone call from Carlton, trying to get a scoop on what was happening in the board room. He deduced that if the CEO leaves while the board is still meeting, there has to be a story. Michael snapped at him and hung up, genuinely distressed that word was already out.

When the board meeting ended late that night, Michael had been ousted, I was the new CEO, and an appropriately worded press release was to be issued by Apple within a day or two. But before we even walked out, the phone in the conference room was ringing: Jim Carlton, hoping to get a statement from someone. Perhaps he was just guessing. (An old reporter's tactic: "I'm not asking you for the story, I already know, I'm just asking you for confirmation." This can be even more effective when the reporter states the opposite of what he thinks is the truth, because someone who might otherwise duck with a "No comment" is more likely to say, "*No*, you've got it all wrong. . . .")

It's possible one of the board members was slipping out of the room to feed information to Carlton. To this day, I don't know what actually happened; Apple has long been plagued by this ailment.

After my return flight west with Mike Markkula, I got home in the wee hours. A sleepy Charlene greeted me and said, "There's a man who's been calling you every fifteen minutes."

"Who is it?"

"Jim Carlton of the *Wall Street Journal*. And he keeps asking me to comment on your becoming CEO of Apple. Do you want his number?"

I went to bed.

Carlton reached me uncomfortably early in the morning, got nothing from me, then called back and got Charlene again as soon as it seemed reasonable I might have left for work. This was badgering; I didn't like it and Charlene didn't know how to handle it. For the next several days, she let the answering machine take messages, and called people back. Some might consider him a go-getter who dug out the story in rain, shine, sleet, or storm. To me, he was the most aggressive one of the media bunch, with a style I always found harsh.

John Markoff of the *Times* didn't play that game. He was the journalist I have the most respect for in terms of sheer intellect and skills as a reporter. But he has the curious trait of rarely showing up in person. Even at our most important announcements, when hundreds of press people would be assembled, I'd get a phone call from John asking for the story, though he lived only ten miles up the freeway. But maybe a *Times*man can get away with that, knowing that almost any CEO would take his call, and that even if he got only a couple of sentences, he could claim hot, exclusive information.

Julie Schmit of *USA Today* was much more civilized, though rather tough on me for the first year or so. I quickly found she would honor a confidentiality if I asked her to. The behavior of Julie and others like her shows that ethical and human values can be the understructure to successful reporting. This isn't a call for a Pollyannaish press, but the media needs people with honor and respect and the willingness to do a thorough job.

Jim Goldman of KRON-TV, who had been covering me since my National Semiconductor days, never went for the jugular. He gave me very fair coverage and I still appreciate that to this day.

Tom Abate of the *San Francisco Examiner* wrote what I thought was one of the best stories that I was to get during those difficult days. Here was an example of thoughtful, considerate reporting rather than just trying to make a name for himself. His talents have been recognized, and he's now at the *San Francisco Chronicle*, where I'm sure he'll have a successful career.

The reports in *Fortune* by Brent Schlender were among the worst. To grant the devil his due, I admit to admiring his writing ability. He fascinates with phraseology ("a paragon of dysfunctional management and fumbled techno-dreams . . . scrambling lugubriously in slow motion") and is a master of modifiers ("shell-shocked employees . . . hapless shareholders . . . queasy Macintosh faithful").

But I deplore the use he puts his talent to. The leading schlockmeister of populist business journalism, he dazzles with language while plying his trade as a literary ax murderer.

I had begun saying to Charlene, "Smile, sweetie, it's the second best thing to do with your lips." It helped me to keep things in perspective, something I was having a hard time doing. At least I have enough sense of humor to laugh over one item Schlender printed. He meant to make me look foolish, and succeeded, but I found it funny nonetheless. Brent attributed this to a nameless Silicon Valley CEO:

Amelio told us: "Apple is a boat. There's a hole in the boat, and it's taking on water. But there's also a treasure on board. And the problem is, everyone on board is rowing in different directions, so the boat is just standing still. My job is to get everyone rowing in the same direction so we can save the treasure."

I looked at the person next to me and whispered, "But what about the hole?"

In response, I offer a Maxwell House Coffee jingle from the forties:

> As you travel on through life, brother,
> Whatever be your goal,
> Keep your eye upon the donut
> and not upon the hole.

As for the *Forbes* people, typified by Nik Hutheesing, who did a cover story on me, they are exactly the opposite of the *Fortune* BS (= Brent Schlender) style of reporting. Hutheesing and his peers are responsible, respectful, and supportive of the best traditions of journalism.

Anyone who deals with the media, and most everyone else as well, knows or has been taught the tacit agreements that cover two specific situations. "Not for attribution" means "You can use what I'm about to tell you, but you may not quote me as the source," and "Off the record" means "This is so you can understand the situation better, but you may not print it."

Therefore, at the bottom of the barrel, I place Jon Swartz of the *San Francisco Chronicle,* who I view as showing little respect for the rules of journalism and representing everything an honorable and professional member of the media should *not* be.

It wasn't just that Jon didn't honor the rules. On one occasion he actually asked me a question and gave assurance, "This is off the record," then used the information anyway. How is what Jon does different from youngsters stealing what they want off store shelves?

Mark Twain once said, "Everybody in the Virgin Islands eats tamarinds. But they only eat them once." One learns quickly with a Swartz, who is to the media what tamarinds are to the Virgin Islands.

With the desire to build readership, a fact I finally understood, it sometimes seemed that the media was simply trying too hard to find any Apple story. In July, *Business Week*'s Peter Burrows did a piece that said I *wasn't* writing a book—as though anyone would care. When the vacation home I had bought on Lake Tahoe became a matter of public record, *Rolling Stone* encouraged their readers to believe I had played hooky from Apple to go house hunting when I had, in fact, bought the house months earlier, while still at National Semiconductor.

Many of the less professional writers could think of nothing better to do than attach importance to the most superficial of things. Remarks about my hairstyle, weight, and clothes are airhead subjects. I couldn't help asking myself if these were the people who genuinely belonged to the institution about which Jefferson said, "Given the choice between a free press and a free government, I would choose a free press."

o   o   o

Time is a villain for most people these days. The American society once called it progress when the workweek went from six days to five and a half and then to five—the standard forty-hour workweek. But for a variety of reasons, a great many people still put in much more than the nominal forty hours. Those with jobs in a fast-growing company, those with high ambitions, those who need the overtime pay or two jobs to make ends meet, rack up considerably more than forty. And it's even more difficult for women, many of whom, in addition to holding down a full-time job, also retain the labor-intensive and emotionally-intensive traditional responsibilities of running the household, raising the children, and getting meals on the table.

I wonder if many people imagine it's different for CEOs—who, presumably, get to make their own rules, hire people to help, and set their own schedules. A glance at any CEO schedule would prove that time is just as much the villain for a corporate leader.

A typical day's routine during my tenure at Apple started between 6:00 and 6:30 A.M., when I would get the newspaper, fill a thermos from the automatic coffeemaker, and take the thermos and newspaper to Charlene so she could begin her day without stress and with some reassurance. Before leaving for Apple, I would spend thirty minutes or so in my library on things that required contemplation, quiet moments when somehow things just seem a little clearer, with no phones ringing, no people running in and out, and I could focus and concentrate. Whenever possible, I resisted the pressure for an early-morning business breakfast or early meetings, because I hated to rob myself of that one little slice of the day.

It's inherent in the life of a CEO that he or she deals with so many varied subjects, inputs, decisions, and conflicts in every single day. There never seems to be a time to pause and reflect. Perhaps that could be said for most people in business, so the issue has more to do with the number of people's lives who are affected by your decisions. I felt the pressure of the many people working at Apple who were depending on me. During a typical working day, if I could focus on something for as long as thirty minutes, it felt like a luxury. I had always handled interruptions with ease, but they were morphing into monsters because of the time pressures.

I had told my staff to keep 50 percent of my office time clear of appointments, so I would have the opportunity for some uninterrupted time to contemplate the major issues. Yet of the sixteen days I was in the office in July, my calendar shows that a total of only eighteen hours was set aside for this "CEO time."

It's not just corporate executives who need thinking time. As soon as a manager gets to a level where the responsibilities go beyond the tactical and begin to involve an element of the strategic, then a period of thinking time every day becomes a necessity.

On arriving at my office, the first act after shedding my suit jacket and changing into a sweater (the same one that the people at National Semiconductor behind my back used to call my "Mr. Rogers sweater") was to give my associate a string of assignments based on the work I had taken home with me—usually enough to keep her busy the rest of the day. She would give me inputs on things we hadn't been able to cover the prior day. And we would go over my calendar for the hours ahead and get synchronized. This start-of-the-day routine is one I've followed for at least twenty years, back to when I was just beginning as a manager.

I've always been amazed at how few managers have the disciplined habit of meeting with their assistants every day. Just those fifteen to twenty minutes can insure a smooth working path, because your associate or secretary can chase down details you label as important and provide the needed facts. If I asked Cindy or Aggie to call some particular person to see if Apple had any data on market elasticity or the number of products we had introduced in each of the last three years, she would be sure that I had the information by the time I needed it.

Managers of a sizable organization also have other staff people who can be given an assignment that involves doing some kind of research. There were times I would ask Jim Oliver, for example, to find out what the quality data were for the Power Macintosh 5300, and I could count on him to collect the data, analyze them, and get back to me with a report.

One of the best reminders of the value of time comes not from a contemporary harried worker but from the ages-old inscription on London's famed clock tower:

> No minute lost
> Comes ever back again.
> Take heed and see
> Ye nothing do in vain.

Despite the ceaseless pressure of too much to do and too little time, I still felt an obligation to read the huge volume of e-mails that continued to be sent by employees; I was still personally responding to as many of them as I could in the several hours I devoted to this each day.

A typical response was one that went to someone who was distressed about a few of the changes made during the reorganization; there was a concern that women were being edged out of management positions and my attitude on this issue was being challenged. I did not consider this a simple issue to resolve, because it's nearly impossible to convince anyone of anything by just asserting a position. So I answered this way:

```
    I realize that there are people who were identi-
fied as managers in the new organization who are
not highly regarded by some employees because they
have not delivered on their projects. Since I
wasn't here until recently, I had no way to assess
whether their difficulties were due to their own
lack of abilities or whether the dysfunctionality
of the organization was the true cause. The only
fair thing to do is to let them perform in the new
organization and assess their performance as
quickly as possible. I can assure you that there
will be accountability; but with accountability
there must also be fairness. But if they do not
perform, then someone else will be given a chance
to lead their group. With your help and patience,
we can sort this out reasonably quickly.
    The matter regarding Sheila Brady is very unfor-
```

tunate. It was my intention for her to be given
even broader responsibility, because it was clear
to me that Sheila was a keeper, a performer.
Following the announcement of the new organization
there were a number of details to be ironed out.
During this period, someone said something to
Sheila that caused her to be very upset but I still
don't know exactly what that was.

Despite the best efforts of George and myself to
resolve this, we have been unable to work through
the issues. I very much want Sheila to be a happy,
respected member of our corporate community. If you
can do anything to help give me insight into what
to do next, I would appreciate it very much. Let me
assure you that under my leadership, there will be
no glass ceiling. If you feel that any manager is
rewarding people on any basis other than merit, I'd
like to hear about it. Over time you will see that
I mean what I say on this matter.

If we are to get this company back on track, it
must be with the full effort of the people at the
foundation of the company. The role of middle managers is to eliminate roadblocks and to do whatever
must be done to help their people be productive.
Promoting their own self-interest is not on this
list. If you or anyone else has a concern regarding
this, please see George or me.

My parents taught me that regardless of the consequences, I should always try to do the right
thing. This was doubly true regarding people matters. If you do this consistently, over time you
will be recognized and rewarded. That's what I have
done my whole career. I avoid politics, I work hard
and I try to do the right thing. To change the
dysfunctional part of the culture at Apple, I need
you (and others like you) to help me by being my
eyes and ears, by being courageous through the
tough transition period. As I put more and more
pressure on managers to perform, some of the incapable ones will try anything to avoid being measured on performance. It is during this period the

people must be the most patient and the most courageous because this is when such managers can be the
most difficult.

Please hang in there! Apple needs the help of
all the good people we can find!

Thank you for writing and for your dedication to
Apple.
Respectfully,
Gil

In all my e-mails and letters to employees, vendors, customers, and
Apple fans, I tried to get across a theme that I consider basic to who I
am and how I want to live and work: If you start with what is honorable rather than what is profitable, you can hope to achieve both honor
and profit.

        o o o

Meanwhile Apple employees were sharing their concerns over mixed
messages about Apple's progress. Sharon Aby, at the time a senior Apple
field sales manager in Chicago, bared her views in an e-mail to a friend:

It's been a tough time to be an Apple account
exec these last few weeks. Oddly, though the big
pressure has come from within the Apple community
not from the Wintel [ie, Windows] camp at all.

A lot of my long-time customers are expressing
major doubts about continuing to support the use of
Apple in their departments. They are dismayed by
the layoffs and our real failure to acknowledge
some very serious software problems that are plagu-
ing our product line. How would you feel if you
bought your Mac 7500 and after three months, you
still couldn't browse the Web with Netscape? What's
worse, what if you call your Apple support hotline
and they deny there is a problem! The general consensus is that Apple's quality control has fallen
apart.

On the good side, even Wintel users acknowledge
that we still have the best, easiest to use
computer on the market.

> I like Gil Amelio's observations in his book
> "Profit from Experience" about business. There is a
> lot of enthusiasm about Gil and a strong feeling
> that Apple will survive and grow.

On balance, not an encouraging scorecard.

○   ○   ○

The search for board members is conducted much the same way as the search for a new member of the executive team—through business associates and executive search companies. We were two people short on the board, and I used both methods. Heidrich & Struggles had come up with a list that included some candidates I thought worth considering—people who I knew had strong values and also the specialized kind of business mentality needed on a board of directors. For additional recommendations, I also turned to an old friend whom I much admire and respect, Harold Burson.

Harold is a founder and chairman of what is probably the most highly esteemed PR firm in the United States, Burston-Marsteller Public Relations. Although he's based in New York, where the firm has its international headquarters, Harold was my first choice to help improve the tainted Apple image I had inherited once I found that the more conveniently located Regis McKenna was unavailable. Harold provides a potent combination of wisdom, judgment, and understanding, honed through many years of practical experience, and is a gentle man and gentleman besides. The quality of his advice and counsel has earned him a worldwide reputation that is unequaled. When he agreed to handle the Apple account, he also agreed to put himself personally in charge.

On one of his frequent visits to California, Harold had asked me, "What are you doing about your board?"

"Looking for new members," I said, and I told him that Heidrich & Struggles had been brought in to help.

Harold said, "I think you should be considering Ed Woolard." I knew the name but not the man. Woolard is the chairman and former CEO of DuPont and, Harold pointed out, had served on the board of IBM, a fact that struck me as a strong positive—presumably he was already familiar with the many challenges and vagaries of the computer industry.

After looking into his background, talking to some mutual acquaintances, and reading some articles Harold sent me, I concluded that Woolard might prove to be a suitable fit for Apple's board. A phone conversation with him boosted my confidence level, and I took his name to the board. They gave me the go-ahead to follow up and do some more checking.

On my next trip to the East Coast, I detoured into Wilmington, Delaware, to meet Ed at the offices DuPont maintains on the grounds of the airport. Over six feet tall and slender, Ed soothes with a laid back, very comforting "Southern gentleman" manner and a boyish charm that, I quickly found, belies a keen intellect combined with a sense of enjoying life. The conversation brought out that with an easier schedule these days, he and his wife, Peggy, both tennis lovers, travel the world to see all the top matches.

As for the matter of Apple, Ed made a special point of emphasizing that he would want to be an active board member, that it was not his way to just sit in meetings and ratify every proposal of the CEO. He implied this had become a problem at IBM; after Lou Gerstner took over, Ed had felt he was getting clear signals that Gerstner didn't want a board to make decisions, but preferred a "representative" group—meaning one made up of people from major companies, the names of which would lend prestige to IBM. He and Gerstner had, it seemed, parted company over this difference.

Ed's description characterized the way I myself prefer to function when serving as a board member of a company, so rather than putting me off, his style was absolutely acceptable, "as long," I said, "as we work in a collegial way."

True to his word, as soon as he was installed on the board, Ed became an active participant—even arranging a two-day visit for talks with working-level people. At the end of his visit, he dropped by my office to report, "I've really come away with a good feeling. People understand what needs to be done, and they're responding well to your leadership."

It was my view that Ed's contribution as a board member was worthy and helpful. On one subject, though, I would yield to his pressure to my own ultimate peril.

With his primary background in an industry that is a great deal less volatile (except with regard to the vaporous nature of some of its chemical products) than high tech, Ed believed in making a plan, announcing the plan, and sticking to it. The adaptations and swift-footed changes required in high tech were essentially foreign to his method of management. When he urged following his principle with regard to profitability—to make a clear statement about when Apple would become and remain profitable—I judged that kind of prediction to be as dangerous as quicksand. But I allowed myself to be convinced. Against my principles and experience, I took the bold step of announcing that Apple would once again become and remain profitable by the winter quarter of 1997.

As I would discover to my great and lasting dismay, I would have done far better to resist Ed's beseeching and rely on my own judgment.

◦   ◦   ◦

It was getting harder to smile even at the amusing quotes passed along by close friends trying to help me keep a balanced perspective. One I still ruefully recall, a Belgian proverb gathered by Malcolm Forbes: "Experience is the comb that Nature gives us after we are bald."

I wasn't balding yet, but I was already visibly grayer.

12

Once More to the Breach—
MORE BAD NEWS,
AND WE COMPOUND THE
SALES PROBLEMS

 Every chief executive in corporate America quakes to hear that Arthur Levitt is on the phone.

The fear is justified: Arthur Levitt is chairman of the Securities and Exchange Commission.

The regulations under which corporations function are so extensive that major businesses spend tens of thousands of man-hours a year attempting to comply, all the time knowing that despite every effort, it's impossible to be certain they've adhered to every rule and requirement. The SEC, an independent agency of the federal government charged with overseeing the stock markets and financial reporting of businesses, has an extensive set of rules about what you may and may not say about how your business is doing and how it will do. Every public statement, press interview, and television sound bite by an executive runs the risk of a slip of the tongue or careless misstatement that can land the individual and the company in trouble; a quarterly or annual report deemed to contain misleading information can be considered a very serious matter.

When something is amiss, routine matters or everyday irregularities are handled by a call or letter from a staff member or, in more serious cases, the head of a division. Matters weighty enough for the chairman to place a call directly to a CEO usually mean a violation severe enough that someone could go to prison. Someone like *you.*

So when my admin came in and interrupted me to say, "Arthur Levitt is on the phone," I turned white as a sheet. *Oh, shit, what have we done now?* I had visions of some securities fraud violation that we committed without even knowing it and could picture endless legal battles, suits by disgruntled stockholders, and a clouded reputation forever.

With trepidation, I got on the phone. Levitt said, "I just wanted to introduce myself and meet you. I want you to know I'm a Mac fan and I really love what you're doing with the company. And, oh, by the way, this has nothing to do with SEC business."

A fan call! From the chairman of the Securities and Exchange Commission! If word got out, I would be the envy of every corporate honcho in the country.

Levitt went on to tell me that he's on a budget for buying Macintosh equipment—his wife allows him, as I recall the figure, $10,000 a year. He described how carefully he makes decisions to keep up with the technology while also staying within his spending limit. He even had a suggestion: "Have you ever thought of creating a special service where power customers like me could call and ask questions, rather than just going through the regular 800 number that everybody else uses?"

I thought it an excellent way to reassure our really loyal customers that we wanted them within a preferred inner circle, and promised to pass the suggestion along to our marketing people. It was eventually added to the support operation. I thought of promoting it as "the Arthur Levitt service." I suspect the chairman would not have appreciated the honor. Or worse, it might have violated some obscure regulation. . . .

(At the time of this writing, though, Apple is still doing only a mediocre job of providing extra service to key customers—another example of a culture problem.)

o   o   o

Bill Gates and I had been hammering at each other since the very first get-together in March to work out a deal of some kind between our two companies. I was hot to nail down terms that would allow Microsoft to openly endorse the Mac platform. Going public with a Microsoft endorsement in my pocket would mean I could serenade the major software suppliers and have a much better chance of keeping them in the Apple tent. The developers were continuing to lose confidence in the future of Apple and the Mac; if they began to leave in large enough numbers, it would be time to turn out the lights and fold the tent.

If I couldn't get an agreement with Bill, at least I wanted an endorsement from him: "The Mac's a great product and we'll continue to develop software for it." Just a statement like that from the leader of the world's greatest software company could be enough to shift the balance for some developers, giving a lot of the Apple faithful confidence that staying with the Macintosh still made sense.

I had already been promised endorsements from John Warnock at Adobe Systems, Jeff Pappas of Lotus, Bud Colligan of Macromedia, and others who comprise the top six or seven people in the industry. But Bill Gates, as he had repeatedly demonstrated to me, never gives anything without getting something in return. When I asked for an endorsement, he said, "Well, I have a request." And it turned out he was back on the Internet Explorer bandwagon, this time fiddling a slightly different tune.

Bill said, "I want Internet Explorer to be bundled on exactly the same basis that you bundle Netscape Navigator. I'm not looking for preference, but I am looking for parity." In effect he was saying, "We don't want you to recommend a browser, we want you to put both Netscape and Microsoft browsers into your packages and let the customer choose." That was the price Bill wanted for having someone stand up at MacWorld and reaffirm their support of the platform.

That seemed reasonable, and a small enough price to pay for his extremely valuable support at this critical juncture. I said, "Okay, we'll treat them both on an equal footing," and then immediately called Jim Barksdale, CEO of Netscape, to tell him what I had been coerced into. Jim wasn't happy with the news. "You know," he said, "those guys are incredible." He asked, "Have you ever thought of talking to the Justice Department about Microsoft?" I admit to being caught off guard by the question.

Jim said, "I'm gonna have my lawyer call you about what legal recourses you have here." His lawyer did call not long after, and we kicked the topic around, but I wasn't about to pursue that course of action. I just didn't see how it would profit Apple; it would only defocus us, distracting us from the business at hand.

So Bill Gates assured me he'd send a Microsoft executive to lend us the promised support, and we scheduled the two Web browsers, Microsoft's and Netscape's, to go into our next major software release.

o   o   o

The issue of licensing Apple's system software had caused outbreaks among company people the way territorial disputes incite wars between nations. Confrontations on the subject of licensing had raged throughout most of the 1990s and strong forces had built up on each side of the argument. In the past, as a relatively uninformed observer, I would have been hard pressed to make up my mind. As CEO, I needed to address the issue and make a considered decision.

But what would Apple be licensing? If you said, "The right to compete against the Macintosh," you're on target. The pro forces argued this would broaden the base of people using the Macintosh platform, encouraging the all-important software developers to create more and better Mac programs, and that only by traveling this path could the Macintosh be saved from extinction. The con forces argued that clone machines would steal Apple customers, further reducing Apple's market share, while the competition would accelerate the already fast-sliding profit margins, and that only by *not* doing this could the Macintosh be saved from extinction.

Many Apple-watchers remain convinced that John Sculley's failure to start licensing the Macintosh was a fatal error, and, soon after I began my inquiries into this issue, I began to accept that notion as a major cause of Apple's foundering. But I was to discover there was more to the story.

Early attempts to launch clone projects—including at least one within Apple itself—had been squelched. Michael Spindler finally crossed the bridge, signing the first deal with start-up clone-maker Power Computing Corporation in 1995. Spindler also set up a licensing group in Apple under Lamar Potts to make other deals.

When I arrived, Lamar was close to new, major agreements with Motorola and IBM. This pleased me—licensing deals with these two major firms would lend credibility to our shaky company.

Motorola left the impression they were just moving ahead with us because we were a key customer—an act of friendship, as well as a way of generating more business for the chip side of their company. But it turned out they were serious about it and brought out a product called StarMax, which they marketed until late 1997.

The giant IBM, always slow to move, needed some prodding. I met on several occasions with Dr. Mike Attardo, who ran the chip part of the company, and, on the business side, Nick Donofrio, senior VP of technology and manufacturing. Mike wanted IBM to jump in with both feet, while Nick was listening to dissident factions within IBM, especially from the IBM PC division, where the attitude was that the company already had a PC line and didn't need another. We finally managed to sign a deal but, despite assurances that they would build a clone, internal politics kept them from going any further than signing third-party deals in which other companies received a sub-license.

I made it clear to each of the companies that were negotiating clone deals with us: "Our reason for giving you a license is for you to develop your own customer base, not take away ours." For example, Apple had never served the low end of the marketplace—except for education, we had at that time no products in the $1,500 to $2,000 bracket. A perfect target for the clone-makers. And in fact, UMAX Technologies Inc. followed just this strategy.

At Power Computing, though, cofounder and CEO Steve Kahng studied the marketplace, found that the most profitable segment was computers for the publishing industry, and set his sights on this high-end market—a customer base Apple could ill afford to lose. Kahng was very aggressive in coming out with high-end machines that were faster than the Macs. He should have never been able to take any market share in that area from us; he should have met a brick wall. But we had left ourselves vulnerable by not creating machines at the cutting edge of the technology.

Apple sales reps were accustomed to losing sales to IBM-PC clones; they didn't like it, of course, but it was the way of the world. Now they were paying calls on customers in an industry that Apple practically owned, to find that Power Computing had taken the sale away. They moaned, groaned, bitched, and complained. And I couldn't blame them.

On the other hand, under the licensing agreements, we made

money each time a clone-maker sold a computer. *How much?* I wondered. CFO Fred Anderson came up with a number, but it didn't make sense—"about $50."

I asked him, "How much would we have to charge just to be profit neutral?"—so we would make the same profit whether the customer bought one of ours or one of theirs.

Fred brought back an answer: As the machine performance went up, the license fee would need to increase. For high-end machines, just to come out even, the appropriate fee would have to be about *ten times* higher than we were charging, an almost absurd amount.

I couldn't fathom how the fees had originally been established or what anyone had been thinking to allow Apple to come out so short. Perhaps after more than six years of fighting the battle of licensing, the war-weary Apple executives driving the program had been so excited about finally getting some licensees lined up that they neglected to ask finance to churn the numbers and see if they made sense. We were caught in a licensing vise: losing sales to the clones, and making a pittance in license fees that came nowhere near balancing the scale. John Sculley had, I decided, anticipated this difficulty when he steered the company away from licensing.

But now the finance people, seeing their own figures, changed their tune and joined the chorus of voices chanting against licensing. Yet we were committed by contracts that would be expensive to cancel or renegotiate.

A way out of this dilemma appeared from an unexpected direction.

The operating system team, now under Steven Glass, was making notable progress on the next software release, unofficially called System 7.7. Thinking about that designation, I realized, *The new version is going to include a number of pieces of Copland, which will bring a dramatic change in the user experience and make it the most stable of any operating system on the market. It's more than an upgrade.* I told Ellen Hancock, "We should be calling this 'System 8.'"

But the change in designation would bring an unexpected benefit. The clone contracts contained a provision that the pricing terms could not be changed so long as we were using System 7. As soon as we had announced System 8 by that name, I sent the licensing team and the finance people back to recalculate the fees to the clone-makers. For the high-end machines, I relied on the principle that a deal isn't any good unless it's good for both parties, so told the licensing team to back off to a less steep formula and settle on numbers that would improve the situation for Apple but not be so painful for the clone-makers as the several hundred dollars per machine that the profit-neutral formula would dictate.

A few months later, when the plan was announced, the press made a big flap over news that Apple wanted to increase the license fees—as if asking to change the rules so we could make a reasonable profit was a major sin. The clone-makers had less problem with the change. After some serious negotiating, Motorola was ready to sign, and Power Computing had given handshake agreement.

It never happened. After I was terminated, Steve Jobs—in one of his I-won't-listen-to-any-advice edicts—reneged and canceled the licenses outright. Although the basic contention over whether licensing is or is not best for Apple can still be argued either way, Steve's high-handed method of deciding, based on his own opinion and without concern for any previous agreements, was another sign of his rigid business judgment.

Or perhaps he had never been taught that a promise should be treated like an unpaid debt.

o   o   o

Back in April, soon after I arrived, we had looked at selling our manufacturing plants. The motivation was raising cash, but more than that was also the goal of moving more toward a model of outsourcing our manufacturing.

Outsourcing would take fixed costs off our books and turn them into variable costs. If sales went down, we wouldn't have that fixed burden to carry; whoever had bought the plant would be stuck with it, but presumably they'd have other customers and so be better able to weather the storm.

But there was another reason, as well: I wanted to keep options open about the company's future. Although this will sound like heresy to legions of Mac lovers, I could foresee the possibility that we might reach the point at some future time when Apple needed to look more toward the operating system as a source of revenue and depend less heavily on hardware—the same transition Steve Jobs had made at NeXT. With fewer manufacturing facilities, we'd be able to make that transition in a more graceful way. I didn't talk to anyone about this possibility, because I didn't want to create more concern. We had enough upset and turmoil already; no sense in creating more unnecessarily.

We had, though, sold the Fountain, Colorado, manufacturing plant in April, and had intended to do the same with the Sacramento plant. But Sacramento had earned a special place in the Apple community. The plant was made up of dedicated people who had really come through for the company a lot of times—when something had to be done on a short deadline or a new model needed to be pushed through the line and out the door.

And I discovered that the people of Apple had an emotional attachment to the Sacramento plant that had never developed for the plant in Fountain—a sense of identity, a bonding. When it became known that we were thinking of selling this facility, I got impassioned letters from employees begging me to reconsider and keep Sacramento inside the tent. The letters had the desired effect—I postponed the decision.

By August, though, people in the company as well as Apple watchers on the outside had reached the point where they realized we had to get still more assets off our plate. The prime candidate was the Sacramento plant.

But we couldn't find anybody to buy the facility. After a diligent search, we had to face the painful reality that getting the costs off our books meant closing the plant. Several hundred people were thrown out of work. We provided termination packages, but I knew many of those people would be hard-pressed to find other companies in the Sacramento area able to use their specialized skills.

No matter what the reason, getting fired always hurts.

o   o   o

We were basking temporarily in the sun of "turnaround" stories and renewed customer enthusiasm. Fortified by the many "attaboy" articles and messages, I made plans for attending the Boston MacWorld convention in August, which would be my first MacWorld in the United States. People seemed quite curious about forming their own impression and hearing what I was going to say.

All the indicators seemed to point toward an upbeat theme, so my plan was to give an informal talk from notes instead of a formal speech. There would also be a video, some celebrity guests, and a series of demos.

On the day of my keynote, August 7, the Boston weather changed from uncomfortably hot and humid into a delightful New England day, which I took as a favorable omen. The room was absolutely packed, and people who couldn't get in were standing in front of TV monitors outside the hall and around the trade show floor. Later reports said there were about 4,000 people in the hall and another 15,000 watching on monitors.

The demos were done jointly by me and Frank Casanova, part of Apple's advanced technology group, who ranks with Guy Kawasaki as one of our most popular presenters. Frank's shoulder-length hair, care-nothing clothes, and intrinsic Apple spirit contrasted with my buttoned-up reputation. He and I enjoyed and respected each other, and we worked well together on these demos; our styles blended admirably and the audience let us know they enjoyed seeing the old and the new Apple coming together.

What an incredible experience to have the audience with you and responding enthusiastically to your words. I fully understood the elated feelings a performer gets when rewarded with applause or appreciative laughter. The show flowed well, I received a standing ovation, and the press reports were generally favorable.

On my way out, a young woman asked to pose with me for a photo, then planted a kiss on my cheek—a reaction I don't usually inspire. Charlene was, fortunately, not with me at the time.

Although I enjoyed the experience on the stage and the subsequent praise from the press, I remember wishing the reports had been more on the content, less on style and the entertainment aspects of the presentation. (A speech I gave shortly after I left Apple to the members of San Francisco's prestigious Commonwealth Club was crammed with thoughtful ideas; the reviews were positive, yet 99 percent of the coverage merely fixed on superficialities and gossip about Apple and me, bypassing a chance to disseminate some concepts that could be truly valuable for their readers to consider. *Is there no room for thoughtful reflection? Does everything have to be showbiz?*)

MacWorld Boston was judged an Apple triumph, but the heady sensation was not to last long.

o   o   o

When a company is underwater and out of breath, few choices a CEO struggles with are more fraught with potential hazard than decisions surrounding the quarterly report. It may sound like a paperwork exercise, but the consequences can be severe. For me, the report for the fall quarter of 1996 would prove another turning point helping to kick-start the downward spiral toward my departure.

Over the previous couple of years, Apple's sales had been rising, followed by a serious dip in the winter quarter just before I took over. My April through June quarter in 1996 had brought sales revenues that were almost a carbon copy of the disaster that had sunk Spindler. Now, in August, part way through the fall quarter, the revenue numbers showed that sales were clearly picking up. It looked as if we had successfully put behind us the horror of the inventory excesses of Spindler's Christmas. Customers seemed to be regaining a little confidence in the company and its products. It was easy to convince ourselves that the downturn of the last two quarters was just a temporary manifestation, that sales were now back on the upswing.

Though I was pleased to see the increases, I had a nagging feeling in the pit of my stomach that they might not be sustainable. I knew we were going to be facing a ticklish problem at the end of the quarter: Do we declare a profit? And if so, how much?

Accountants will tell you there is no wiggle room here, that you have no latitude and are confined to reporting the numbers the way they actually are. That's what any auditor will claim: The rules spell out what you must do and what you must not do.

The reality lies elsewhere.

Management does, in fact, have some prerogative to shift things a little more one way or a little more the other in how results get calculated and reported. Corporations are sufficiently complicated that a spectrum of equally defensible realities exists.

For example, how much inventory reserve should a company take in a particular quarter—$10 million? $20? $50? It's a judgment call. If in the current situation it makes sense to be conservative, management decides to take a bigger number; if they're in position to be a little more aggressive and it's in their nature, they take a smaller number. Any large company faces a thousand decisions like this as they drive toward closing the books for a given quarter.

I said at a late September meeting of the executive staff, "We're going to be facing a decision soon as to what kind of results we want to report for the quarter. Our sales are strong enough and our prices are strong enough that we should be able to report a profit."

But I pointed out we could be slammed with serious consequences by making the wrong choice in this position. I said, "I need your guidance. If there's a chance sales are going to be down again in the following quarter or the one after, then we should not report a profit." Investors and customers already knew we were experiencing losses and had heard me publicly say that the company did not expect to be profitable for two or three more quarters; the market had already digested this expectation, so we stood to lose very little by reporting a loss.

On the other hand, news that we had made money sooner than expected would be a great shot in the arm, helping restore confidence. But what if we reported a profit this quarter, then followed up with more losing quarters. We would have built up confidence, trust, and hope and then shattered it; we would be considered erratic and unreliable, and be in a far worse position than if we didn't report a profit to begin with.

I told the staff, "If there's a chance the sales increase isn't going to be sustained, what we should do is be extra conservative, declare a small loss, and keep working on the long-term problems that need to be fixed."

By the time of the next meeting, Fred Anderson had taken a poll of the executives in operational roles. The consensus was that we had turned the corner, sales would continue climbing, we would have a sensational Christmas quarter. Fred recommended declaring a profit; not a single voice was raised to dispute Fred's numbers or his reasoning.

In hindsight, we were misreading the market. We had done well in summer because we had exceptionally strong education sales. But education is highly seasonal, peaking in the summer as school systems get ready for the fall start of the school year. We looked at the totals instead of the breakdown, which would have shown that the increase was not much due to increased consumer or professional sales.

The day came when we had to close the books on the quarter. Fred was recommending that we show a profit of approximately $27 million. I told him, "I'm still not comfortable about this—I'm uncertain about the sales ahead."

"I have the forecasts from all the salespeople," he said. "I've talked to the controllers in all the divisions. Everyone says we're going to make a profit in the Christmas quarter, and therefore I recommend you report a profit for this quarter."

We reported a profit. Julie Schmit's article in *USA Today* was headlined "Apple turns a profit—and a corner." The *New York Daily News* proclaimed "Apple Shines as Losses Dip." And other newspapers and magazines all across the country wrote about Apple's "comeback."

But I had just made one of my worst decisions ever.

o   o   o

As if we didn't already have enough bad news to contend with, on September 5 the *Wall Street Journal* ran an article by Alex Markels headlined "Companies Dump Macs as Loyalists Lose Faith." The article quoted people like Jeffery Blade, identified as a Dow Chemical computer specialist who "sang the [Macintosh's] praise far and wide" since his college days and who had become a Mac programmer, but was now saying, "It's just not worth fighting for anymore."

Calling the Mac "no longer state of the art," the article listed the number of Macintosh computers that each of several well-known companies were said to be "dumping"—Ernst & Young and Monsanto, 2,000 each; Eli Lilly & Co., 7,000; Northern Telecom Ltd., *30,000*. And so on.

Enough to give a strong man heartburn.

o   o   o

Following the close of our fiscal year at the end of September, it was time to calculate annual bonuses. This experience, which in most companies is a time for smiles and rejoicing, at Apple in 1996 produced some smiles and, I'm afraid, a heavy dose of cynicism.

Not long after arriving, I had revised the bonus plan for employees at the vice president and director levels for the six months remaining in the fiscal year. A bonus plan only makes sense when it serves to stimulate focus on those things most important to the company, and I structured a setup that would get these top managers thinking about improving the cash position, reducing excess inventories, increasing revenues, and reducing costs.

Apple wasn't out of the woods, not by a long shot, but we had done well on every one of the measures. Sale of the debentures had at least temporarily resolved the critical cash situation; inventories had been written down and sold off; the cost-reduction targets had been met. And the executives had unanimously been in favor of declaring the fall quarter profitable. (Was this decision motivated by the favorable impact it would have on their bonuses? By the time business managers reach these high levels in a major company, I expect them to be able to set personal considerations aside in decisions carrying so much weight. If I misjudged, it proved to be a very serious error—another of those that rank among the worst of my career.)

As a result of meeting the criteria that had been established, the company's twenty top managers and executives, except for me, received bonuses equal to 175 percent of their bonus targets.

A boon to them, of course. But to many employees—including, I understand, many of the people receiving the bonuses—it looked like greed, a calculated gouging of an ill company. I was on one hand pleased that Apple's top management had been rewarded for the success of their efforts and given a generous reason to stay; on the other hand, had I anticipated the outcome and the reaction of employees, I would certainly not have set up a plan that resulted in such lavish payouts.

o   o   o

With Charlene at my side, I stepped onto the deck of the 150-foot power cruiser *Highlander* in response to an invitation from the Forbes brothers for a one-day Hudson River cruise. Their father, the late Malcolm Forbes, had started the tradition as a way to afford chief executives a chance to casually share ideas and exchange experiences in an off-beat setting, while Forbes himself took the pulse of his guests' thinking. Many stories in the pages of *Forbes* magazine I'm sure sprang from topics of discussion on those several-times-a-year outings.

We had been invited for the last Saturday in October, along with some sixty or so business leaders, including Jim Unruh of Unisys, Bob

Crandall of American Airlines, and other top executives from all over the globe. Leaving from a Manhattan pier, the yacht headed north up the Hudson, past a colorful landscape of trees just beyond the full glory of their showy fall splendor. Our destination was the Poughkeepsie area, where a tour had been arranged of the Hillwood Art Museum. The three Forbes brothers, Kip, Bob, and sometime presidential candidate Steve, circulated to make sure the staff was attending to guests' appetites and thirsts.

Gathering people with diverse interests and experiences together in this setting was enormously successful and the sharing of ideas and concerns a rewarding experience for me. Bob Crandall and I bonded by commiserating with each other at length about the difficulties our two industries were experiencing. Crandall was especially interested in my battling with Bill Gates and was surprised at my expression of real admiration and fondness for Bill.

The presence of a wandering magician added a Fellini-esque touch to a memorable day. At one point on the return trip downriver, I noted that a card game had gotten started (for what turned out to be a very modest stake—a mere ten cents a point). And I discovered a crowd had gathered to watch as a lady and her partner cleaned a bunch of big-shot businessmen out of their coins. Charlene!

Kip laughingly warned me that in ensuing years I would have to leave Charlene at home or keep her out of the card games.

As we went ashore about 6:30 that evening, the Forbes brothers handed out going-away gifts—*Highlander* caps and a box of a packaged product.

The product, when I opened it at home, turned out to be the Forbes software. I had been given a Windows version.

In my letter of thanks, I chided Kip, "My machine won't run your software"; he promptly sent back a version for the Mac.

o o o

There's a superstition among airline pilots that major accidents happen as a result of three compounded errors. At Apple, the threes were coming in groups of threes, and small miscalculations were springboarding into major calamities.

I came across an observation written by a young philosophy student: "Socrates was a philosopher. He went around pointing out errors in the way things were done. They fed him hemlock."

Apple's annual sales conference has in most years been an extravagant event, a gathering lasting several days, held in some lush location, designed with a lavish hand, planned by people experienced in throwing a memorable party, and featuring live music, top-dollar entertainment, dancing girls, laser shows, celebrity performers, and multimedia extravaganzas.

Most companies have these events, in good times and in bad, despite the enormous cost. It's the best single opportunity for bringing the sales reps together, introducing the new sales strategies, showing them the new products and promotional materials, pumping them up for another great sales effort, and sending them home rarin' to go.

My new COO Marco Landi, in his second role as head of Apple's sales organization worldwide, came up with an idea that would let us hold the sales meeting at a considerably lower cost. But it proved disastrous.

Landi and John Floisand, who had been promoted to running worldwide sales for Marco, decided to hold not one conference, but three. To eliminate the expense of flying sales reps from around the world to a single city, they would instead stage three regional conferences—one week in the United States, the following week in Europe, and then a week in Hawaii for the Asia/Pacific people, all to be held in October.

One look at his plans and I felt like taking that hemlock. At the limit of my patience, I called Marco and said, "You're going to keep the executives and product managers out of the office for three weeks—that's crazy." And I pointed out that he had scheduled me to make speeches at times when I wouldn't even be available.

As everyone in retailing knows, October is a critical period for getting product through the channel for Christmas. We weren't just going to have each sales rep tied up for a week at the most critical sales period of the year, but were also going to have the senior executives and the product managers out of the office and on the road for three brutal consecutive weeks to attend the meetings.

Every company at any given moment has ongoing efforts and short-term goals. If the lights are out in the entire executive suite, there's nobody driving these programs or providing the leadership to get things done. Product introductions slip, meetings with customers don't happen, important phone calls aren't returned. And while the sales force would like you to believe they are solely responsible for all sales, most of the biggest orders don't get placed without the involvement of some senior executive. If Sears or Fry's is going to place an order for $50 million worth of Macintoshes, they first want to speak with someone in senior management to get the comfort level and reassurances they're looking for. Sure, the transaction will be initiated through a sales rep, but a major buyer wants to talk with a senior vice president, as well. Marco's decision to take senior execs out of their offices for three weeks seriously compounded the problem of taking the sales reps off the street.

By the time I learned of all this, changing the dates would have cost a fortune and upset thousands of people's schedules. I should have done it anyway. The sales for October proved to be a disaster—we booked hardly anything. The first week in November, we looked at orders and they were barely above zero. I was livid.

In the Christmas quarter, Santa Claus *again* stayed home for Apple. We had expected $2.4 billion in sales but did only $2.1 billion. Worse, the sales force had pulled off another round of channel-stuffing, despite my earlier direct orders that this was never to happen again. We took a $120 million bath for the quarter, another triple-digit loss—meaning we had reported a profit in one quarter and followed up with a huge loss in the very next. And as if that wasn't bad enough, we lost all the sales momentum we had begun to build.

As I had feared, the profitable quarter rallied expectations, and the following unprofitable one sunk us. Newspaper accounts started to accentuate the negatives. Our good news was blithely mentioned in passing, our bad news racked up column inches everywhere. The snowball effect took over—a negative story runs, customers decide to stay away, sales decline, which triggers more negatives stories. . . .

This was another of the turning points, a triggering event for a lot of what followed, a painful trap from which I would never shake loose.

13

To Be or Not to Be—
WHETHER 'TIS NOBLER TO CHOOSE BE OR NeXT

When we evaluated Jean-Louis Gassée's software, we found much to admire; the possibilities were very real. Yet we began to recognize that the Be software treasure chest was partly water-filled. Gassée's software developers at Be had so far created zero support for file sharing. They hadn't ever printed even a single page of a document, because they had yet to write any printer drivers (the software that tells the computer how to format a page so it makes sense to the printer). The BeOS concept was, indeed, an elegant system worth bragging about, but a massive amount of work was yet to be implemented.

My conclusion, after looking at the software and hearing the due diligence reports of my engineers, was that Jean-Louis was offering Apple a great concept that was still three years and megabucks away from solving our problem. I began to see his enthusiasm for selling to Apple in a new light: Could he be running out of money, investors, and time, and viewing Apple as a potential savior? Wrong reason for buying his company. Still, BeOS was solid and certainly offered one road to the answer we needed. My team and I listened to this very experienced, smooth, polished, and brilliant French technologist trying to sell us a package that in many ways was tempting and worthy.

Jean-Louis added a sweetener that I believe was heartfelt: "I really want to see Apple succeed. If we make a deal, if you like I'll come in and run the software organization for you." He didn't waver at the fact that Ellen Hancock was sitting at the conference table with us, that she was Apple's new head of product development. I admired him when he glanced at her and amended his offer: "I'll even report to Ellen." This magnanimous suggestion shouted down the warnings about his self-centered, egotistical negotiating; it was wise, gracious . . . and right on target, since I would not have wanted yet another person reporting directly to me.

The meeting broke up with both sides agreeing to continue the conversations. I knew that Jean-Louis would be pressing his team harder than ever to make headway on some of the technical issues that concerned us.

o   o   o

All through the negotiations with Jean-Louis, I continued my frequent phone calls with Bill Gates. He remained excited and eager to conclude an agreement, repeating his promise to throw a huge amount of resources at overcoming the technical problems.

If we did it cleverly enough, we could get something that still looked and felt like a Mac, yet would overnight become compatible with the entire Windows world and could run on Intel processors. I kept thinking of the appealing advantages, and key advisors pressed me nearly every day to do the deal with Gates. Still, I was nagged by the technology hurdles; despite Bill's reassurances, they still looked as intimidating as ever. I continued using delaying excuses with Gates, and the search moved forward.

o   o   o

Over at Sun Microsystems, Scott McNealy has a very stable operating system called Solaris that had proved itself through years of use at some of America's largest and most demanding firms. In terms of a solid foundation, Solaris offered probably the best alternative available.

The problem was that Sun had spent zero energy on the user interface. To give a copy command on the Macintosh, it's easy to drag the file icon to the new location; to discard a file, you just drag its icon to the little symbol that looks like a trash can. So incredibly simple that it's dazzling, much of the Macintosh interface is immediately obvious or so intuitive that once it's learned, it's never forgotten.

Solaris, on the other hand, is based on a programming language called Unix that only a highly skilled software engineer can know and love. Sun workstations were designed to be used by techies and devotees of Unix, so there was never any compelling reason for McNealy to insist on making Solaris easy to use. The fact remains that Solaris customers are still burdened by arcane, complicated commands that are a challenge to learn and remember, making even DOS commands like "copy c:\msoffice\msword\address.doc a:\backup\letters" seem brilliantly obvious.

My conclusion was that though the foundation of Solaris was solid, Apple would be left to create an entire user interface, which had to represent a massive undertaking. Ellen Hancock didn't agree with my take on Solaris and went to bat for this as the best choice. Throughout the evaluation process, Ellen was a highly vocal exponent for making a deal with Sun.

o   o   o

With weeks between discussions, no wonder Jean-Louis got the sense we were drifting. He couldn't know I was spending more of my time on operating-system concerns than any other issue. From his perspective, things were going nowhere, and he was getting impatient. He called and said, "Gil, we have to meet."

"I'll be glad to get together, but I'm just on my way out of town for a series of trips. I won't be back for two weeks."

"Where are you going to be?"

"First stop is Hawaii."

"Will you have any time to talk?"

"I'll make some time."

"Then I'll fly over there to meet you."

When we sat down at the hotel in Kauai, Be continued to hold center stage as my leading option, with the others still hovering in the wings. I was genuinely pleased that the two of us had the chance to talk things through, clearly the best way to get a deal wrapped up.

Jumping right in, Jean-Louis said, "I have great love for Apple and I want to help," and then without hesitating he went on, "The best way I can do that is by contributing this operating system." He referred again to some of his earlier deal closers, assurances that he would come aboard and work as an Apple employee, and "It doesn't matter who I report to." Again, he was saying all the right things.

"What about price?"

"Money doesn't matter to me," he said. "I'm an engineer, I don't get involved in price. I just leave it to the backers. Whatever the backers say is fair is okay with me."

Whether I was ready to accept that or not, I let it go. By the end of the meeting, Jean-Louis left to fly back to the mainland, assured that if the price was agreeable, we would move forward toward a deal.

Before I even got back to my office, the press had enough details of our meeting to make me uncomfortable. Worse, the stories quoted Jean-Louis as saying I had demanded he fly to Hawaii for the meeting. I saw this as typical Gassée, until I got a conciliatory e-mail from him that said, "I was distressed to discover the quotes attributed to me by the *Chronicle*. I feel terrible about the tone and timing. In particular, I know very well you have several alternatives before you, internal and external, of which we are but one. While this was both a distortion and a misuse of a background conversation, I feel the need to accept responsibility and apologize for this unfortunate incident."

I still thought he had talked to the press as a way of forcing my hand, and was not pleased. (My theory about all this is that Jean-Louis had learned from John Sculley this trick of using the press for leverage to get what you want; Sculley had used it to shoo Apple employees back into line.) Later, when Jim Carlton was researching his book, Jean-Louis reverted to the original story he had tried to disclaim. The book describes how "Amelio telephoned him one day in late October and asked him to fly to the Hawaiian island of Kauai immediately."

Gassée is personally charming, and the Be technology offered one viable solution for the future of Apple. On the other hand, what would be the dynamics of our long-term relationship? The answer wasn't very appealing, but I filed away my reaction until we heard Be's price.

CFO Fred Anderson rushed in brandishing some papers—the response from Jean-Louis's board and backers. They would sell us Be and all its assets in exchange for shares worth 15 percent of Apple

Computer. I've dealt with some tough negotiators, but I was stunned. And what gave me such a distinct impression the price was an amount Jean-Louis had personally decided on? So much for the backers making all his money decisions.

It's expected that a seller will name a high price at the start of negotiations, but the figure needs to be reasonably defensible. At the time, Apple shares were depressed; when investor confidence returned and the price came back to an even modestly realistic level, 15 percent of Apple would be worth something well north of $500 million.

Our due diligence placed the Be value at about $50 million.

Without waiting, I placed a call to Jean-Louis and said, "You have zero sales, you've got an operating system that's three years away from any reality, and you want 15 percent of the company. That's not in the cards. That's not even within the realm of possibilities."

Over the next few weeks, Jean-Louis dropped his demands to about $300 million and we negotiated up to about $125 million. I knew that was really overpaying, and it was as far as I was going to go.

Two months later, the matter still wasn't settled. But the heat was on in the press, with stories every day speculating about what Apple would do, what deal we'd make, fueled no doubt by Jean-Louis, who has his supporters in the media.

There was still one option on the list we hadn't yet explored.

○　○　○

I needed the Bard himself to write my opening lines for a conversation with Steve Jobs. How should I approach the option of his company's software, especially after my past disastrous meeting with the high-tech kingpin? I could hardly phone him and say, "Hey, buddy, this is your ol' friend Gil, I'd like to buy your operating system."

I was asking around among my top people: Does anyone know Steve well enough to call him on this; does anyone know any of his lieutenants? In late November a phone call from a NeXT marketer reached Ellen Hancock while she was in Europe on a business trip. Steve had apparently learned what was going on through his still effective pipeline into Apple. Ellen phoned me to say that Steve was reaching out to open the door.

No doubt Steve knew his company was on our OS option list. And we knew—it was common knowledge—that his company, like Jean-Louis's, was in trouble and facing the very real possibility of never fulfilling the destiny they had worked so hard to attain.

In an industry so extensively crisscrossed by close personal relationships (most people still have friends at the two or three or several companies they previously worked for, and many have a spouse or significant other working for a competitor), and an industry so thoroughly covered by the press as high tech, secrets are nearly impossible to keep.

For me, the phone call with Steve was like inhaling the flavors of a great bottle of vintage wine. He said calmly, "I'm on my way to Japan, but I'll be back in a week and I'd like to see you as soon as I return." And he had a request: "Don't make a decision until we can get together and talk." I was delighted to give him my reassurance.

o   o   o

CFO Fred Anderson came in and said, "We've made some progress with Jean-Louis. I think they'll settle for two hundred million."

I threw a full-fledged executive tantrum, calling the figure "Outrageous!"

Fred asked for the time to give me his thinking in full, so I calmed down and heard him out. Finally I said, "Okay, I'm not saying I'll sign, but you can go back and test the waters at two hundred."

Jean-Louis responded with a $275 million bottom price. Fred came back really disappointed. "We thought he was ready to make a deal, but maybe he isn't."

I later heard that Jean-Louis had been prepared to take the $200 million, but thought he could put on the pressure for even more; I was told he said, "I've got them by the balls, and I'm going to squeeze until it hurts."

A skilled negotiator recognizes critical moments and our offer of $200 million was that critical moment, his last chance to nail a deal on the spot. He didn't, and the tide turned.

Talk about frustration. The search for an operating-system solution had by now been going on for nearly five months. The press stories intensified that Apple was about to strike a deal with Be, the reporters beating a drum that had already fallen silent. I was feeling older and grayer but not much wiser.

o   o   o

Six months earlier, already looking beyond the Apple campus for other operating-system concepts, I heard from Ike Nassi about the work that had been going on at Carnegie-Mellon University in Pittsburgh. They had developed a new class of kernel that they called the "Mach." A kernel resides at the core level of an operating system, and enables the hardware and software to "talk" to each other. The Mach offered a powerful advantage: It was "cross-platform," meaning it could run in a relatively straightforward way on different kinds of hardware—a major conceptual breakthrough at the time.

An enormous number of hours had been spent at Carnegie-Mellon and other universities to develop this kernel, yet it had never been adopted for commercial purposes. So the Mach was still just a worthy university development that hadn't been promoted into the reality of business.

That was the negative. Nonetheless, when I started seriously looking for alternatives to Copland, the Mach offered a compelling appeal. One way to port Copland into a new environment could be to abandon the kernel that Apple had developed and build Copland on the Mach kernel instead.

Nothing comes free. There would have been a lot of "backward compatibility" problems trying to make it work on older Macs. But I wasn't convinced we had an obligation to make a new OS run on every machine we ever made—I thought it was just too high a price to pay. Although we had never pursued the Mach kernel, its possibilities made a lasting impression.

Now it was six months later and the Mach kernel began to look very interesting. And who was already using it? Characteristically, Steve Jobs—out in front of the rest of the industry, as he had so often been. He had recognized the advantages of the Mach nine years before and had seduced one of its creators, a brilliant Ph.D. named Avie Tevanian, into leaving Carnegie-Mellon and joining him at NeXT—over a competing offer from none other than Bill Gates. Because of this foresight, the Mach kernel had been made the foundation for the NeXT operating system software.

Getting revved up for Steve's return from Japan, I spent time delving into our research on the NeXT software to discover what else it might offer us. His people had spent a lot of time thinking about key issues like networking and the world of the Internet—much more so than anything else around. Better than anything Apple had done, better than NT, and potentially better than what Sun had.

And the work they had done on WebObjects, their object-based software for developing Web-based applications, was world-class. An award-winning software concept for developing Web sites, WebObjects looked to be clearly one of the jewels of the NeXT software. It's going to factor importantly into the future, because it allows developers to write applications in a true Web-based environment, creating a user experience that's completely acceptable on the Web. I still can't figure why it isn't getting more attention from the press.

∘   ∘   ∘

With a lingering bad taste in my mouth after the Be fiasco, this time I was determined to move ahead with logic as my drill sergeant. *Sidestep the charisma associated with these silicon stars and ignore the gossip,* I said to myself. Easier said than done.

Given all the technology points for Steve's operating system, NeXT was looking better and better. On the other hand, Steve's company came with a visionary agenda, and I judged that it was the wrong agenda for Apple. But I was definitely interested in his operating system. Was one available without the other?

Steve got back from Japan and on December 2 came in late in the afternoon to meet with Ellen and me in the conference room next to my office, a room still haunted by the lingering ghosts of the deal-gone-sour with Jean-Louis. He said, "It struck me that there might be an opportunity for NeXT to help Apple." Very much how Jean-Louis had started. Were the ghosts feeding him their lines?

"I have no idea whether you guys will have any interest in this at all, but let me just tell you what I think is appealing." A refreshingly modest approach, especially for Steve Jobs. "It's probably a totally crazy idea," he went on, "and I don't even know why I'm here talking to you, but let's see what it feels like."

He launched into a pitch that began by knocking the Be operating system as a disaster for Apple. Gradually he got around to his main theme: "If you think there's something for you in NeXT, I'll structure any kind of deal you want—license the software, sell you the company, whatever you want."

I was sure at the time and I'm still sure that the approach was carefully calculated to set the perfect mood. I was already more interested than he knew, but I was relieved that he wasn't coming on like a high-speed train. There were spaces in the presentation to think and question and discuss.

Before he was through, he had changed his tune a bit: "When you take a close look, you'll decide you want more than my software. You'll want to buy the whole company and take all the people." I was willing to keep an open mind, and we agreed to set up a meeting of engineers from the two companies to examine technical issues.

o   o   o

Emotions too often stand in the way of logic. I had all but crossed Be off the list because of my annoyance at Jean-Louis's unfortunate manner in dealing with me and his feet-in-cement position on price. But this wasn't a moment for allowing myself to be ruled by emotion. I gave Ellen the assignment of having her engineers do a rigorous scientific analysis of how we would fare in using software from Microsoft, Solaris, Be, and NeXT. Wayne Meretsky and his team drew up a set of fifty-seven parameters for measuring each solution.

For me, the central issues were: How certain are we that the solution can be made to work on the Mac? Does it provide a strong base not just for today but for the future? How soon could we have it ready to offer for sale to our customers?

Wayne's scientific analysis and my notepad criteria both produced the same answer: NeXT. Runner-up: Be.

This could have been a situation of "Where does the elephant sit?" (to which the answer, of course, is "Anywhere it wants to"), because obviously as CEO I could make a unilateral decision. It's slower and tougher to decide by consensus, but I wanted Apple's executive team to reach a decision jointly . . . and some of them still favored the Solaris or Microsoft solutions.

Members of the Supreme Court consider not just what's on paper but remain open to be influenced by oral arguments. I determined that we would do the same: We would invite Steve and Jean-Louis each to appear before me and the executive team, and make his case. I would then take the decision of the executives to the board for approval.

o   o   o

With the press so avidly following this story, the Apple campus was much too visible a place for the shootout. We booked the upstairs meeting room at the Garden Court Hotel in Palo Alto. Steve would present on the afternoon of Tuesday, December 10, and Jean-Louis would follow.

Steve's sales pitch on the NeXT operating system was dazzling. He held nothing back and praised the virtues and strengths as though he were describing a performance of Olivier as Macbeth.

This was a different Steve—pragmatic, specific, precise . . . a sharp contrast to the man who had been selling himself to me on that first occasion, more than a year earlier, when he had come to National Semiconductor cajoling me to support him for the post of Apple's CEO. This time he knew exactly what he was talking about, he made listening very easy, and I was impressed.

Then Steve turned the floor over to Avie Tevanian, who he had brought along to handle the technical explanations. Smart decision, since Steve's technical understanding only goes a micron deep. And Avie had a laptop with him so he could demonstrate the software, showing it as a working OS, not just a concept. Steve's only setback came when senior engineer Meretsky asked questions revealing some shortcomings for Apple in using the NeXT software, but Steve recovered quickly and made light of the issues. Between them, Avie and Steve were a very compelling duo.

Jean-Louis, appearing as Act Two, made a grave miscalculation, for which Ellen or I may bear at least part of the responsibility: He did not understand that this was a shootout, or else still thought he had the decision locked up—even though stories had been appearing in the papers for ten days about my conversations with Steve.

He came alone, and he came with nothing in his hands. He said in effect, "Your technical people have met with my technical people, so you know the strengths of our solution."

There was no formal presentation, no technical discussion, not even a sales pitch. He seemed to assume it was obvious his answer was the best, and he already had the order, so why waste time explaining it.

Everything pointed toward Steve Jobs and NeXT, but Jean-Louis had made it a no-contest. The vote for NeXT was almost a foregone conclusion.

○   ○   ○

For the board meeting a few days later, where I would propose the purchase of NeXT, I invited Steve to come and make his own presentation. Steve's arrival offered a dramatic moment, one of those memorable instants that the legends of the industry are built on: Upon entering, Steve walked over to Mike Markkula and the two shook hands. These old friends, whose mutual support had been essential in building the great Apple Computer from its birth, had been avoiding each other for many years, since Mike's role in forcing Steve out of his own company. However difficult the moment may have been for Steve, he wisely recognized this was no time to carry an old grudge.

Even without Avie, Steve did his usual highly skilled job with the presentation and demo. The board was not happy about spending the money that would be involved, but understood the necessity and authorized me to enter negotiations for the purchase of NeXT Computer.

○   ○   ○

I called Steve and said, "We need to get eyeball-to-eyeball and see if we can put a deal together."

"Good."

"We can't meet at Apple, because it would be all over the company in twenty minutes, all over the Valley in two hours, and all over the media by the end of the day. We can't meet at any public place, because we're both too well recognized. So we're down to two choices—it's your home or mine."

He said, "Come on out," and I said, "Fine."

Almost as much as I enjoy flying a jet, I still enjoy driving my classic 1973 Mercedes-Benz, especially when the freeways aren't jammed with rush-hour crowds. At ten o'clock on a late fall morning, the sunlight and shadow on the hills play tricks on your mood.

Steve's wife and children were out when I arrived, so he started some water boiling while he showed me around, and then we sat down in the kitchen like a couple of cronies to negotiate over a cup of tea.

I had no hidden agendas and he seemed just as determined to be forthright as we went through the key points of a deal. Will it be for cash, stock, or a combination? How do we handle the people? What do we do about the stock options that the people of NeXT are holding? How do we handle the publicity? And what would Steve's long-term relationship be with Apple?

I said I wanted him to come in as part of the management team, to be an employee of the company again, and he acknowledged that he understood.

Why did I want him? It's been said that the world is made up of follow-the-pack marketers, like Bill Gates, who wait for necessity to mother invention, while Steve Jobs creates inventions that mother necessity. His is one of those magnetic, charismatic personalities that light up a room. But his invaluable contributions can be largely overshadowed by the dissension he sows.

I had to make a conscious choice to think about his potential role at Apple intellectually, not emotionally, which meant ignoring the unpleasant pressure his personality could cause, overlooking the friction he creates. The gossip did not escape me, and I had shuddered at stories of his treating brilliant, dedicated people like idiots. I preferred instead to value him as someone whom many people admire, learn from, and owe their success to. I was convinced that if I could keep him focused on the one project—the operating system—which was going to be carried out almost entirely by NeXT people, that I could contain the negative behaviors from infecting the rest of the company.

As it turned out, that was wishful thinking on my part. Cornering a tornado might have been easier.

Steve's first issue was with his backers and what they would be willing to settle for. He himself was the largest shareholder; the other major investors were Ross Perot and Canon Corporation. Together the three owned about 75 percent of the company.

Steve started out at about $12 a share.

That was high, but I was figuring, *We're picking up an existing operating system, we're picking up $50 million a year in additional revenues from NeXT sales, we're picking up WebObjects, and I'm getting a team of about 300 very* *talented people.* All of these were things I wouldn't have gotten in a deal with Jean-Louis; this was obviously worth more . . . but how *much* more?

There are two kinds of good-value acquisitions. One is when you see a property that's suddenly become available below market or a solid company in your industry has run into management problems and can be bought out at a discount. These are essentially opportunistic.

This, on the other hand, was a *strategic* opportunity, one you go after because there's some asset you really want or need, an asset you believe will ultimately add to the corporate wealth. In the strategic situation, the price is largely irrelevant. One hundred million dollars more would represent only three days of sales for Apple.

We had done our due diligence on the numbers, but it wasn't a terribly important part of the process. (After the fact, critics and the press would cavil for months over the final price, unable to grasp the long-range significance to Apple, the critical nature of the purchase.)

Still, I told Steve, "That isn't possible. I can't see that kind of money, it's more than I want to spend. I don't think I can meet it."

He asked, "What's the number you're looking at?"

"I think I have a shot at convincing the board to take $10. I don't think I can get a penny more than that."

He agreed. We tentatively settled on $10 as the number. (And it stuck through to the end, representing a total of about $400 million; $12 a share would have made it closer to $500 million.)

Steve brewed fresh tea as we moved on to the issue of stock options. Much more widely used for workers in Silicon Valley than elsewhere in corporate America, stock options—which give the employee the right to purchase shares in the company at a pleasingly discounted price—are one of the basic inducements to attract strong people, especially valuable for startups that can't afford to compete on a salary basis.

Basically what I wanted is what all buyers want: not to be obligated to make good on the stock options held by NeXT employees. For options that had already "vested"—that is, come under the control of the employee—Apple would hand the person a check on the day of settling the buyout for the full value of their options. But all other options would be wiped out, and we would replace them with Apple options, priced as for other Apple employees.

Steve didn't like it. Protecting the interests of his people, he wanted stock options to be converted on a dollar-for-dollar basis to Apple stock. I estimated that would have added about another $70 million dollars to the cost—too pricey. While the arrangement is sometimes customary in deals like this, Steve could see I wasn't going to go for it. He pushed, and then sized up the situation correctly.

We found a middle ground: The options would be converted in a way that maintained the bargain element. So if the exchange ratio was two shares of NeXT equaling one share of Apple, we would convert the options at the same ratio into Apple options. And we agreed on maintaining the same vesting date, so if a particular employee's options at NeXT didn't vest for another year, he'd have to wait the same year for his Apple options to vest.

(Later on, this would prove to be a problem with some of the NeXT employees, who latched onto a story that all the options were going to accelerate so they would get all their money on the day of the transaction. I would have to call Steve and say, "You've got to talk to your employees and tell them *you* made this deal, it's not Apple trying to give them the shaft." It would bother me that I was forced to tell Steve he needed to say it straight to his people; he should have done that on his own. When you make a deal, you ought to have the courage and integrity to stand up for it. If it looks like your people are drifting beyond what you've agreed to, a leader doesn't wait for someone to tell him what needs to be done. When your integrity is on the line, you've got to do what it takes to preserve it.)

Unlike Jean-Louis, who had wanted all stock and no cash, Steve didn't want *any* stock. He wanted all cash, and so did Ross Perot and Canon. I said, "For the other investors, I don't care. If they want cash, they can have it. But Steve, you have to take some in stock." I told him, "This deal is not credible if you don't take part of it in stock."

I felt he had to have some skin in the game, some money at risk. The deal had to give Steve the motivation to work for the benefit of Apple. I knew he loved the company but I insisted that he show it, and started out asking him to take two million shares in stock and the rest in cash. He came back with one million, and we compromised on a million and a half.

We also agreed that Apple would register the shares for him, but that he would not sell them for at least six months. I had wanted it longer than that, but I saw I wasn't going to get it, so backed down. I said, "It's important that you own the stock and that you keep the stock. Your selling it would send entirely the wrong message. As powerful a positive as this deal is, that's how negative it would be if you turned around and sold your stock. It's a double-edged sword." So, still at the breakfast table with our now-cold tea, we agreed on this point, too.

How about jobs for his people? We agreed I would bring across all of the NeXT employees except his CFO and his head lawyer, because we already had strong people in each of those positions.

Then Steve asked, "Would you like to go for a walk?"

It seemed a most unusual idea for a business meeting, and most appealing, except that I later found out this is a standard technique of his. We started walking around his Palo Alto neighborhood, making me a little nervous about it, because I didn't want anyone to see the two of us together. I figured I could always come up with some cock-and-bull story: *We're friends and I was just visiting,* or something equally dumb. But I was hooked in by Steve's energy and enthusiasm.

We walked around the block twice and talked about. . . . I can't remember a word! I do remember how animated he is on his feet, how his full mental abilities materialize when he's up and moving, how he becomes more expressive.

We headed back for the house with a deal wrapped up—Apple would buy NeXT for $377.5 million in cash, plus one and a half million shares of stock. Steve's personal ownership in the company would bring him about $120 million in cash, plus the stock worth about $25 a share, for a total value of roughly $157 million.

The two of us reached his home just as Steve's wife arrived with the children—the timing was theatrically perfect. By then it was past the lunch hour, and I was starving. I said my good-byes and headed back to the office.

o   o   o

The only way to present this to the board was to be totally forthright: "I'm not going to stand here and tell you this deal is worth the money we're proposing to pay. But since we've managed to get ourselves into this situation where we do not have an operating-system strategy, we have very few options."

The board members finally agreed. Their attitude was "It's an outrageous price, but we have to do it."

The process of reducing an agreement in principle into a legal document ordinarily takes, in most deals I've ever done in the corporate world, about three months. It's not a simple task and the lawyers, bless them and their good intentions, make it intricately complicated.

But I had told Steve we needed to get it wrapped up in ten days. Susan Thorner, an Apple lawyer who was very heavily in the middle of this, moved into overdrive; I think she could not have slept more than two or three hours a night. We worried about her health, we worried about the details, we worried about the press—but we got it done, and without a leak.

○ ○ ○

On December 20, with the Christmas holidays already well on us, we saw the contracts would be finished, signed, and blotted by early afternoon, and called a six o'clock press conference for "a major announcement." Three o'clock came, six o'clock came, and we still didn't have a contract.

The problem? Steve's role. He'd been implying all along that he would join as a hard-working member of the OS team, but in reality, his heart was at his movie company Pixar. He had never intended that the deal would include his giving Apple any more than some portion of his attention.

I finally had to confront him. "Steve, do you just want to take your money and leave? Because it's okay if that's what you want."

No response.

"Do you want to be an employee on the payroll? An advisor?"

Still no response.

"Steve, I can't get up to announce the purchase of NeXT without this piece of information—it's going to be the first question the reporters ask."

It seemed like an easy question, a no-brainer, not something to get worked up over, yet Steve was visibly irritable, as moody as I had seen him up to that time. He seemed cornered by some inner monster.

The eminent Menlo Park attorney Larry Sonsini was representing Steve, so I took Larry aside.

"I know it's not kosher for me to be talking to you, but what's going on?"

"Beats me," was all I could get from Larry, who couldn't fathom Steve's behavior any more than I could.

I went back in, closed the door so it was just the two of us, and said, "Steve, what's on your mind? What are you feeling? What are you reacting to? This doesn't seem like a big deal, but obviously it is to you. Please, I need a decision now—one that you can live with and that I can announce."

"I didn't get any sleep last night."

"Why? What's the problem."

"I was thinking about all the things that need to be done and about the deal we're making and it's all running together for me. I'm really tired now and not thinking clearly. I just don't want to be asked any more questions."

That just wouldn't do, so I pressed forward. "Do you want to be head of engineering?"

"No." At least he was answering.

"Do you want to be an advisor to the company?"

"No."

And then, finally, he said, "Look, if you have to tell them something, just say advisor to the chairman." *Okay,* I thought, *that will do it.*

At eight o'clock, I was finally able to tell the assembled media that Apple had "picked Plan A instead of Plan Be."

When they heard Steve's role, some members of the media decided on the spot that when Steve really started playing with Apple, I wouldn't know what hit me. I was getting used to fighting off the worriers.

◦　◦　◦

If you looked at the NeXT buyout strictly as a financial deal and forgot all the other factors, you could, with some stretching, probably have justified in the neighborhood of $200 million. But then you say, Okay, if it can save Apple, what's that worth? Is it worth $100 million? $200 million? $500 million? Twice the $200 million figure was justified, because we were a $10 billion company that didn't have an operating-system strategy worth a damn. And that extra $200 million was a drop in the bucket if it could help preserve the larger company. Since it needed to be done, it was worth doing at a premium. The Jean-Louis negotiation collapsed because, with an operating system that was still a long way from being finished, there wasn't as much stretch in the price as he calculated.

Such decisions are very subjective. I trust to intuition, so long as it's based on firm knowledge plus experience, and with the added ingredient of sharp-edged personal judgment. Hard to predict when moving forward, but easy to measure when reviewing the past.

In a sense, Jean-Louis had the last word and showed a degree of class I had not suspected he had, with this e-mail:

```
Subject: Congratulations
Sent: 12/20/96 1:17 PM
Received: 12/23/96 10:42 AM
From: Jean-Louis Gassée, jlg2@be.be.com
Reply to: jlg@be.com
to: amelio.g@apple.com
CC: hancock@apple.com
    solomon@apple.com
    Congratulations for all aspects of an extremely
well-crafted deal. Clearly we were not in the same
technical and financial league.
    Thanks for having considered us. Happy holidays
to you and your loved ones.
JLG
```

14

Much Ado—
MACWORLDS LAMENTABLE, LAUDABLE, AND LAUGHABLE

 The holiday season should be a time of joy and laughter and frivolous things. My holidays got off to a bad start.

The hardware part of Apple's printers, such as the inexpensive, immensely popular StyleWriter, had been made for us in Japan by Canon, a company that had succeeded in being a reliable prime supplier for Apple. But as our engineers saw it, Canon hadn't been spending on improving their technology, while Epson and others were charging past them. HP, in particular, was gobbling up market share.

In July, I had made the decision that we should leave Canon and change to a different printer-engine supplier. We went into negotiations with HP that turned out to be protracted and intense, at times almost hostile. They wanted a minimum volume commitment of a million and a half units a year, but I was nervous about whether we could meet that number.

Since we were willing to take the basic HP printer and just add Apple software and an Apple case, they were going to have virtually no development costs. But the HP people were hung up on the guarantee; finally the situation got to a crossroads where their people were threatening to abort the deal.

We had already announced the change, so canceling would have been awkward. Just before Christmas I set up a conference call with Lew Platt, the CEO of HP, and the project people on both sides. My position with Lew was, "You guys are already making this engine, just make the additional units for us." I said, "I don't understand why you're talking about guarantees—on an incremental basis, even ten units is good for you because it's ten more than you'd sell without us."

The conversation quickly descended into finger-pointing and "who struck John," with their project people and ours getting very heated. The HP project man said, "If Apple isn't going to meet the volume commitment, we're backing out." I said to Lew, "We're already committed on this, you can't back out on us now."

Meanwhile I was picturing myself having announced a product that would never materialize, further eroding Apple's credibility and my own. It would also mean having to do an about-face with Canon, which would have been very embarrassing.

Lew, on his side, was picturing a lawsuit from Apple for breaking the agreement. This was a nightmare for both of us; all we wanted to do was get it settled with an understanding that made good business sense all around.

Lew could simply have shouted and stormed and said, "We're going to do it *this* way," and his people would have shut up and fallen in line. There are times when I almost envy the obedience that style produces . . . except that it also produces fear, a reluctance to present crucial information, and the death of innovation. Lew is a calm man, I'm a calm man, and the two of us were playing peacemaker between the fiery project people who were at each other's throats.

Still, it took well over an hour before Lew and I had managed to get the Apple and HP project managers calmed down and willing to work together, with an agreement that we would guarantee to purchase one million units.

A few days later, Lew and I ran into each other at a Christmas dinner party. Looking elegant in his dinner tuxedo, the only slightly graying Platt came over to me and said, "I couldn't believe the animosity on both sides in what should have been a fairly simple deal."

"I felt the same way," I said.

"You know," Platt said, "thirty years in business, that phone call was the worst I ever had."

What a way to begin the holidays.

◦　◦　◦

Getting to my Lake Tahoe home for the vacation offered respite and a bit of relief from ceaseless pressures, but little of the exercise I was so sorely missing. In the ten months since arriving at Apple, I had played not a single game of tennis, had rarely gone bicycling with Charlene, and hadn't even found time for taking walks with her. But hopes for challenging flabby muscles on the ski slopes would be dashed by the weather: a 100-year snowstorm followed by torrential rain that brought major flooding, shutting down all the ski resorts and snowmobile trails.

Family members arrived through the storm in shifts. First my side—Todd, Lisa, and Ryan—then Charlene's half—Brent and his wife Mandy, and their sons, Logan and Griffin, Tina and her husband Dan, and Dan's parents. Forget exercise; we mostly huddled around the fireplace, stuck in the cabin for days on end. Even our adult children were climbing the walls.

For me, there was no escape from work, though I would now and again force myself to relax, and feel a smile coming on. One smile came from downloading e-mail of a lyric that was making the rounds on the Internet and was forwarded to me by several people with instructions that it was to be sung to the tune of "Santa Claus is Coming to Town":

> You better watch out,
> Absurd as it sounds,
> 'Cause Apple's about
> To lose a few pounds—
> Gil Amelio's coming to town!
>
> He's making a list,
> And trimming the rolls
> Of projects that missed
> Their revenue goals—
> Gil Amelio's coming to town!

He knows what's losing money,
Like eWorld, PowerTalk . . .
You'd better make your project work
Or prepare to take a walk!

Though you follow his lead
Right out the back door,
You know he'll succeed—
He's done it before!
Gil Amelio's coming to town!

I well remember how this simple silly spoof finally brought forth my hearty laughter and expunged some Scrooge from my soul. I needed help to maintain perspective.

The HP issue was resolved, but a sullen pair of other issues stalked me, making it acutely difficult to fully enjoy the time spent with family. In the midst of a Christmas carol, I would think about difficulties that would face me as soon as the holidays were over: the terrible sales results for what should have been Apple's best sales quarter of the year.

And unwrapping gifts and flaming desserts became merely background blur to my worries over the unreasonable difficulties I had begun to encounter on preparations for my upcoming MacWorld speech.

o   o   o

I had known at the time of the three weeks of sales meetings in October that we were not making our sales numbers for the quarter. This was calamitous news—not just that we were on our way to another losing quarter, and not just that it was the holiday quarter, supposed to be Apple's biggest selling season of the year, but that I would have to report a down quarter following the profitable one. I had predicted the pain and was dreading the coming confrontation with reality.

The fact that Apple had again been manipulated by some of our channel partners—who had once again held off on ordering, hoping for the last-minute panicky price drops they had been accustomed to—would not excuse us from blame; the fault ultimately was our own and I would take the bullet.

We should have responded six weeks earlier to the drop in demand, should have taken drastic steps as soon as we saw sales dip below the normal trend line; we could have spent less on the expensive ad campaign and cut back on travel, which would alone have saved the company as much as $55 million. Had I clamped down on expenditures more vigorously, the numbers of this vital quarter might have been good enough for the report to satisfy the board, the press, and the stockholders.

And to save my own reputation as well as the company's, I should also have taken into consideration the strange psychological factor of the way the market and the opinion-makers work. If you issue warnings in October that you're going to experience a disappointing Christmas, customers and analysts tend to say, "Too bad they're going to have a rotten Christmas." But waiting until late December to announce the bad news makes management look weak and disorganized, and the financial community tends to think, "Those guys are out of control." So this has become today's strange rule: Predict doom early and come through alive.

To my horror, I would discover the situation to be worse than the previous channel stuffing. Although I had repeatedly laid down the law "Never again," I would be shocked to find those instructions once more totally ignored. When the sales reps saw they weren't going to make their quotas and get their commission bonuses, the old methods were dredged up and my orders were set aside without a blink.

I think this was the nadir. I finally realized that I was not being well-served by key members of my executive team; I had left them in place far too long. Even when we know difficult truths about ourselves, it's painfully hard to give them up. Priding myself on nurturing and mentoring, I have in the past kept people long after it was evident they weren't going to make it. Now I had done it yet again; but no longer.

If I was going to face problems with either the board not supporting me or the stockholders not supporting me, then I damn well would rather do it making my own mistakes than suffering for the mistakes of others. Time to start laying my plans for the all-new next phase of Apple's transformation, with some new faces replacing old.

    o   o   o

I saw the January MacWorld in San Francisco as a time and place to gain renewed momentum—a chance to *show* change rather than just talk about it. I was planning to use the event for unveiling to the Macintosh faithful the story of Apple's acquisition of NeXT, what it would mean and why it would be so important to them. Insuring that Steve Jobs would be willing to take part was an important ingredient in the brew; his return to the MacWorld stage would evoke enormous excitement and Apple's image would brilliantly benefit from the enthusiasm he can be counted on to generate. And while System 8 had been covered extensively by the computer magazines, the public hadn't yet seen it operating. Steve would handle Apple's image and support the promise for the future of the company; I would introduce and demo an early version of System 8 and lay out the advantages it would bring to users, developers, and the company. These were the main messages that needed to be clearly articulated and confidently presented.

Early in December I had held an initial meeting with the two men who had been selected to put together the MacWorld event—the writer, a sometime stand-up comic; and a top-level Apple PR executive as producer. At first it seemed likely that they would get the mood and the messages right. As plans started to take shape, it began to sound like the team had an entertaining, upbeat approach—the very positive feeling I was hoping for. Their plans called a big opening by playing off the Apple tie-in with the blockbuster movie *Independence Day*. One of the film's stars, Jeff Goldblum, had already agreed to be on hand to open the session and introduce me. I thought, *Great—just the kind of surprise that MacWorld audiences have come to expect.*

I was presented with a list of other megastars from the worlds of computing and entertainment, and the names seemed to guarantee a memorable experience for everyone in the audience, plus lots of photo ops and stories for the press. Major players from the computer world would convey the message that developers were not fleeing from the Apple platform. We had to build the certainty that buying a Macintosh was still a safe, secure investment.

The developers would each do a tight five-minute spot to show off their new software, demonstrating their continuing support for the Mac. Musician Peter Gabriel had agreed to show how he composes music using the Mac. Aircraft designer Burt Ratan would demo how he uses a Mac in the cockpit to fly an airplane. And creators from a fascinating assortment of other fields would briefly show their own unusual Mac uses.

When I was told that the incomparable Muhammad Ali would appear and take a bow, even though I never got the connection of his appearance quite as clearly as I would have liked, I was, admittedly, delighted. Who would say no to this superstar? Over time I would have the opportunity to better discover the innate greatness of this fine man.

The MacWorld outline assigned me a total of twenty minutes, and that was all I needed. The role I had taken for myself would be to present the key introduction of the soon-to-be-delivered System 8, and set up Steve Jobs's presentation of the operating system that would be based on the NeXT software, which we had already begun working on. Following the recent trend at Apple to assign musically related code names to our OS development projects (Copland, after Aaron, and the now defunct Gershwin), this one was being called Rhapsody.

I decided that it would be best to do all this near the end of the session, providing a natural lead-in to introducing Steve, who, with a flash of his charismatic smile plus about twenty minutes or so for his message, would wrap up an impressive session.

I told the team, "I'm going to speak from notes. I don't need a whole speech written, just get me a tight, strong outline. And make sure it times out right." They agreed to have a first draft for me by December 18.

The eighteenth arrived, but no speech notes; all I got was a hazy promise: "It's coming together." I called the writer and said, "It's getting close to Christmas, Apple is about to close for the holiday vacation—when am I going to have the speech notes?" He said, "It just needs more editing."

As we got even nearer the beginning of the holiday break, I continued to get only excuses and promises. A draft finally arrived—so disorganized and so poorly done that nothing would serve but to tell them to start over.

I said to the writer, "I must have these notes by the day after Christmas. Before if possible, but no later than the twenty-sixth."

The twenty-sixth—nothing. In a phone call, the writer promised, "I'm just sending you a disk. It's on its way."

He sent it that same day, as promised. By U.S. mail—at Christmastime! I should have known then that I did not want this man doing any work for me.

When the disk finally arrived, it contained only a file of designs for the backgrounds of the slides—no speech notes, no text, no main points, no outline, no ideas—nothing, not one single element that I could begin with. His excuse was, "It just hasn't come together yet." I was furious at having been assigned this person to work with me.

I thought, *Perhaps he was rebelling because he wanted to do a word-for-word text that he could get acknowledged for, instead of an outline on which the spoken words would be mine instead of his.* I had worked with speech-writers so many times before and was appalled at the disorganized mind of this man.

So I cut my vacation short and headed back to Cupertino. Like so much of what was going on at Apple at the time, just getting to the airport serving Tahoe proved a trauma-filled adventure that dragged on interminably. Only highway 267 was open, and the fifteen-mile drive took six hours.

Back in Cupertino, I pulled together a team including VP Doug Solomon and my aide Jim Oliver, and we got the notes done. Another example of waiting too long; I should have acted earlier to bring in a writer I confidently knew could do the work in a way that would support me and be a credit to Apple.

o   o   o

January 7. MacWorld was upon us, and things were continuing to go wrong. My speech notes were still being worked on and, without material to practice from, I skipped the one rehearsal that had been scheduled for me. The team had been so disorganized and so dreadfully inefficient that nobody had consulted with Steve Jobs about where he had been scheduled in the program.

Used to being the star act, it hadn't even occurred to Steve that he would appear anywhere but near the beginning of the main session; he was blithely unaware that I had chosen to build up to his appearance as a climax. He was backstage ready to be called on when he learned he wasn't to appear until after the whole crowd of people he saw waiting with him. I can understand his fury; I wasn't there to reassure him, and no one else had the courage to explain.

Yet his behavior was another issue, a full-fledged "Steve-trum": his personal version of a tantrum that I was told come on quite frequently to one extent or another. This one was both inappropriate and ill-timed.

My speech notes were still being massaged up until minutes before the starting time. As soon as the final changes were entered, my executive assistant David Seda took the disk and hurried backstage to have the file loaded into the TelePrompTer; under the last-minute pressure, he did not realize that the wrong draft was transferred, nor that large portions of the text had become garbled. I was set up for a disaster and had no clue.

But that wasn't all. I would later learn that the event manager for this landmark MacWorld had not scheduled a single complete walk-through of the demos. The guests and presenters, I was told, had never been directed which way they would enter and exit, or how to stand so they'd be visible to the video cameras beaming their image onto the huge overhead screens. Their demos had never been timed or rehearsed. The entire production effort had been focused on technology; no one had made any effort to work with the people. It was as if the company had never staged a major event before; no wonder Steve was fuming.

Although I knew I had not been supported professionally, I didn't know the extent of the disorganization; I did not yet fully realize I was about to suffer one of the most embarrassing and unforgiving experiences of my life. I waited, trying to gather courage by recalling the feelings of success I'd had at MacWorld Boston just six months before.

My cue came, I walked out, and began. I quickly discovered that the slides were in the wrong order and realized that the TelePrompTer was showing me an earlier, outdated version of the script. As I searched for my place in the hard copy of the show flow I had fortunately brought out with me, I tried to remember in what order the people waiting in the wings were expecting to be called.

Then I reached a place where the text on the prompter was totally garbled. There was an awkward silence, I could hear my own heart thumping as I tried not to look distraught; the notion of being relaxed and spontaneous flew out the window. This was going to be an ordeal.

And then I began to see that the people I was introducing were each speaking, not for the expected five minutes, but closer to fifteen. Or more.

The session started at noon and was scheduled to take an hour and a half. One-thirty came, and we were only halfway through. Backstage there seemed to be an unending line of people still waiting to give demos. Because their appearances had not been scheduled, timed, and rehearsed, because a carefully timed show script had never been finished, I became like the man with the hook in old-time vaudeville, the villain who had to disappoint those still waiting in the wings for their time onstage. But I did what the situation demanded: With one eye on the clock, I jumped into my operating-system portion.

My work on honing the System 8 and Rhapsody messages paid off, so that I was able to finish within the twenty minutes allocated. That done, I proudly flowed into my introduction of Steve, who came onstage to the expected warm reception and loud applause.

I thought to myself, *He's such a showman, he'll realize that time is a big problem. I bet he'll know how to do his part in less than fifteen minutes.*

But he cozied up in the warmth of the spotlight for thirty minutes or more. And, when finished, he ruthlessly ruined the closing moment I had planned—although what he created was a more dramatic ending than any writer could have scripted. For the finale, I was to join Steve on the stage, thank him . . . and then, for a moment no one in the audience was likely to forget, I would bring out Steve Wozniak.

PR had assured me that the two Steves, together again, would make headlines. Fifty photographers in the front rows would get smiling, historic photos of the two of them and the three of us—"perfect photos to go with positive stories about Apple Computer."

I introduced Woz, catching the audience by surprise . . . and he came out to the biggest ovation of the day. Woz back in the spotlight, where he deserves to be—a stunning moment.

But as soon as Woz appeared onstage, Jobs walked off. And there was no coaxing him back. His own feelings were more important than good press for Apple; he had decided not to cooperate—and that was that.

o   o   o

We had taken three hours, twice as long as scheduled. TV channels that had booked satellite time to air live coverage of my operating-system presentation and the Steve Jobs remarks had been forced to broadcast filler. Reporters from the East had missed their deadlines. Photographers went away without their shots of the two Steves.

When I visited the MacWorld show floor that afternoon, some people griped about how long it had taken, but there were many positive comments—perhaps from people just being polite and kind, but they seemed quite sincere. When the news reports appeared, my staff attempted to protect me from the scathing reviews. Dan Gillmor wrote in the *San Jose Mercury News* that I had looked like I was "ad-libbing like crazy, and ineffectively" and that "about 10 minutes after he started, [Amelio] had a look on his face that said, 'Uh, oh, I'm bombing.'"

Fortune described me as appearing "uncomfortably pseudo-casual in a sport jacket and banded-collar shirt" and reported that I "rambled" and "droned on for hours."

One audience member on his way out had asked an Apple employee whether I had had a stroke.

And those were just some of the kinder remarks.

The key members of the event team tried to explain what went wrong, but I was reacting in the way I do when seriously furious—I tend to shut people out. I had heard about Apple's memorable shows, videos, and product introductions; this team didn't measure up. And instead of learning from the experience, these two ill-prepared and disorganized people would later badmouth me and try to shift blame for their failure.

I often think how wasteful it is that those with real capabilities should doubt their abilities, while bunglers seem so damn sure of themselves.

o   o   o

Bill Gates and I, despite continued frequent phone calls, didn't seem to be getting any closer toward settling a technology-exchange deal between the two companies. He still seemed to think he could get an agreement from me without giving anything important in return; I was still sure he would eventually see I was adamant and give enough ground to reach an agreement that made sense on both sides.

The series of deal-making calls was interrupted by one of very different character. Like many companies in high tech, Microsoft is always trolling for talented people they might be able to hire, and they've never been shy about sending out recruiting pieces to Apple employees. Just the way a carpet-cleaning firm buys a mailing list and saturates a community with junk mail, Microsoft somehow gets hold of Apple employee lists and sends "We'd like to offer you a job" messages.

Apparently they don't always screen their lists well: To my great amusement, I received an e-mail solicitation to consider the opportunity of working for Microsoft.

I responded with a seemingly annoyed message to Bill Gates—a complaint, as if I had taken the message seriously and was demanding a retraction. Bill called me directly and launched into an effusive apology: "Gil, I'm so sorry, you have to understand in a big corporation how things like this happen, I'm really embarrassed by this . . ." and so on.

I sat there, leaning back in my chair, letting him pour out a long list of apologetic words. Finally I felt a bit sorry for him and interrupted his spiel in mid-sentence to say, "Bill, I was just teasing you, I'm really not upset."

Silence. And then a burst of full, unchecked laughter, an *explosion* of laughter. He had been duped, and had thoroughly enjoyed the experience. It was the only time I ever got a true and deeply responsive laugh from Bill, the only time I ever heard him enjoy himself so thoroughly. And it says something admirable about a man who can laugh at himself but is quite respectful and careful about laughing at others.

Yes, I believe Gates is not often enough given his due as a human being.

o   o   o

When I first arrived, trade-press journalists had written articles asking, Should Gil dump Newton?

A year later, Newton the product was looking much rosier; Newton the division was still a large cash drain.

We had over a billion dollars in the bank, but the company was existing on borrowed money. The time had come to think about selling some family treasures. I told Fred Anderson, "We better see if somebody can find us a buyer for Newton or Pippin." Fred reluctantly agreed.

Under a cloak of secrecy—because the news that these product lines were for sale would have destroyed morale among the Newton and

Pippin employees—we once again called on investment banker Eff Martin of the Goldman Sachs office in San Francisco. Every day I would read the papers fully expecting to see a story about Apple's search for a Newton buyer and was shocked that we actually managed to keep a lid on this story for as long as a month, something of a record run for an Apple secret.

On February 3, Lee Gomes broke the story in the *Wall Street Journal*, but all he could report on were whispers ("The struggling personal-computer maker has talked recently to venture capitalists . . . "), with no confirmation, no names of venture capitalists supposedly involved or of buyers who might be showing an interest. And, of course, "Apple declined to comment."

In those days, instead of talk radio, I drove to and from my office playing a mind game I had named "How much is Newton worth?" The Newton division was generating revenues of $200 million a year and running up operating and manufacturing costs of about $260 million a year. Under normal circumstances, the asking price of a going product is some multiple of sales; that formula didn't apply to Newton, since there was no assurance of when the division might turn profitable. The secret number I had arrived at as the lowest price I would accept—a number I shared with no one, not even Fred—was $50 million.

While I was convinced its intrinsic value was much higher, I would at that point have been willing to get the cash drain off our books for that figure. Any lower and we would have been suggesting the product was probably not viable; any higher, and I thought the deal would be seen as too costly.

I need not have spent much time thinking about it. We got bites on Newton from the Korean giant Samsung and from Ericsson in Sweden, as well as two or three smaller players. But they wanted to open discussions at price levels well below my bottom-line number, enough below that I did not take the offers seriously and broke off the effort.

When that fell through, I decided to spin the Newton group out as a wholly-owned subsidiary. Later on, as the product became more successful, we could offer stock in Newton as a subsidiary company and we'd then be able to use shares of the stock as leverage to help retain key employees and lure new ones of the same A-list caliber.

I called all the Newton people together in a meeting at Town Hall and told them I thought they were ready for this first step toward independence, and ready to be measured and rewarded on the basis of their performance instead of the performance of Apple as a whole. Not everyone seemed enthusiastic, but perhaps nine out of ten appeared pleased with the idea. That was encouraging—it meant that most had confidence in their own ability to make Newton a success.

o   o   o

Apple shareholders were showing more patience than typical investors do. With the annual shareholder meeting coming up, I would have almost no welcome news to share, so would concentrate on talking about plans, forthcoming products, and expectations. I hoped they'd show even more patience and give us the time to see my plans through.

What could I do to take a little sting off the bitter taste of their experience? Perhaps an appropriate show of dedication by the executives would help—not in a verbal form but expressed in terms most investors best understand: money.

My first trial balloon, quickly shot down, was a suggestion that the senior management team all accept a reduction in salary. It's hard for most people to understand that these executives were living up to the level of their income—their salaries ranged from $375,000 to $500,000, on top of which they were receiving performance bonuses ranging from 50 to 100 percent. So even the worst off of the group was taking home well more than half a million a year before taxes.

Most people have personal experience with what happens when the family income goes up: We buy a better car, some new clothes. If income goes up dramatically, we move to a better neighborhood, put the children in private schools, become more generous supporters of the church, the temple, our favorite charities. And in no time, the monthly spending is as close to the monthly income as it was before the increase.

So the reluctance to take a salary reduction wasn't unexpected. I suggested another approach: keep base pay at the existing levels, but suspend executive bonuses.

This time everyone agreed. It would only be a gesture, a drop in the bucket, representing a saving of a few million dollars a year in a company with multibillion-dollar revenues. But I hoped it would be seen as a positive commitment and perhaps deflect a little of the criticism.

∘ ∘ ∘

I had now been working for a year with no employment contract because of that damned provision added by Ed Stead requiring that the terms had to be ratified by the stockholders at the annual meeting.

With that meeting finally just ahead, the last bit of misery I needed was gratuitous negative publicity; there was enough bad news to keep us all miserable. But over at *Business Week,* Peter Burrows was still finding ways to break into print at my expense. His newest episode, yet another attack on my salary and bonus, appeared in the January 20 issue under headlines of "Executive Sweets" and "At Apple, Pay that Defies Gravity." Very clever, these headline writers.

The inequity of my being required to work without contract was overlooked by Burrows as he in three slick paragraphs reminded everyone that my pay packet was on the line. "Because he signed on after the last annual meeting, . . . shareholders only now get to vote whether to grant him a million stock options and up to a million shares." Sounding as if he was suggesting how investors should vote, he went on, "Although no opposition to Amelio's pay has surfaced, his tenure has yet to produce the turnaround investors hoped for." To me, this clearly smacked of pot-stirring disguised as reporting; I thought stockholders reading the piece might get a message that "no opposition has surfaced *yet,* but if you're smart, you'll realize things haven't gotten any better and rethink the promises in the Amelio contract." It certainly made me question whether Burrows cared at all about the value of living up to honorable agreements and deals arranged in good faith.

The article included a clever quote that, despite my annoyance, brought a smile: "Quips pay expert Graef Crystal: 'I'd love to short Apple and buy shares of Gilbert Amelio Inc. Now, that would be a terrific investment.'" But I couldn't help but wonder if some stockholders might decide how to vote on my contract based on those smart-aleck innuendos.

The *San Francisco Chronicle* had a lead story in its business section that carried the head, "Apple Gets Sicker Under Dr.'s Care." A photo caption read, "Gil Amelio has touted himself as a turnaround expert."

Although my short-term performance at Apple left reporters a fertile planting field for their poisonous seeds, I was by this time growing hardened to their criticism and attacks. But with the pressure of the annual meeting just ahead, the blatant and ill-timed pounding from the press caused me to feel brutalized, and I began to conjure up worst-case scenarios.

o　　o　　o

To counter the fantasies, I worked long hours on a cold-hard-facts speech to the shareholders. I expected a considerable amount of moaning, hand-wringing, and blaming as a result of the terrible report we had recently issued for the Christmas quarter. Some shareholders would be angry, and attending reporters would be looking for, even hoping for, sparks and fury; a meeting of shouts and disruptions would provide them with better copy than a straight-forward speech and an agreeable audience.

Two days before the meeting, Harold Burson flew out from New York to personally review my speech draft. With fifty years of experience and the judgment you would expect from someone who has helped to shape the PR industry, Harold has the touch of a master. His skillful changes and additions—though probably no more than half a dozen phrases—captured the sensitivity of what I was trying to communicate and had a major impact on the impression I created. In the hundreds of speeches I've given, only Harold and one other speechwriter have shown the unique ability to capture the content of my thoughts and blend it with my personal style to advantageously package my intrinsic best. Some people *are* writers; many who claim to be writers, merely write.

On the morning of February 6, I drove to the Flint Center remembering the annual meeting of a year earlier, when a stoic and pained Michael Spindler appeared at a loss about how to handle challenges from irate, dissatisfied stockholders. I would handle myself better . . . but would the crowd be any less unruly and contentious? I tried to thrust all negative thoughts from my mind but couldn't help imagining my contract being rejected, a motion being introduced to fire me, or distraught employees or stockholders shouting at me from the floor. Could things get *that* out of hand? I wondered if Spindler had anticipated the rancorous questions he had to endure. *Walk at least a mile a day in another man's shoes.*

I found a parking spot easily at Flint Center and took it as an omen. The meeting was begun by our new legal counsel, Jack Douglas, who went through some of the required business. Like the beginning of a storm with just a few heavy drops on a tin roof, one of my fearsome scenarios began playing out—Jack was being heckled by the audience. Should I have arranged for security people? Could things get *that* out of hand? Too late to worry about it now.

But I realized with relief that the heckling was from only one person, a man who kept interrupting, demanding to know why Amelio wasn't making the presentation himself. Was he hiding? Jack ignored him and the presentations continued as planned.

Charlene remarked later that the irrational behavior of the disruptive audience member may actually have done me considerable benefit. His words were outrageous and his style so offensive that "By the time you came out, Gil, the audience wanted to hear a factual message in a rational voice."

The advance abuse I had received from the press over my compensation clearly did not express the view of stockholders, who seemed to remember and take seriously my three-year estimate for transformation.

The vote on my contract was brought up and passed easily. A final tally would show some 90+ percent in favor.

I wanted to share the facts of the Apple situation carefully and thoroughly, and had hoped that by being forthright, explicit, and open, they would give me the time I needed to follow through on my strategy. There is nothing like the truth to give one confidence, and I was ready to take the bull by the horns: When it was time for questions, I walked to the front of stage, looked directly at the man who had been making Jack's time at the podium so miserable, and said to him, "I'll take your questions now."

Rather sheepishly, I thought, he politely replied, "I'm satisfied."

The presentation was regarded as one of the best I had ever given—even the press grudgingly awarded me a reasonably thumbs-up report card. Another hurdle behind me . . . but another big one to face in just two weeks.

o o o

February 17 brought me once again to Japan for MacWorld Tokyo. I had eliminated all the extraneous elements that had caused delays and frustrations at MacWorld San Francisco the month before, stuck with my OS remarks and the key demos, and nailed it—finishing five minutes ahead of schedule. To the obvious delight of my staff.

The entire event received a highly gratifying approval from the audience, but it was a somewhat hollow success. I knew that it was the San Francisco debacle people would remember, not the successes at the shareholder meeting and in Tokyo. Such is human nature.

But for me personally, the supportive applause at the shareholders' meeting combined with the approving MacWorld Tokyo experience brought affirmation I sorely needed.

o   o   o

More because of timing than any other reason, we had decided that my appearance in Tokyo would be the launching pad for announcing three new products. This was a high moment—these were the first new products to be developed under me, meeting the new standards and criteria I had set.

Over the years, Apple had achieved worldwide fame for innovation and technology leadership, but word had never gotten out (Where was the press on *this* story?) that management had let R&D run wild. Apple's R&D had long been suffering in secret from an absence of thoughtful and wise decision-making, and there was an almost eerie absence of plain common sense in the design process. The product-development situation when I arrived was the opposite of what anyone could have anticipated. Many of the projects then in work were ill-defined, ill-conceived, or unmarketable and had to be abandoned.

One prime example: a new laptop computer code-named Hollywood. The basic concept was brilliant. Designed to be used by field salespeople and others who need to give small-group presentations, the computer's screen was detachable, so it could, for example, be turned around to be viewed by the customers, while the sales rep controlled the display from the keyboard in front of him. What's more, like the old Radius monitor for the Macintosh, the user could choose to project the screen image for either a horizontal or a vertical orientation, and the screen was designed so it could sit on a desk or table either way.

Great concept; big problem. No one seemed to have paid any attention to the fact that the heavy part of the computer was in the screen, not the base. During a presentation, there would be no difficulty, but when a user attempted to use the machine as an ordinary laptop, the overweight screen would cause the whole unit to topple over. I could only gape and wonder by what process a group of intelligent, innovative, and experienced engineers could delude themselves into thinking this defect would not be a drawback. Did they think users wouldn't notice!? Unless I had canceled the project, work on this disaster would have continued. I still shake my head over that one.

Even as a newcomer, I could see glaring mistakes. A recently introduced desktop machine, the Performa 6400, had for cost-saving reasons been designed with only one serial port. This meant the customer could not be connected in an AppleTalk network to other machines and direct-connected to a printer at the same time. It was expected that the 6400 would be a big hit, but, for this and a whole series of similar reasons, sales were very disappointing. Why would these experienced people wait until told, "Go back and clean up the mistakes"?

I theorized that the design process had become bent out of shape in Apple's crusade to increase market share. During that phase there were no customer surveys, no hard marketing data, barely any focus groups. To meet demands for lower-cost products, the thinking of the development people had been redirected from "What features do we need to sell this machine" to "How much will this feature cost us." Customers traditionally expected quality from Apple; the cranking process that emerged during this era was giving them cheap and dirty.

Apple designers had had their thinking pounded into a strange shape and until it was changed yet again, Apple products couldn't achieve our traditional "insanely great" ideal. And the thought process didn't begin to change until I discovered, to my dismay, this excessive dollars-and-cents orientation to product design, which was being done at the expense of customer satisfaction. Designing for cost is a valid engineering principle, but it only makes sense when you keep the customer at the center of your focus. We weren't doing that.

But on February 17 in Japan, with the two new desktop machines and a dazzling new PowerBook, I could proudly say that Apple products were back on the quality track.

The two desktop computers, the 8600 and 9600, featured an ingenious concept. To add memory or other internal elements, the user pushes a lever on the side and the box *unfolds,* exposing the innards so the installation can be done in moments, even by a novice. That concept had been sitting in the industrial lab for a long time, and with just a bit of coaxing and prodding toward the DSUV concepts, the engineers were able to bring it into the foreground; it eventually won for Apple a series of awards for industrial design.

For the new laptop, I had said, "I want a world-class machine with a big screen and blazing speed, but don't get exotic." They came back with the PowerBook 3400, offering a 12.1-inch screen and an operating speed of 240 megahertz, and it's been a big seller since day one.

Adding to the excitement, we would very shortly introduce a 300 megahertz desktop model.

With these new machines, even *Red Herring* magazine, not one of my greatest admirers, would be telling its readers that "the world's fastest laptop and desktop computers both carry the Apple logo."

I'm sure many people got tired of hearing me say, "We need to make products we can be proud of." But the words sunk in; the admonition was working and Apple would again be proud of its products.

o   o   o

Although I agreed that the products were beginning to be impressive and it looked as if we were gaining ground on all three of the most important elements for selling computers in the consumer marketplace—processing speed, size of the hard drive, and price—I perceived a seriously weak link. Fortunately, though, it was out of sight of all but the most sophisticated buyers, so would not hurt short-term sales.

All computers have a "bus," which channels information from memory to the processor. Each time the processor is ready to perform the next step and needs data from memory, it sends out a request and gets the data back through the bus.

In the Macintosh, the bus was a narrow tunnel that hadn't been widened in years, passing data back and forth at speeds of 40 or 50 megahertz. The processor, regardless of how fast it is, has to sit there waiting until the bus can send in the next batch of data. At some point a limitation is reached where no matter how much faster you make the processor, the user doesn't perceive any increase in speed. So Apple could boast that we had 250 and 300 megahertz machines, but that didn't mean that high-end users who upgraded were going to get any sense that they had gotten their money's worth. And in the end, what really matters about computer performance is what the user perceives.

From early on, I had been leaning on my head of R&D and the engineers themselves to improve bus speed, and getting explanations instead of results; our brilliant new machines still chugged along at the same old bottleneck bus speed. But now, at last, the engineers were able to show me demos in the lab of the next generation, due out before the end of the year, with a new, much faster bus design.

R&D was designing world-class machines again. Another wonderfully encouraging sign.

o   o   o

Concerned friends told me that Steve Wozniak had expressed his disappointment with Apple's education program. I knew Woz holds a strong dedication to the education of youngsters; he deserves much of the credit for Apple's early and generous impact on placing computers in schools. After leaving Apple, he had unashamedly pursued his degree and, teaching certificate in hand, had gone into the elementary school classroom—a stunning career change for one of the founders of the personal computer industry. Woz is a singular man with a singular purpose—in my book, a true visionary.

He and I shared a dedication to education, although my efforts have been primarily centered in serving on boards of universities and education-focused groups like the Wingspread Commission.

I called Woz and invited him to come see me. When we sat down together, he responded to my invitation to "tell me what you think we're doing wrong" by openly sharing his concerns that Apple was not putting enough energy into education, which he saw as a lost opportunity for Apple, as well as a failure in meeting a vital need of young people. He pointed out that we were depriving the company of a lucrative market and also depriving youngsters of the obvious advantages of the Macintosh.

Here is a guy who still loves the company. He's thoughtful, and he cares. I knew at once that it would benefit the company if Woz would agree to serve in a no-pay advisor capacity, as Steve Jobs already was.

I put that to him and he seemed willing to give it a try. But since it would mean he and Steve Jobs attending meetings together, he thought there was some background I needed to hear.

I may not be recalling a few of the details accurately, but as near as I can remember, the story went like this:

"Back when Steve Jobs and I were still just kids hanging out together, we were looking for ways to make some money. Before Mike Markkula, before the Apple in the garage, Steve managed to get an assignment from Nolan Bushnell of Atari to do some circuits for one of their electronic toys. I'd do the designs and build the circuit board, and we'd get $1,000. Nolan wanted it fast—it was on a real short deadline.

"It took some all-night design sessions, but I got it done on time and gave it to Steve, who took it in to Atari. He came back and gave me $300. I said, 'I thought we were getting $1,000.' Steve told me, 'No, they talked us down to $600, and I figured, you know, it was better than nothing.' So I said, 'Okay.'

"Years later, I found out from a guy who had been at Atari that they had really paid Steve the full $1,000. I did the work; he kept $700 for himself and gave me $300.

"When Steve knew I'd found out, that sort of ended it. We've never been close since."

Woz admitted to a bad feeling in both directions, but he thought they could manage to serve together for the benefit of Apple, and agreed to give it a try.

I would come to build a true and lasting admiration for Steve Wozniak and to respect his integrity. I was glad he had told me the story; otherwise, I would always have wondered why there seemed to be such animosity whenever these Apple founders were together in the same room.

The adage says that time heals all wounds; the parody says that time wounds all heels. In this case, neither version seems to have worked.

15

Discontented Winter—
A REORGANIZATION I DON'T WANT BUT MUST DO

In an ailing company, I set as one of the first goals getting very quickly back to the other side of break-even. Expense reduction should be deep enough and fast enough that you need to do it only once. Nobody likes a massive layoff; as I wrote in *Profit from Experience,* a major corporate layoff is usually a sign of ineffective management.

The longer new management continues chasing the break-even number without crossing it, the more serious the situation becomes.

When pushed to forecast the return to profitability back in May, I had announced what our plan said, that we would break even in the winter quarter of 1997. Now we were into that quarter and my promise was looking empty. I shared the bleak news with Ed Woolard that profitability wasn't going to happen; he did not receive it well. Highly aggravated, he said, "You've taken a public position on the break-even and now you're going to have to come up with a new forecast."

My gut reaction was that by making a further prediction I would run the risk of landing the company and myself deeper in the pit. *Miss once and you look bad, miss twice and you look incompetent.* I was twisting on the end of a hook and wondered what to do.

But Woolard, joining forces with Fred Anderson, persuaded me to issue a release announcing a new forecast. Fred and I agreed that it would be safe to predict break-even in the summer quarter, based on the fact that this was always strong for Apple because of education and back-to-school sales.

Although I've always been comfortable with risk-taking, forecasting a timetable for Apple's success was like flying an aircraft in which I hadn't been checked out: I wasn't sure what to expect.

o   o   o

Apple's gross margins when I arrived were 14 or 15 percent; we managed to inch them up to 19 to 20 percent and stabilize there. In the long range plan, we were aiming for 23 percent.

What does that translate into? Suppose Apple did $2 billion of sales in a quarter. Gross profit represents what's left after deducting the cost of manufacturing the goods and selling them. A gross profit of 20 percent on $2 billion would represent $400 million in Apple's cash register. To break even for the quarter, the company would have to run the entire rest of the business on $400 million; spend less than $400 million and we would show a profit.

The expense rate I had inherited—that is, the operating cost exclusive of manufacturing—was about $650 million a quarter. At that rate of spending, Apple would lose money even on sales of $3 billion a quarter. In fact, sales had reached that level in Spindler's final quarter, but had started to plummet right after Christmas.

But why were sales so bad? The company had been cutting its own throat by a series of dangerous miscalculations and judgment calls— building low-end machines when customers wanted more performance; stressing cost and volume but sacrificing quality; designing machines that lacked features offered by competitive products.

Apple had been losing customers who were defecting to the Windows platform, buying machines from Gateway, Compaq, Dell, IBM, and the rest of the competition. But there was another reason as well: The company was being punished by its own success. A Macintosh owner could continue using the same reliable machine for five or seven years, and often did . . . while consumers on the "Wintel" side, using DOS/Windows machines, needed to buy a new computer every three years. (I was receiving letters from users who would praise the Macintosh and bless the company: "It's amazing, I've got a ten-year-old Mac and it's still running today's software." We could take pride in that, yet the business side of me would shudder as I thought, *This customer should have bought two or three new models in that time.*)

Meanwhile—as if we needed any more bad news—the whole industry was experiencing a decline in the number of people buying computers.

The combined effect of these negative forces: The sales forecast dropped to $8 billion for the year, and I was fast coming to the conclusion that the true level was closer to $7 million. To survive, we would have to shrink our costs to $350 million a quarter or less. I had already knocked expenses down from $650 million down to about $430 million, but another $80 to $100 million needed to be cut in order for a profit to surface. (Though I never told anyone, I had Fred beginning to work on expense models reflecting revenues as low as $6 billion.)

There was no escaping: We would need to reorganize into a less costly operating structure.

A constant frustration from the first was that no one seemed to be able or willing to tell me, with any degree of accuracy, what sales revenues were likely to be. It would have been pretty frightening if I had known the truth up front, but at least we could have sized the company correctly the first time.

Now we would need another round of layoffs.

∘ ∘ ∘

To achieve the successful turnaround of various divisions and companies in my career, I've had to downsize a number of times; none of them has been without pain. At Apple, I would feel it harder and deeper. The company reorganization announced in February 1997 affected me emotionally more than any. For the sake of the company's survival, I would have to lay off many excellent people; Apple could not afford to retain these talented, devoted, faithful, hard-working folks and remain in business.

At the same time, we announced a change to a *centralized* organizational structure that I fundamentally believed was neither appropriate nor suitable for this company. I've always preferred a decentralized structure to keep strategic decision-makers closer in contact with the results of their decisions. Especially at Apple, where the culture has always championed the individual and stressed freedom to act unilaterally, I knew the centralized structure ran counter to twenty years of history.

Yet we could no longer afford the duplication that is a typical byproduct of a decentralized company. In the reorganization, we would move away from the structure of business centers, such as a PowerBook division, a high-end desktop division, and so on, in which each of these managers had P&L responsibility. The new structure would bring the company to a dull, simplistic hierarchy organized along functional lines—manufacturing, marketing, engineering. More traditional, less entrepreneurial, less encouraging to innovation . . . but far more manageable and definitely less costly.

I knew that some day, when the company was once again in the black and thriving, we would return to a decentralized organization. I reassured myself: *This reorg is a temporary expedient until we bridge the profit gap.*

I also knew that when we reached that point, Apple would have to go out and find people just like the ones I was letting go. It was a painful time for those being laid off, for Apple, and for me.

Out of a workforce now down from 16,000 to 13,000, another almost 3,000 people would lose their jobs, and many would suffer even more than the financial trauma a layoff causes. Once again, I was impressed by the fine qualities that Apple people exhibited during this sad phase. Many wrote letters of thanks for the years of experience at Apple, others wrote poems and eased the pain with gallows-humor jokes and stories.

Typical of the many letters was one sent by a respected company VP, Jim O'Neil, who had set up and then successfully managed Apple's Support Center in Austin, Texas. Jim had returned to Cupertino to accept a position in the Fred Forsyth manufacturing organization and had done such an effective job of outsourcing logistics that he had virtually done away with the need for his position. His name didn't appear on the new org chart. Yet his dignity shows in the letter he sent—a letter that quotes his former boss, the legendary Bill Coldrick, who at one time had been Apple's president of U.S. sales.

Folks,

Bill Coldrick, not a big believer in debating decisions, used to love to say to those who might nevertheless venture a contrary opinion, "You can say anything you want on your last day at Apple." Well, for me that day has come, though I don't intend to abuse the privilege.

After 11 years, I'm moving on. But before I do so, I would like to thank all of you for sharing your time, talents, and patience with me. I genuinely appreciate it. Despite the challenges, Apple has been, and I'm confident will continue to be, a uniquely rich work environment which presents a tremendous opportunity to learn and grow. I know that I certainly have. Although I'm genuinely excited about plotting a new individual course, I can't imagine that I will ever work amidst so many intelligent, passionate, dedicated, and entertaining people.

To those of you who remain, I trust that you can set aside what you read in the media and rebuild in yourselves the faith in Apple that so many of our customers continue to carry to this day. I know this sounds preachy, but I hope that you'll have faith in the future, embrace change for the positive and natural stimulus that it is, and keep in mind that life is, after all, mostly attitude and timing. And for those of you who cannot find it in yourselves to do so, Bill had yet another pet expression, "Working at Apple is not a life sentence."

Best Wishes & Regards,
Jim

Under the smoke screen of reorganization, I did something much too long in coming: I maneuvered several executives out of their jobs or out of the company.

With one exception, these were all people I admired and genuinely liked. They had been unswervingly devoted to Apple and had given the company their very best efforts. Perhaps their inadequacies were merely a lack of needed skills and experience, but to some degree they were too deeply imbued with an arrogant Apple style that needed to change, yet they were unwilling or unable to relinquish. I had to face it: the most serious failing was mine—in not acting sooner. It's unfortunate to have to replace a top executive, even worse when it's done a year late.

As I play back my relationships with people, I've observed my own behaviors and realize that I need to pay attention to whether, over time, my esteem for a person is rising or falling. It now seems to me that's a much more reliable way of measuring than first impressions; perhaps I need to set a trial period of, say, three months, and see how our relationship works out. I continue to think about this issue because, although I've always considered myself an accurate judge of people, the Apple experience has shaken my confidence in that area.

In short order, four executives were replaced, a formidable step to take all at once, but one I was not willing to delay any longer.

o　o　o

Fred Forsyth, senior VP of operations, was a hard worker and extremely loyal to Apple. My initial impression had been, *What a great guy, we're lucky to have him.* But as time went on, I realized that Fred's enthusiasm and caring for the company were not matched by skills needed to translate what had to be done into results on the factory floor. He definitely understood what was needed, he could explain it, but when it came to making it actually happen in the trenches, he was less effective. Attitude is definitely important, but you also have to have the follow-through.

Fred was also a victim of the "your-order-is-only-a-suggestion" school of Apple thinking. In any well-run business—and you don't need to have a business school degree to figure this out, it's just common sense—what the factory builds is based on what the company forecasts it will be able to sell.

At Apple, it didn't work that way. We would create a plan but the factory would build different products, in different quantities; no wonder the company never achieved plan. Never mind that the forecast was usually worthless anyway.

In 1996, for example, we anticipated very respectable sales of the forthcoming PowerBook 1400. This was in the financial forecast, which was based on input from the executives; each of them received a copy, and we discussed it in executive staff sessions. But Fred, I believe, didn't take it seriously; he treated the financial forecast like unreliable crystal-balling from Sales. Whatever the reason, his people never placed orders with the suppliers to build the quantity of 1400s that were in the forecast.

I didn't uncover the problem until autumn; by the time our suppliers could respond and the factories could gear up, build, test, and ship, we had lost three months. Which meant that Apple missed the lucrative Christmas selling season. PowerBook sales were backlogged; had those units actually been sold and delivered over Christmas, there would have been enough revenue to show a vastly better quarter, which would have made an enormous difference both to Apple and to me.

Simply stated, this failure was caused by an arrogant attitude traditionally held by Apple executives. Fred acted as if he alone had the authority to decide how many units would be built, instead of following what the financial projection called for.

I came to understand that this company had never rigorously insisted that the financial plan be the governing document on which all the other plans—for manufacturing, distribution plan, and the rest— were based. Instead, each manager had come to rely on his or her own judgment and did what he or she thought best.

The blame didn't rest with Fred or the others; they had been allowed to run wild. I wondered, *Had there ever been the leadership to insure that all the pieces would come together and be reconciled?*

To replace him I tapped Jim McCluney, a very able manufacturing man who had once run our Cork, Ireland, plant and who still talked with a substantial accent. Jim made notable progress in cleaning things up during the coming months, but it wasn't enough to rescue my job. (After I left and Steve was making the decisions, to my consternation, Jim was among the top-quality people Steve dismissed, leaving me to fear for Apple even more.)

o   o   o

In a marketing setting where the channel partners weren't as important, John Floisand would undoubtedly have done better. Unfortunately this fine man didn't seem to be a match for the tough channel partners he had to deal with, and they pretty much controlled the relationship.

As a person, John would make a wonderful friend. As an Apple executive, we needed someone who could manage these relationships better than John appeared capable of doing.

We had a candidate I thought fit that description: Dave Manovich, who had been with the company for nine years, but had left during the final days of the Spindler era. A man full of Western charm from his native Montana, Dave had earned the reputation of being adept at managing the channel. He, too, was let go in the early days of the Jobs reign, another big loss for Apple.

∘   ∘   ∘

Satjiv Chahil's promotion to senior VP of worldwide marketing by Michael Spindler just before he left Apple came as a result of the successful tenure Satjiv had enjoyed in Japan, where he was credited with a significant upturn in Apple sales. I initially responded like the Mac loyalist I was to what I call the old-school approach of Apple advertising, which is founded on the principle that "you should buy a Mac 'cause it's cool," rather than promoting the Mac on the basis of the specific values it offers to benefit a user.

But the marketplace had changed, and I tried to convey to Satjiv that we needed to give people harder, cutting-edge reasons why they should be buying our products. And as a basis for doing that, we needed scientific marketing research. I couldn't get Satjiv away from being Mr. Feel-good. He was a world-class cheerleader at a time when the team needed some tough offensive linemen.

I think the fault was not his; Satjiv had been asked to fill a job that required a professional knowledge of marketing. The sales team needed support and some very specific tools that could build their sales. As time went by and the company's fortunes declined, Satjiv was subjected to a lot of pressure and criticism from the other executives: "Marketing guys are supposed to be out there stimulating the market, our sales are going down, and Satjiv is spending his time in Hollywood making deals with Tom Cruise." Gradually he lost the respect of his colleagues and there was no recovering from that.

What we needed was someone who could move marketing in a direction of being more professional, more scientific, more cause-and-effect oriented, someone experienced in using primary research to define everything from ad campaigns to the products themselves.

I sent for Guerrino De Luca and told him, "You can't have that nice cushy job running Claris anymore; you've got to come help solve the Apple problems. This time I won't take no for an answer. I need you here." It would be like a demotion in several ways—from CEO of Claris to a senior VP title at Apple, from heading an independent organization to heading a division within corporate. But at least I was able to make the offer attractive financially. Guerrino agreed and became the new head of marketing for Apple. He, too, would be let go during the early purge of Steve Jobs's reign, but would land as CEO of Logitech International.

o   o   o

Reporting to John Floisand in her job as VP of Americas sales, Robin Abrams had been performing remarkably well in an incredibly difficult situation—made more difficult by the unruly and often out-of-control Landi, who often went around John and tried to tell Robin how to do her job. She had brought more discipline to the organization and had a solid recognition of her responsibility; Robin had the analytical abilities to make sure the decisions she made were of benefit to the whole company, not just the sales force. Here was an executive who could solve problems across boundaries in the way I had been trying to get the other executives to do.

When Pat Sharp, head of human resources, came in to say, "Do you know we're losing Robin Abrams?" I was stunned.

Hesitant to talk against anyone, Robin finally related how Marco Landi had brutally said to her something like, "In this downsizing, there's no future for you here, there isn't going to be any role for you to play." Naturally she had been both disappointed and upset, and so had immediately called in a headhunter.

I said, "Robin, I don't understand where in the hell Marco got that thinking, he certainly didn't check with me. And it's not true. You're doing a superb job and we really need you to stay."

But by that time, several weeks had gone by. Robin was on the point of getting a job offer. I tried to talk her into staying; the die was already cast.

It was another Landi story that I found impossible to reconcile with sensible business practices.

o   o   o

In many ways I admired Marco Landi, although I freely admit that appointing him was probably one of the biggest errors of my 500 days.

Again and again I asked myself how I had been convinced into putting absolutely the wrong person into the second most powerful job in the company.

Marco had a highly autocratic style of management. Forget participatory management, this was an "I speak, you do" way of running an organization.

But the worst part was his highly emotional nature that too often triggered an explosion. Marco in a rage would ridicule and demean people in front of others, using language that should never be used publicly, much less in a business setting. According to one manager who was there, Marco stopped one executive vice president in the middle of a presentation and "filleted" him in front of a large group. I spoke to Marco several times about the many complaints that were reaching me, but never saw the slightest iota of evidence that he had the capacity to change.

I waited too long again, but finally decided, *I don't want to deal with this anymore. I just don't want Marco in this job.* At the time I was attending meetings in southern California, and Marco was getting ready to leave for an extended overseas tour. To wait until he returned would have been a big mistake, so I decided to tell him immediately. This meant doing something I dislike and had probably never done before: I presented him the bad news by telephone. Worse, it was on Valentine's Day that I called to say, "This just isn't going to work. When I gave you the job, you said that if I wasn't happy in six months, you'd gracefully leave. Now I want to call that option."

I was expecting an unpleasant explosive reaction, but to my surprise, he accepted my decision calmly and was very gentlemanly about it.

The amazing truth about Apple alumni is that they land wonderful jobs and perform very well; Apple people, even ones who have been fired, are the star performers at many companies in Silicon Valley and across the nation. But at Apple, they were too undermined by the dysfunctional culture.

I regretted these executive layoffs, but in some cases it launched people who needed to get on with their lives into new careers. Some of the executives took a nice long sabbatical, got their handicaps down, and then set out in new directions.

As an Apple alumnus myself, I now know how they must have felt.

o   o   o

On a happier note, there were rare, memorable, upbeat experiences that I recall with a smile.

Apple had agreed to do a Webcast on the Aspen Comedy Weekend, put on by HBO at the Colorado ski resort, which led to an invitation landing on my desk. The Webcast was coincidentally scheduled to be held on my birthday weekend, and I easily convinced Charlene that it would be a fun and well-earned change of scene for us.

I could never have predicted that I would be greeted by high praise and enthusiasm for the Macintosh from a gathering of comedians—not a group one might consider heavy computer users. On Friday night, backstage after a Dennis Miller performance, Sinbad described himself as "a big fan of Apple," and proved very knowledgeable about the Mac. He asked to borrow a new QuickTake electronic camera, which was on display at our booth, and I wondered what he had in mind—it had to be funny.

Later in the weekend I saw him on the dance floor with *three* ladies simultaneously, hilariously cutting up while taking photos at the same time. (With a letter of thanks, he later sent me prints of the pictures; his singular sense of humor surely wanted to suggest some great ideas, but when back within the serious confines of my office, I could not imagine how he imagined Apple might use these madcap photos.)

Jerry Levin, the TimeWarner chief, offered what sounded like a compliment: "I admire what you're trying to do. Not many executives would take on that Apple challenge." Revealing, I guess, that he wouldn't have. If so, perhaps he had the better idea.

At dinner, Chevy Chase joined us, and because his vibrant personality attracts people, we were soon joined by Dennis Miller, Martin Short, and that other Martin—Steve. They took turns telling jokes, trying to outdo each other, and I wish I had been taking notes.

A highlight of the weekend was a sales slogan that Rob Reiner insisted we should adopt: "A computer so easy, even an adult can use it."

Should I have sent it to our ad agency as a sample of a level they should be aiming to achieve for us?

16

A Very Palpable Hit—
STEVE JOBS REVEALS HIS HAND

When I don the cloak of historian and look back over the events of my relationship with Steve Jobs, I wonder what I might have done differently.

I had begun getting fervent warnings from people I trusted back as early as when I first started the conversations with Steve.

Pat Sharp, my VP of human resources, had said to me just after we had announced the deal for the NeXT acquisition, "I think you've just done one of the most courageous acts I've ever witnessed, but I don't think you know the extent of your bravery."

"What are you talking about?" I asked.

"Reengaging Steve with the company takes real guts. I agree it's the right thing to do; I think the company will ultimately benefit. But there's a lot of personal risk in that decision because of Steve's reputation and style. And because of his emotional history with Apple."

I told Pat what I'd been telling everyone: "This company has got to come first before any other objectives or concerns. And that's what all my decisions will be based on."

Pat, a sixteen-year Apple veteran, was one of many who predicted I'd encounter problems by including Steve in the deal; she thought as I did at the time that the positive value would far outweigh the negatives.

But she was still driven to warn me. I had been getting warnings from many people who had worked with or near Steve; like an innocent teenager, I was sure it would be different for me.

o   o   o

Bill Gates was another who wasn't exactly enthusiastic about my prospects when I called to tell him that we had selected NeXT instead of Microsoft or Be. He went into orbit.

He said, "Do you really think Steve Jobs has got anything there? I know his technology, it's nothing but a warmed-over UNIX, and you'll never be able to make it work on your machines."

The more he talked, the more heated he became. "Don't you understand that Steve doesn't know anything about technology? He's just a super salesman. I can't believe you're making such a stupid decision."

He wasn't finished blasting me. I just waited for him to continue. "Damnit, Gil," he said, "Steve is pure salesman, that's all he is, he's not an engineer, he doesn't know anything about engineering and 99 percent of everything he thinks and says is wrong. What the hell are you buying that garbage for?"

Gates carried on and on, blowing his stack for twenty or thirty minutes before he finally calmed down.

I still wonder what the computer world would have turned into if our decision had gone the other way and Bill Gates had gained effective control over the Macintosh operating system.

o   o   o

My thoughts turned back to the Steve Jobs I had negotiated with for the purchase of NeXT, our sitting in his kitchen, Steve making tea for both of us, introducing me to his wife and children, the Steve who could be completed trusted, who had made me feel like a lifelong friend.

I still believe he had been forthright that day in the kitchen, even letting his feelings shine through. In the midst of our negotiations, he had impulsively asked, "Can I be on the board of directors?" He was being real and open, not devious and hiding—I liked that.

At the time I had replied, "Probably anything is possible, Steve, when the deal is done. But I won't make any promises about a seat on the board. My take at this time is they won't invite you to be a director—there's too much history. Let's complete the deal, get some time under our belts, let people see how well we work together, and then I will personally revisit the topic of your being on the board. I think right now it's premature."

"Gil, that really hurts," he admitted. "This was my company. I've been left out since that horrible day with Sculley. But Apple has always been a part of me."

"We should try to make that happen for you," I said.

"I understand," Steve said. "But I want you to know how much this really hurts."

I admired him that day and I still do—being so candidly open is neither easy nor comfortable for most men. I was caught off guard and thought that despite the stories I had heard, here was a true look into the real Steve. As I would painfully discover, it was merely one facet of an extremely complex personality.

◦   ◦   ◦

Attorneys always take forever. Weeks dragged by from the time we cemented the deal with Steve, while the legal staff wrapped up all the minutia and drafted the final papers for signing. Steve gradually got worked up, until he was on the phone with me two or three times a day. "How're we doing on this, how're we doing on that?"

Every now and then in the middle of those conversations, he would take the opportunity to throw in some advice. One day he said out of the blue, "I think you ought to kill Newton."

"What do you mean, 'kill it'?"

"Shut it down, write it off, get rid of it."

I said, "Steve, do you have any idea how expensive that would be?"

"It doesn't matter," he said. "It doesn't matter what it costs, people would cheer if you got rid of it."

"There's a crowd of people out there who really love the Newton. Maybe some of the financial analysts might cheer because they know it's a drain on Apple resources. But I've looked into Newton and it's going to be a moneymaker. I don't support getting rid of it."

The answer didn't satisfy, but at least he moved on to another topic.

Finally the attorneys finished their nit-picking. On February 15, we gathered in the board room for the official signing of the papers and a makeshift feast—coffee and bagels to celebrate a $400 million deal. The NeXT employees could now get their stock, the investors their cash, and Steve his $120 million cash and a million and a half shares of Apple stock.

With the deal closed, Steve reverted to behaving like my friend again. He bounced around like a schoolboy on a trampoline. "Gil," he bubbled, "you and I need to go out and have a great bottle of wine to celebrate closing the deal."

"That sounds good to me, I've got a wine cellar with some decent bottles waiting for a party; I'll bring the wine."

"With our wives," he suggested.

He was back to the old-college-chum feeling again. And that's the way it went with Steve—flip-flopping from a soaring high, when he was an absolute delight to be around, to a mood of extreme anger or intense gloom that excluded any rational or civil conversation. I would get to see so many varieties of moods that I never knew exactly who I would be facing.

If I had been more sensitive to the nuances, perhaps I would have sensed that I was already living on borrowed time.

o   o   o

Steve's suggestion of serving as an advisor was one I looked forward to setting in motion. We spoke often and he came in to share his insight and experience once or twice a week. For ten months, from September 1996 to the following July, I talked to Steve more frequently than to my children—perhaps for more hours than to my wife, though I shudder now to realize that fact.

When I was wrestling with a problem, I would walk through the issue with him. We talked about networking, Java, Rhapsody, and many other subjects on my list; nine times out of ten we would agree, arriving at a decision we were both comfortable with.

I was in awe over the way Steve's mind approached problems, and had the feeling we were building a mutually trusting relationship based on a comfortable working style and respect. But the layers of the onion had not yet begun to peel away.

To a reporter who asked, "Are you trying to take over Apple?" Steve replied, "I get along real well with Gil, I think he trusts me." The reporter took it as a denial of his intent to power his way into a controlling position, and so did I. The reporter and I were misled by a typically Jobs diversionary statement.

Steve Jobs, a master at the politician's gambit of diversionary statements, may seem to agree with or endorse a position, but in fact he's answering a totally different question, which effectively serves to mask his real intent. Many of Steve's forthright-sounding answers only give a Houdini-like illusion of reality. I would become excruciatingly aware of his magic with words.

o   o   o

From the day Steve had been violently torn from Apple's womb by the board, he must have become obsessed with the notion of again taking over the company. How else explain that visit to me at National Semiconductor? So one of the strategies he could be expected to pursue was arranging to get people loyal to him placed into key positions and shoving out or moving aside people who weren't willing to accept "Stevie Wonder" as their maximum leader.

It's possible to read the history of those few months exactly that way, and there are journalists and Apple folks who will tell you that this is just what happened. I don't see it like that.

Steve did, in fact, pressure me very hard to put Avie Tevanian in charge of all software. He said, "Look, when you bought NeXT, one of the assets you bought was Avie. He's been with the company for nine years, almost the entire life of NeXT. And if you had to pick five people who are the best systems software engineers in the world, his name would certainly be on the list." All true.

"It just seems to me," Steve argued, "that the smart thing for you to do is put him in charge of the software program."

Anyone buying into the scenario of Steve scheming for control would have viewed Avie as a pawn that Steve wanted in a critical position. If I had subscribed to that view, Avie would have been given a nothing job in the depths of the company, which would have pushed him to resign. But that would have been disgracefully narrow-minded. Putting Apple first was more important than protecting my territory. I had met Avie, I knew what he could do, and I completely agreed with Steve's assessment of his worth and value for the company. Talent like

Avie's is rare, his qualifications spoke for themselves. Steve didn't need to convince me.

But who would he report to?

Ellen Hancock, my head of R&D, was an outstanding journeyman manager. Even though she hadn't written software in a couple of decades and wasn't on the cutting edge of the field, she was the logical choice to be Avie's boss. Steve had begun working on me about this a month in advance, taking a very strong position that she was not qualified to manage Avie and that he would leave if told he had to report to her.

It turned out that wasn't true at the time, as Avie himself later told me.

Steve, it seemed, had a problem with Ellen as a result of a single blunder she had made. We all slip occasionally and even smooth-tempered Ellen had unfortunately ruffled some feathers. At a meeting of the key software players, a question came up about the Rhapsody operating-system project. Avie, who was there in visitor status (since the deal with him hadn't been finalized), made some comment about the software at an engineering level. Ellen got up and refuted what he said, handling it in what to Avie was a clumsy put-down that he found embarrassing, and he called to talk to me about it.

He said, "Gil, if you ask me to work for Ellen Hancock in this job, I will do it, but . . ." I reassured him of my support and thought I had resolved his concerns. Unfortunately, Avie also told his friend Steve, who latched onto the incident like an angry dog on the leg of an intruder. He wouldn't let it go.

Another aspect of Steve's personality, especially when it comes to being loyal to his friends: When he makes his mind up about somebody, he never changes it. If Ellen had walked on water the next day, he still would have counted her a loser. He even told a reporter that Ellen was a "bozo," which got into print.

But Steve was right about where Avie belonged in the organization. System software was and is so very critical to the company's survival that I needed to telegraph its importance throughout Apple. The best way to do that, I decided, was by having the person doing the work report directly to me.

In my special effort to get close to Avie, he and I frequently met for an hour or so, sometimes over lunch. I called him up one day and said, "If you're free, I'll come over to R&D and we'll eat in the cafeteria." Before lunch, he showed me a box he had set up that was running the Rhapsody kernel—very exciting, like seeing a dream begin to come true.

Over lunch I asked, "How are you doing, is there anything on your mind we should talk about?"

He said, "Everything is going great. There's a lot of work to be done and I'm putting in the hours but . . ." He paused, uncertain whether to continue, and then said, "Working for you is really different than working for Steve. When Steve would call me up and say, 'Let's have lunch,' I'd panic."

"Why was that?"

"Because Steve only suggested lunch when he had some important message to deliver. And I never knew what kind of message it would be. I always expected the worst."

And then he said something that was only a small compliment but stayed with me: "Working for you is really nice."

The other top executive from NeXT that Steve wanted me to use was also a no-contest. Jon Rubenstein is a Cornellian, a brilliant engineer who had run hardware engineering at NeXT, then gone on to start a business of his own, which he sold to Motorola.

And the timing couldn't have been better for Apple. Engineers had previously been scattered in the PowerBook division, the Performa division, Power Mac, and so on. When reorganizing, I had pulled together operations that had been spread among different operational divisions. The engineers were now all in a single engineering group . . . but I had no one qualified to run it.

I asked many people for their suggestions of a candidate for the job. When I asked Steve, he said, "I have the perfect guy." I met Jon, checked him out, and agreed that Steve had again delivered top talent.

Maybe Steve really was just setting me up, putting his own people in place, ready for a palace coup. If so, the decisions I made were bad for me. But they were beneficial for Apple, and I would likely have made them even had I known for certain that Steve was being guided by ulterior motives.

o   o   o

Was Steve Jobs planting takeover rumors with his friends in the media, building support for a takeover from early on? Nobody was naming their sources when *Red Herring* asserted, "It's no secret at Apple that Mr. Jobs has little faith in Mr. Amelio's ability to turn the company around" and claimed to have been told that "Steve could finish Gil at his convenience." Told by whom?

A piece in *Fortune* asserted that the acquisition of Steve Jobs's company "is beginning to look more like a NeXT takeover of Apple. Never mind that NeXT Software was a boutique with revenues that would amount to less than a rounding error to Apple. . . . [T]o the Machiavellian eye, it looks as if Jobs . . . might be scheming to take over Apple for himself."

And like a softening up before a military invasion, laudatory articles were being posted on the Internet, like this one about Steve from "Doc Searls" of the Searls Consulting Group, which read in part:

> Steve's message was no different than it was at Day One: All I want from the rest of you is your money and your appreciation for my Art.
>
> Steve's art has always been first-class, and priced accordingly. There was nothing ordinary about it. The Mac "ecosystem" Steve talks about is one that rises from that Art, not from market demand or other more obvious forces.
>
> See, Steve is an elitist and an innovator, and damn good at both. His greatest achievements are novel works of beauty and style. The Apple I and II were Works of Woz; but Lisa, Macintosh, NeXT and Pixar were all Works of Jobs. Regardless of their market impact (which in the cases of Lisa and NeXT were disappointing), all four were remarkable artistic achievements.
>
> The simple fact is that Apple always was Steve's company, even when he wasn't there. . . . In the end, by when too many of the innovative spirits first animated by Steve had moved on to WebTV and Microsoft, all that remained was that righteousness, and Apple looked and worked like what it was: a church wracked by petty politics and a pointless yet deeply felt spirituality.
>
> Now Steve is back, and gradually renovating his old com-

pany. He'll do it his way, and it will once again express his Art.

These things I can guarantee about whatever Apple makes from this point forward:

1. It will be original.
2. It will be innovative.
3. It will be exclusive.
4. It will be expensive.
5. Its aesthetics will be impeccable.
6. The influence of developers, even influential developers, will be minimal. The influence of customers and users will be held in even higher contempt.
7. The influence of fellow business artisans such as Larry Ellison (and even Larry's nemesis, Bill Gates) will be significant, though secondary at best to Steve's own muse.

Should be interesting.

Just as there are a great many Apple watchers, there are also a great many Jobs watchers, the more perceptive of whom are able to see the genius behind the manic mask and the manic behind the genius mask. I came to know Steve as smart, excessively selective about the people he wants as friends, impatient, lacking in integrity, and very controlling.

The media, thrilled at the possibility of having Steve Jobs back at Apple, was stirring up a ground swell equivalent to one that would be created for a resurrected Evita Perón.

17

A Pound of Flash—
PEOPLE WHO WANT
A PIECE OF APPLE

Never in my wildest dreams would I have conjured up an image of an Arabian prince investing over $100 million in Apple (I pictured a caravan of heavily loaded camels trekking bags of riyals across the sands) at the same time that a Silicon Valley billionaire is attempting to buy the company, while a popular, charismatic idol pulls strings behind the scenes. Siskel and Ebert would give any script with those plot lines two thumbs down, would compare it to the Beatty/Hoffman desert fiasco *Ishtar;* even preteen fans of Jim Carrey would consider the plot too far out.

Very little about this real-life fantasy made any sense to me, and the true motives of some of the players were beyond understanding.

The Larry Ellison buyout scenario made the least sense, but was built into headline proportions. On March 27, in a routine newspaper interview, Ellison suddenly began talking about taking over Apple. He blurted out to a reporter for the *San Jose Mercury News* that he was forming an investor group and would decide soon whether he would move for control of the company. The *New York Times* then picked up on this claim to note that Ellison's company, Oracle, had in the past maintained these matters to be Ellison's personal business, but that the company had recently "taken the unusual step" of becoming involved—whatever that meant.

Ellison is arguably the most successful businessman in the San Francisco Bay area, certainly in terms of self-enrichment: He is often acknowledged as the wealthiest man of Silicon Valley. Despite the offensiveness of his remarks, my reaction was that if he had some valid ideas I could adopt to speed up the transformation of Apple, I would eagerly hear them.

But when I called him to say, "Let's sit down and talk," he failed to return my calls or give an okay to set up a time to meet. I was to be deprived of hearing the many great ideas he claimed to have.

The plot continued to thicken with another slam-crash article in a *Fortune* March issue. They had almost no story to match their theme ("Steve Jobs . . . could make Apple his once again") but lent credence to Silicon Valley rumors. Steve "might be scheming to take over Apple for himself," they wrote. And, "If anyone doubts he could do it, all you have to do is ask his best friend, Oracle CEO Larry Ellison. . . . Says he: 'Steve's the only one who can save Apple. We've talked about it very seriously many, many times, and I'm ready to help him the minute he says the word. I could raise the money in a week.'" According to the article, Ellison maintained that he and Steve even had a technology plan for Apple.

Faced with even a remote possibility of a hostile takeover attempt, I decided it would be best to put up a defense, and we hired both Goldman Sachs and Solomon Brothers to help. The consensus, it turned out, was that if Ellison was willing to pay a reasonable price for the stock, we were dog meat. Ellison's access to trainloads of money made the outcome very clear.

I called Steve to see what he had to say about the irresponsible remarks being attributed to his "best friend" Larry. He said, "I really don't understand what's going on, Gil. I think all this is crazy. You and I have a good relationship, I don't see any reason to make any changes."

I said, "Great, I'm glad you feel that way. What should I tell the press? And Steve, make it something definitive—something I'll be able to quote you on."

In the all-too familiar way I had by now come to expect, he sidestepped; despite my repeated requests, he would not give me a straight answer that could be attributed to him.

Even before then, I would learn much later, Ellison had been conniving over Apple. Joe Costello, CEO of Cadence Design Systems Inc. and a longtime friend of Ellison's, has acknowledged that Ellison approached him in January with what could only be considered a wild proposition: to crash the Apple shareholder's meeting and demand changes. And he wanted to put Costello's name forward. Former Wall Street financier Michael Milken, a buddy of Ellison's, was named as one of the plotters Ellison was lining up in his efforts to gain control of the company.

Yet despite a series of similar manipulative behaviors, I somehow didn't want to give up on this relationship with Steve. But the conversation about Ellison convinced me that my trust was misplaced. I finally absorbed the fact that I had been too eager and too willing to believe he was on my team. At the first real test of our developing friendship, he let me down. He could have gone to Ellison and said, "Larry, cut this shit out," and the entire charade would have come to an end. Steve was clearly in position to help add strength to my image; all it would have taken was a quote that I could honorably give to the press.

When reporters asked Steve what has happening, he'd fall back on the same oblique style with statements like, "Well, I'm giving Gil the best advice I know how." Or like, "Gil has done a good job of fixing the financial structure of the company." *What the hell does that mean?*

Hindsight reveals it all as a series of tactics to discredit me before moving ahead with a carefully planned strategy. Steve played his part by working his way into the confidence of board members, while Ellison's takeover remarks undermined confidence in what I was doing. It doesn't take a genius to understand how the board would soon be very willing to listen to arguments about getting rid of me. I had been directly warned by many people that Steve in his Machiavellian mode could readily devise such a plot.

The sequence of events was no coincidence. After negotiating to buy NeXT in December, it took until February 15 to actually close the deal; Steve got his check and his stock soon after. That was the signal for Ellison to kick off his campaign to shake confidence in the Apple management, which started within weeks.

Larry Ellison was hit with criticisms from every direction for the way he handled himself in this. Charles R. Wolf, an analyst with C.S. First Boston, told the *Times*, "They are redefining craziness here, taking it to a new level." He called Ellison's behavior "unique in the annals of corporate takeovers." Richard Shaffer, publisher of the *Technologic Computer Letter*, was quoted as saying, "People who are serious about buying companies keep it as quiet as possible."

The whole affair left the impression of a man looking, not to buy a company, but to shake confidence in its management enough to permit a takeover without having to spend any money—a tactic that only brings a value if you have someone in a key position inside the company, placed to bore from within. Surprise! Would that person be Steve Jobs, who had already captured the attention and friendship of board kingpin Ed Woolard?

I was becoming trapped in a web of plotting as intricate as the Wars of the Roses.

o   o   o

Mike Markkula had been riding me in board meetings that we should be running more ads, while I had continued to insist that it never makes sense to spend lots of money on ads until you have products that buyers want. Mike felt so strongly about this that I had several times asked for a vote by the board, and they had always voted him down.

But now, with the Apple engineers having so brilliantly responded to my challenge of creating a totally new product line within a year, the picture was looking bright. Spartacus, the startling computer that looks like nothing more than a flat screen, had been announced at MacWorld in January as the Twentieth Anniversary Macintosh. We were already selling the new PowerBooks, including the super-high performance 3400, as well as the 8600 and 9600 desktop machines with the unfolding cases that broke new ground.

By July, we would be ready to introduce computers running as fast as 350 megahertz, which would make them the fastest personal computers on the market. Right behind that would be yet another wave of machines with a new processor chip from Motorola and IBM, called the G3, which would, finally, deliver a faster bus, greatly increasing how speedy the computer seems to the user.

And consumer confidence was rebuilding. A survey by *HomePC* magazine found Apple ranked by home computer users in the top three for customer support and tied with Hewlett Packard as number one in reliability. Ingenuity was thriving: Apple had been issued more than 130 patents in 1996, more than twice as many as Microsoft. We were still losing good people, including some brilliant engineers, but those we had were doing stellar work, in the old Apple tradition.

Now with the product line shaping up, the time had come for turning our attention to marketing. It was time to start a campaign aimed at building sales.

I had been shaping a new ad campaign concept with our in-house advertising man David Roman, insisting we needed a hard-hitting campaign that would tell people in no uncertain terms why they should buy a Mac. Our agency, BBDO, came up with the ingenious "Just Ask a User" tack, which combined eye-catching graphics with copy that told people straight out why buying a Mac was a smart decision. Research made it clear that we had to answer the question in the minds of consumers, "Why Mac, why now?" I think it was one of the best campaigns the company had ever designed in terms of giving consumers the answers.

Earlier, the board had approved spending an extra $20 million for advertising in the upcoming summer quarter, over and above what had already been budgeted. That would be a promising start, but would give us a hit for only about three or four weeks. Could we afford an in-your-face advertising effort to insure Apple's exposure in a consistent way over a much longer term? The agency, Roman, and I put together an aggressive plan with an advertising budget that would involve increased spending at the same rate—$20 million over the current ad budget in each quarter for an entire year.

Now if I could only convince the board to okay the increase . . . in the face of another round of bad news.

o   o   o

When the board of directors gathered for dinner at Valeriano's restaurant in Los Gatos on March 24, I couldn't enjoy any of the social conversation, knowing full well that the next morning I would once again have to deliver some very bad numbers to these same people.

As much as I tried to put negative thoughts out of my mind, I couldn't quite escape the pressure, couldn't relax enough to enjoy an evening with these people I both liked and admired. Around the table was Mike Markkula, in any group a source of lively conversation, and

Bernie Goldstein, whose contrarian views had often been a thorn in my side, but who always had experiences to share that were worth my attention. And Del Lewis, who was always giving me encouragement, and whom I had come to like and respect.

With Jürgen Hintz and Peter Crisp both having resigned, their replacements were relatively new, people whom I looked forward to knowing better.

Kathy Hudson, CEO of the packaging firm W.H. Brady Co., a former Kodak executive, was always professional, thoroughly businesslike, and I came to admire the fact that she insisted on answers to a series of well-thought-through questions before making up her mind on any issue. More often than not she would in the end see the question the same way I did, leading me to believe her own way of thinking was very much aligned with mine. I considered her an ally even though she was decidedly her own person.

Gareth Chang was running Asia for Hughes Electronics when I recruited him to serve on Apple's board. He's a man who, I think, dislikes confrontation and the stress associated with it. When he missed board meetings or "attended" by phone, citing scheduling conflict, I suspected he was just as glad to avoid potentially unpleasant scenes.

I had one small run-in with Gareth. His background is in sales, and he thinks like a sales executive. He called one day and said, "Nike is thinking of dropping the Mac and going over to Windows machines. You should send Phil Knight a new 3400 PowerBook to show him how good it is." It turned out the company had plans to buy only a few Windows computers, but I gave instructions to send a machine anyway.

Gareth called back a week later to complain that the machine hadn't arrived. Being the salesman he is, I'm sure he expected me to fly to Nike headquarters and deliver it personally, while I saw it as more important for our sales rep in Portland to do this himself as a way of helping cement his relationship with the company.

From this one incident, I believe Gareth concluded I wasn't much of a salesman, a view that he would hold against me when the chips were down.

But that night in Los Gatos, none of the issues or politics mattered. Past tensions melt away under the influence of pleasant surroundings, rich food, and full-bodied wines. Although it was impossible to keep company business completely out of the conversation, each of us made a special effort to maintain a social tone. All conflicts were being postponed until the next day; to say I was edgy is putting it mildly.

o   o   o

When the same group gathered in the board room at 8:00 the next morning, the topic of advertising once again provoked heated debate. Now I was asking for approval to spend $80 million for the year above the $130 million we were already spending; even though this only represented a return to about the level of the ad budget when I arrived, the request was not received well.

The discussion was one of the most animated and intense this board ever had. The Markkula camp, now supporting my stance, said, "Regardless of the cost, we have to do it, we have to get out there to let people know we have confidence in our products. Therefore we have to run this campaign, whatever it costs."

The opposition, articulated primarily by Bernie Goldstein, said, "You can't advertise your way back to success, the number-one priority is making the business profitable. No ad can be as good as a profitable quarter, and that's more important than running a good ad campaign. So therefore you can't afford to spend the money."

It ended with a nay vote: The board decided not to support an increase in budget for additional advertising beyond the summer quarter. I experienced the decision like a strong punch to my solar plexus that took the air right out of my lungs. They had expressed extreme displeasure with sales revenues, but then refused to agree to boosting sales through advertising—even though we all knew that advertising was our best chance for getting the sales problem turned around. Mixed messages from a board of directors is not a good sign.

It was time to present some upbeat news before the big downer. I announced that the winter quarter just ending would mark a record for Apple of the strongest PowerBook sales ever in a single quarter.

Before anyone felt like patting me on the back, I laid the rest of the story on the table: Despite the great PowerBook sales, total revenues for the quarter would be well below expectations. "Compared to the same period a year ago, we'll be reporting revenues down by 27 percent."

I hurried on before they could disrupt my presentation with premature questions: "I feel obliged to give you my insight into where we're headed for the rest of the year. It does not look good. We are simply not getting the sales volume we have to have for the business."

There was no real quarrel with the strategy. For the most part, the board members understood that if in my shoes, they would likely be doing the same things.

Yet instead of thinking and working together, a hammering began.

Ed Woolard began to throw out ideas like, "What we really need is a great marketing guy," and "Gil, why don't you give more of the day-to-day responsibility of running the company over to Fred Anderson so you could spend time out with customers, marketing the products?"

I tried to reassure him by answering, "Ed, there are just too many other issues that need attention for me to be out of the office. The problems aren't just operational or financial." I reminded them that, even without the additional ad budget they had just turned down, we would soon be launching a bright new ad campaign as planned. "In the fall we'll allocate a lot of money for both print and TV advertising, and hopefully that will help us have a better Christmas. That's what we've got to shoot for."

But the seeds of dissatisfaction had been planted in Ed's mind. He became fixated on the idea that "You gotta be spending your time marketing, you gotta be spending your time driving sales, that's the only work you should be doing." Every pilot knows that when flying on the gauges, you can't concentrate on a single instrument, you have to keep scanning the entire panel. It's the same for a CEO: You have to keep watch over every aspect. Concentrate on just one area and the company is likely to crash.

Ed kept insisting, and the session was getting tense. "I hear what you're saying," I told him. "I don't agree that I can just turn the business over to the CFO. But you have my word I'll do everything I can to increase the level of attention to marketing."

The other board members were squirming, as well. "Is there daylight out there?" "Do we have reason to believe sales are going to improve?" "What makes you think this company will ever be profitable again?" They were feeling embattled, frustrated, not knowing where to turn. And I knew in the backs of their minds they were worried about their own reputations and potential of shareholder lawsuits if things didn't soon start looking more hopeful.

It was following this meeting, I believe, that Ed Woolard started complaining to Steve Jobs, "What are we gonna do to get the sales up?" and "Steve, what would *you* do?"

Things were unfolding exactly as Steve must have wanted; it couldn't have been playing out better if Jobs had written the script himself.

∘   ∘   ∘

Just over the horizon loomed the July MacWorld in Boston, and I realized that Apple could enjoy enhanced glory if a deal was announced with Microsoft. No amount of money spent on marketing and advertising could get the company the positive exposure and believability that such an announcement might bring. I tortured over this, recognizing that if in my eagerness I accepted a deal that wasn't right for Apple, we might achieve short-term gains but lose heavily in the long run.

The crux of our negotiations now turned on a relatively new issue: I had been counting on a commitment from him to develop a version of Microsoft Office that would run on Rhapsody, our forthcoming operating system based on the NeXT software. This seemed to me absolutely crucial; without the availability of major, front-runner applications like Word and Excel, we would have little hope of selling the Rhapsody operating system to the world of Macintosh users.

For his part, Bill presented every possible reason why Apple should adopt the Microsoft Internet browser, Internet Explorer, as our default browser . . . and, of course, in the Gatesian manner, wanted my buy-in on one or two other things as well. Making a commitment on the Internet Explorer was, I thought, not the best choice for Apple. Nonetheless I was willing to agree—*if* he would make a commitment in return to produce a version of Microsoft Office to run on Rhapsody.

He refused even to consider it.

I said, "Bill, you're asking me to do this, this, and this, and I'm agreeing to do it all, but I ask you only one thing, to put Office on Rhapsody."

"I can't make that commitment," he said.

"Then how do I explain to my customers that you're serious? We have mutual customers, and the question they always ask these days is whether Microsoft is going to put Office on Rhapsody."

We ended the conversation in a stalemate.

o o o

I told the executive staff, "We all want to announce a deal with Microsoft at MacWorld, but let me tell you what it looks like to me: It ain't gonna happen. He knows I want to do this before MacWorld, and he's using that as leverage. The only way it could happen," I said, "is for Bill to realize Apple will not be ramrodded into doing this just because the clock is ticking down on MacWorld. And the only way I'm going to convince him that I'm holding out for a good deal is if we just miss MacWorld and get a deal later."

The message would sink in on Gates, I thought, when MacWorld came and went, and no deal had been made. He'd then see we weren't going to fall on our knees to get the deal at any cost and would start negotiating seriously. By August or September, a month or two away, we'd have an agreement. We would wait.

I could envision any number of things that might delay or alter this expectation. The actual outcome was one I would never have been able to imagine.

o o o

In April, Fred Anderson called to tell me he had been advised by investor relations that someone had just bought $115 million worth of Apple stock, gaining approximately a 5 percent stake in the company. The someone turned out to be an oil-rich member of Arabian royalty: the forty-one-year-old Prince Alwaleed bin Talal bin Abdulaziz Alsaud, a nephew of King Saud.

Described as one of the world's wealthiest and most powerful investors, Alwaleed has in a few years accumulated substantial holdings in retailing (Saks Fifth Avenue), airlines (TWA), entertainment (Euro Disney), an empire of five-star hotel chains (including various Four Seasons, the Plaza in New York, and the George V in Paris), and many other areas. And all of that is just part of his portfolio.

But Apple was his first drilling into the black gold of high tech. The prince told *Bloomberg Business News* that he would examine the company's management strategy and the takeover plan proposed by Larry Ellison who, he said, was a good friend.

Later I would learn that Alwaleed had been invited to a late-night meeting at Ellison's San Francisco apartment, where the discussion focused on a number of specific high-tech companies as possible investment opportunities. "Things could be resurrected [at Apple]," the prince was quoted as saying, "and we could have the old Apple back." The remark had an ominous ring, suggesting a hands-on investor who might want a lot of attention and who might want a voice in company decisions. "I will listen to both sides," the quote went on. "I need to see which one convinces me more." Could this well-heeled, astute member of royalty be the partner Larry Ellison had been looking for?

The photogenic prince also proved to be a reporter's dream, a man of exotic contradictions. One curious *Business Week* journalist who trailed the prince into the desert found a scene to inspire news copy that read like fiction. "40 or so robed Bedouins [sitting] on carpets around a huge log fire, sipping tea. . . . Nearby a camel is being milked in the dark. At 3 a.m.., the desert is silent. Well, almost silent. . . . As huge TV monitors erected on the sand drone out Wall Street's closing prices, . . . Alwaleed is on the phone with his lawyers in Washington, ironing out a Securities & Exchange Commission filing. . . ."

The prince had said he wanted to infuse strength back into Apple. Ellison might have expected me to find that off-putting; instead, it struck me as an invitation to reach out. I immediately wrote to Alwaleed, inviting him to visit for a full review of our plans to get Apple back on its feet again. His reply explained that although he couldn't just then come to meet me himself, "rather than let any more time go by," he would send his banker, Michael Jensen, head of corporate finance for Citibank Private Bank in Geneva, along with a relative and business advisor, Mustafa Al-Hejailan.

We had been working on a presentation almost from the day Prince Alwaleed's investment had become known, anticipating a visit. The representatives arrived mid-morning on Thursday, June 19. This was too important for me to say some polite hellos and then leave the rest in the hands of the executive committee members; I had my appointment schedule kept free for the remainder of the day.

Although these were men who must have sat through many long business presentations, I didn't want our people to drone on at them with the usual dull dog-and-pony show of one speaker after another. Instead I had a set of charts prepared and we worked it out that all the presenters would remain seated at the table; each time we moved on to a new chart, whoever was the most knowledgeable about that particular subject would talk about it. Others of the group would join in to expand on an idea or offer another cut on something that might not have been clear. So instead of doing a formal presentation, we would turn it into an open discussion—very Apple, very conducive to sharing ideas.

As I had hoped, it proved a bright way of keeping the session on a friendlier footing. And it also communicated a sense of people working as a team.

After lunch together in the board room, the visitors met the other executives, and then we took them on tours of the facilities, where they saw demonstrations of a number of the major new products soon to be introduced.

When the two were getting ready to leave at the end of the day, Al-Hejailan said it was the most impressive presentation and demonstration he had ever witnessed. He believed we were doing the right things, and he would go back and tell that to the prince. He had been especially captivated by the E-Mate, a nifty, pint-sized computer for schoolkids. I think he was imagining all the children in Saudi Arabia learning to read, rhyme, and reason with the machines.

The report must indeed have been a favorable one. Prince Alwaleed did not join with Ellison to take over Apple, as many people had expected, and he did not ask for a seat on the board. It was a vote of confidence and couldn't have come at a better time. But perhaps it would have been better if he *had* been given a seat on the board; I would soon be in need of directors who were not sitting with hair-trigger panic buttons.

◦　◦　◦

Apple wasn't just losing customers; we were losing the loyalty of long-time supporters. What could we do to show old Mac fans that we were coming back?

Through the experiences with Whoopi Goldberg, Arthur Levitt, and a great many others, it had struck me that while lots of people use the Macintosh, it was also true that lots of *famous* people use the Mac. And, I had begun to realize, people who were leaders in many fields not only use the Macintosh but are highly vocal about their enthusiasm for it.

Movie stars, Nobel prize winners, astronauts, and composers are Mac addicts.

By tapping into their enthusiasm, I felt sure that some of these people would be willing to come together in an advisory council that could meet once or twice a year, providing us the benefit of their ideas and suggestions about what the company should be doing to keep the Apple products ahead of the market. I intended to be forthright about asking those who agreed to allow our PR to do some name dropping.

The answer from many of the people we asked was a resounding yes, they would be glad to participate. This was the origin of what came to be called the AppleMasters program, and the first gathering took place early in April, beginning with a dinner at the Silicon Valley Capital Club in San Jose, which agreed to let us take over the entire main dining room.

It would be appropriate to call this a stellar occasion. Twenty-five world-class masters of their fields flew in to be with us for the launch of the program: Nobel prize–winning physicists Dr. Donald Glasser and Dr. Murray Gell-Mann; astronaut/scientist Dr. Mae Jemison; mountaineer and writer Sir Chris Bonington; environmentalists Amory and Hunter Lovins; and from Hollywood, Jennifer Jason Leigh, Richard Dreyfuss, Gregory Hines, and Kathleen Kennedy, the producer of *E.T.* and *Jurassic Park*.

The fact that one of the most celebrated sports figures of all time, Muhammad Ali, was an Apple user and had agreed to be an AppleMaster produced a memorable moment when he walked in to join us. Before dinner, he talked with me about his recent travels in connection with his humanitarian work around the world.

Michael Crichton, author of runaway best-sellers like *Jurassic Park* and *The Lost World*, is, as might be expected, an engaging dinner conversationalist. He made the extraordinary statement to me, "When I sit down in front of a Windows machine, I can't write; when I sit in front of my Mac, I can write. So I only use Macs." Other creative and thinking people describe using a Macintosh in similar terms that those who use a Windows machine don't fully grasp and might consider a gross exaggeration. But around this table, I was hearing the power of Macintosh described by people who think differently, in words that I hoped would one day, when the budget allowed, become advertising copy.

It was, to say the least, an animated dinner conversation, with Macintosh the unseen but ever-present guest of honor.

But Macintosh was very much in evidence the next morning. Each AppleMaster received a new desktop computer and a new PowerBook, as part of the company's way of saying thank-you (and, too, as a subtle but valuable promotion for the Macintosh). The morning was devoted to an intensive training session to bring the Masters up to speed on the bells and whistles of their new machines. I was intrigued as I wandered among the group, listening in and kibbitzing with them, and even offering some help in the learning process.

At midday many employees gathered in Apple's Town Hall to meet the Masters and to pick up on any ideas they might offer that could help the company. We wanted the maximum number of people to take part in this session and had arranged to have it televised around the campus and to other Apple locations.

Apple's Kanwal Sharma handled the MC duties, introducing each of the Masters who volunteered to speak. Harry Marx explained how he used Apple technology for the movies, giving a demo that blew everyone away. Kathleen Kennedy, the *E.T.* producer, talked about how the Apple products have been used in film production. She described some effective tactics she had used in promoting her films and bridged into some clear suggestions on how these same promotional ideas could be adapted by Apple.

Michael Crichton's carefully expressed contribution was memorable and Richard Dreyfus poignantly described the importance of saving Apple; each message was worthy, heartfelt, and memorable.

But then suddenly the intellectual mood changed. Gregory Hines took the stage, planted his feet, looked at the audience, and grabbed everyone's attention: "I don't need to make a speech, I just thought I'd do a dance for Apple." His eloquence was then clearly expressed in a ten-minute performance—a breathtaking tap routine, interspersed with verbal captions. A remark about how fast the Macintosh is, for example, would then be illustrated for a minute or two with a blur of dazzlingly fast steps. Apple people were enthralled and let him know it. Their excitement was obviously felt by Hines who went on beyond any routine he might have planned. He successfully communicated his feelings in the best way he could; it was one of those magical and memorable performances that artists and audiences carry with them for a lifetime.

Over the next days, many folks stopped me or wrote me to express how very moved they had been by the heartfelt expressions they had heard and seen at the Town Hall Masters session. Both in language and dance we had all witnessed appreciation, commitment, and loyalty to Apple.

Since that initial meeting, AppleMasters has expanded to include novelist Tom Clancy, actors Harrison Ford and James Woods, Monty Python refugee Terry Gilliam, and Oscar-winning director Sydney Pollack.

That these people are all enthusiastic Mac users was encouraging; that they were willing to spend time traveling to Cupertino for this event was a testimonial to the dedication that the Macintosh inspires. I was thrilled to have brought this group into existence, privileged to have spent time talking to the individual members of this august group and being inspired by them. Definitely one of the brightest highlights of my 500 days.

And the group did, indeed, lead to a strong marketing impact at the corporate level.

Time spent with people who have bigger ideas or smaller fears leaves one renewed and refreshed. I returned to my office with heightened enthusiasm for tackling the roadblocks still in my way. Apple's restored health remained my number-one concern and priority; I would take inspiration from the AppleMasters I had talked to: Don't give up and keep your eye on the long-term win.

18

Bullets Wrapped in Fire—
I AM DISMISSED

On June 16, six months after an exuberant Steve had suggested we celebrate the buyout of NeXT as a foursome over a bottle of wine, we managed to schedule dinner together. By this time our relationship had gone over some speed bumps, but I still hadn't given up.

The sun was still bright in the evening sky when the four of us gathered in Redwood City, a bayside coastal town near the San Francisco airport, on Monday, June 16, one of those brilliant days at the end of spring, beautiful almost anywhere but especially magical in the Bay Area. My wife Charlene had never met Steve before, and I had met his wife Laurene only once.

Gaylord's was a new restaurant for Charlene and me, but as Steve and his wife prefer vegetarian cuisine, I had agreed. And it was apparently a popular restaurant with them, because Steve was able to order without looking at the menu; I said, "Whatever you're eating, just order for the table." Which he did without hesitation.

Here we were—the perfect team: He ordered the food and I had selected the wines from my cellar. The white was a fine Montrachet, the red a 1964 Cheval Blanc—each bottle worth well over $300. Probably both were too sophisticated for a vegetarian meal but I, for one, enjoyed them more than the food.

We started dinner on the early side, around 6:30, and talked and drank amiably for the next three hours. The animated conversation, the sharing of wines, and the not totally unenjoyable experience of being introduced to vegetarian foods would have convinced any onlooker that these two couples were the closest of friends. The appearance of four people appreciating each other in a simple setting could surely be conclusive evidence of the joys of true friendship. Appearances and perceptions are often more real than reality.

Mellowed by the wine, I reached for the check and couldn't believe a total of $72 for four dinners. I thought I'd finally figured out why so many smart young people had become vegetarians—healthy and really inexpensive. I wondered if Charlene would want to return to Gaylord's and if dinner would have tasted quite as enjoyable without the expensive wines and lively company.

As we broke up, Laurene gave me a big hug and kissed me. "Gee, it was so great meeting you folks." I wondered what Charlene would have to say about the evening.

She couldn't wait to tell me how charming and natural both Steve and Laurene were and expressed real surprise at what a wonderful evening it was.

"I think he's just great—I mean, he's such a charmer and his wife is, too." She commented on how wrong people are about Steve, because he seemed so sincere and real. She repeated, ". . . simply charming."

Charlene's descriptive word was right on the money; it's easy in hindsight to see the dinner as another diversionary tactic, even as his scheming for invasion of my territory was taking place. While the other vegetarians at Gaylord's had thought they were observing four jovial friends dining together, Steve's plans to manipulate my termination were charging forward.

o   o   o

Twelve days after the dinner, as part of his scheme, Steve Jobs took an action that caught me and a lot of other people off guard, and would leave a mark against him in the memories of many people in the investment and business communities.

During negotiations for the buyout of NeXT, once we had compromised on his million and a half shares, I had said, "Steve, we'll register these shares, they'll be yours outright, but you have to understand it's very important that you not sell them. It would damage the company very badly."

He had assured me, "I've got all the money I need, I'd have no reason for selling."

In June, one block of a million and a half shares of Apple stock was traded in a single day. Rumors started to circulate that Steve had sold his shares, newspapers ran stories speculating that Steve had sold out, industry watchers conjectured that Jobs was sending a message of mistrust in Apple's management.

When I called him I said, "Steve, am I right? I'm telling people that the shares sold were not yours, that you wouldn't trade your stock. Remember, you and I had an understanding that you wouldn't sell any without advising us first."

He simply said, "That's right."

So after our conversation, when people asked what the story was, I told them exactly what I thought he had said: "Steve assured me those weren't his shares." Although I believed him, I must admit that I did have suspicions, but held them just below the conscious level. *"That's right,"* I began to wonder—*what* was right?

When large blocks of stock are traded, the federal government requires that details be disclosed in the company's next Quarterly Report. When the next one appeared, it listed Steve's name next to the infamous 1.5 million shares—less one share he kept to be sure he stayed on the mailing list for reports.

I said, "Dammit, Steve, I asked you point-blank about these shares and you denied it was you." All he had to say in his defense was "Yeah, I didn't want to fess up to it because I was a little embarrassed. I was sort of in a fit of depression at the time and I just felt the company was hopeless and so I just did a spontaneous thing and sold my shares." Like a little boy caught with his hand in the cookie jar, Steve said, "I feel really bad about it."

Selling the stock was a slap in my face, a punch into Apple's midsection, and I anticipated more trouble ahead. Steve's lie about the sale aggravated the situation and left a taint of sordidness.

Still, if he was depressed when he sold the stock—at about $14 a share—how did he feel three or four months later when the price hit twice that amount?

o   o   o

My early decision to cut back on advertising and maintain a lowered profile until the product problems were fixed, plus the board's rejection of a long-term increase in the ad budget, now came back to haunt me. I heard loud and clear that sales revenues were not improving fast enough to please the board. Particularly vociferous on this issue was Ed Woolard, the very person who had urged I set a timetable for profitability. "Gil, you said you'd be profitable by now and you didn't do it. How are we going to maintain credibility? How can you continue to be a leader if you're not credible?"

Talk about being trapped between a rock and a hard place!

Forcing myself to stay calm and cool, I challenged Ed's logic: "In my experience, the top line doesn't grow until virtually everything else is fixed. You have to get your quality right, you've got to get the product line right, and all the rest. The top line is the last thing to respond."

It was not the last I would hear from Ed Woolard on this subject.

o   o   o

I think of it now and will remember it always as *the weekend that was*. I will never again experience fireworks in the same innocently joyful way.

Early on Friday morning of July 4, Charlene and I joined forces to get ready for an extended family gathering. We had been anticipating a first chance to introduce two of our grandchildren to Independence Day traditions like fireworks and hot dogs. Joining us at Stonewood, our Lake Tahoe house, were Charlene's daughter, with husband; her son, with wife and two young children; and friends of theirs with two more youngsters in tow; altogether we would be eight adults and four children aged three and under. Charlene accurately accuses me of finding ways to avoid any duties except for providing the wines and piloting the water-ski boat.

We had agreed on relaxed, unstructured days of water sports and barbecues, promising each other to stay calm when the littlest ones turned raucous. We envisioned a weekend of mellow conversation, light-hearted laughter with the warmth of family and friends to reset our overwound emotions. And it began well enough, exactly as planned. There were neither phone calls nor faxes to spoil the laid-back mood of the day for Charlene and the children, while I managed to find or invent an amazing number of ways to disappear into my second floor home-office to put the final words on an almost-completed deal I had been trying to forge with Bill Gates.

Bill had continued to hold out on the one term I considered make-or-break: committing to develop applications for Rhapsody. Without his agreement, Apple's new operating system concept would prove entirely hollow, a benefit only to Steve Jobs for the amount of money he had pocketed. So much depended on this one aspect of the agreement. But now Bill was getting closer to saying yes.

I'll always remember how fragmented my attention was that weekend as I quietly interchanged roles between host, husband, friend, and CEO. There was no way I was willing to let this Gates letter slide— it spelling out the details remaining to be settled and had to be finished and sent to Gates first thing Monday morning. I used every minute I could snag. But Charlene's voice would seek me and I would soon chase downstairs again to pitch in.

Friday night the entire group of us strolled out to the end of our pier. The only sounds to mar the evening calm were our warnings to the children to stay away from the edge; the only distraction I felt was that letter to Bill left unfinished on my desk. But when the sparklers we set off for the children resulted in their shrieks of sheer delight, my mind shifted to the moment at hand and I felt myself relax into the occasion. We soon needed to bundle up against the night chill off the lake as we huddled together to watch other more formal and impressive fireworks, impressed and awed at discovering we were able to see three different displays simultaneously.

Charlene and I caught a flash in each other's eyes. It had been one perfect day. I should have known that days like this don't often come very many in a row . . . at least, not for the CEO of Apple Computer.

Saturday night, the fifth, after a too-long day of activities—too much socializing for me, but rated as near perfect by family and guests—we enjoyed dinner at a nearby restaurant on the lake. On returning, most of the crew decided to make it an early night. I merely glanced at my desk, shuffled a few papers, changed a few sentences on the Gates deal, and went to bed.

I was ready for an early start on Sunday morning, but was summoned by the ring of the phone. There was Ed Woolard's most official-sounding voice, "Gil, I need to talk to you."

I thought, *It's Sunday on the Fourth of July weekend. Ed is in England for the Wimbledon tennis matches. What could be so urgent that he's got to call me from there?*

"Charlene, I'll take this call in my office."

Woolard jumped right into the topic: "Gil, the board has been meeting by telephone on and off for the last thirty-six hours and I'm afraid I don't have a very good message for you."

I wasn't ready for this. Was I was really being fired? I couldn't think of any other bad news that deserved this trite preamble.

"We think you need to step down. You've done a lot to help the company, but the sales haven't rebounded."

I managed to respond, "Ed, you don't realize how much more work needs to be done at the grass roots of this company before you're going to start seeing the top line grow." And I repeated the theme I had been drumming on: "The top line is the last to grow, virtually everything else must first be set right. This company is not in that situation yet."

Before the shot is fired, the victim is offered a blindfold. Ed's version of the blindfold was "We need somebody who's going to drive the sales, and we know sales and marketing isn't your primary strength."

I hoped Charlene wouldn't come looking for me. I was sure the color, including the suntan I had nurtured during June weekends, had drained out of my face. It sure felt like that.

I needed to fight on: "Ed, we've just finished a quarter with results that were better than the analyst predictions. You want me to step down just when things are beginning to look better!?"

He answered, "We want to find a CEO who can be a great marketing and sales leader for the company."

"Remember, Ed, I told the board it was going to take three years to get this company back on its feet again. I'm not even halfway through those three years. I recognize how much pressure we're under from shareholders and customers and everyone else, but we all have to pull together, deal with reality, and rise above it."

He countered, "The board is at the place where we don't want to discuss it further."

"If that's the opinion of the board and it's not something you're willing to talk to me about or have an exchange on, then I will of course step aside."

He said, "We're going to treat you with the utmost respect, and we'll make it as gracious and cordial a transition as possible."

But I was mad as hell. "Ed, it really bothers me that if the board members were having these kinds of concerns, they should have brought me into it. As a member of the board, I should have been a part of the discussion even if the discussion was about me. I'm disappointed in that behavior; I can't believe you would exclude me."

No response, just, "We merely ask that you cooperate and be supportive of this important transition."

It was a *done deal*. I felt like fighting, I could have fought; I could have marshaled my forces and waged board room warfare. That's not my way.

But our conversation could not be over and leave me wondering how all this had come about.

I asked "Ed, who knows about this?"

He said, "Well, of course, all the board members know." And then he hesitated for a moment and added, "Oh—and Steve Jobs knows."

"Steve knows?"

"Well, Steve was one of the people we talked to about this. We wanted to get his viewpoint. And I'm sure you'd agree that Steve is very knowledgeable about things like this. His view is that you're a really nice guy, but that you don't really know much about the computer industry. He advised that we need someone with more knowledge of the industry—that the company would stand a better chance of doing well."

"Ed, why in the world would you involve Steve in a decision like this? Why was he even part of a discussion about me?"

Ed gave me no answer, but I easily supplied my own—a scenario that would later be supported by fact.

"What's the next step?"

"Gil, as soon as we finish, I'm going to call Steve and tell him we had this conversation and what the result of it was."

Perplexed but still trying not to show it, I said, "Listen, Ed, Steve is not even a member of the board of directors, so what the hell is he doing in any of this conversation?" I was fed up with the conniving and didn't really expect a truthful answer.

The shot had been fired—my time at Apple was over—and I thought, *May as well let him talk to whoever he wants.*

I sat there dazed, looking at the work I had been doing on the Microsoft deal. I wondered how to tell Charlene. I heard sounds that signaled my sister saying her good-byes. I needed something sweet to get the bitter taste out of my mouth.

Ed had managed to ruin my weekend but I didn't intend to spoil it for everyone else.

o   o   o

I broke the news quite calmly to Charlene as we drove home from the airport. I couldn't predict with certainty how she'd react, but she was unemotional about it and, of course, very understanding. As we walked into the house about 6:00 P.M., the phone was ringing and I heard the mellow tones of Steve's voice—the last person I expected to hear from.

He began a sort of speech that started with "Gee, Gil, I just want you to know, I talked to Ed today about this thing and I feel really bad about it."

I let him talk. "I want you to know that I had absolutely nothing to do with this turn of events, it was a decision the board made, but they had asked me for advice and counsel."

Then he felt the need to say, "You're a man with the highest integrity of anyone I've ever met. You're a real classy individual."

I remember grunting something meaningless, and he proceeded to give me some advice. "Take six months off, don't do anything, don't try to find a job, don't work on anything, just take six months off and do nothing."

"I'll probably do that, Steve."

He said, "When I got thrown out of Apple, I immediately went back to work, and I regretted it. I should have taken that time for myself. I wish I had."

I mumbled, "That sounds like good advice."

Then he made an offer that sounded genuine. "When you start to think about what you want to do next, please feel free to call on me, I'd be happy to act as a sounding board on what might make sense for you. If you just need someone to talk to, I'm here."

Hanging up, I sensed it was just another one of those "my closest friend" kind of conversations. Yet I don't think it was insincere. I think there are two people inside the body of Steve Jobs, and you can never be quite sure in advance which one is going to be talking to you.

Charlene interrupted my thoughtful mood to ask, "Was Steve Jobs the reason you're being let go?"

I said, "He says getting me thrown out wasn't his doing, but I don't believe him. In ways, I still like the man, but I don't believe him."

Charlene agreed, "I don't believe him either. I've always thought I had a sixth sense about people. I've never really been taken in by anyone before, but I was totally taken in by Steve Jobs, and I really feel like an idiot." I knew exactly how she felt; I had, along with many others, also been trapped by the charisma and boldness of this unusual man.

"Join the crowd," I said. "Steve has charmed more people than you and I will ever know."

When asked by reporters, I would say, "Steve told me that he had nothing to do with my being fired." I had learned from Steve how to say something without saying anything.

o   o   o

From Steve's narrow perspective as a salesman and marketer *extraordinaire*, he probably concluded that most of the major problems facing the company had been solved. I had managed to build up the amount of money in the bank; my insistence on cleaning up the quality issues had resulted in the problems being addressed and set to rights; I had forced a complete retuning of the product line; and due to the NeXT acquisition, Apple had an operating-system strategy most people were genuinely excited about.

To me it was just a beginning, but to Steve it must have looked like the opportune time to make a move toward achieving his primary goal—to take Apple back for himself. He surely realized that in a few quarters I'd have the company making money again. Successful numbers plus quality products, excellent service, and a new operating system would bring cheers, bring customers back to Apple—at which point the board would not be interested in changing management. By forcing the board's hand when he did, he could achieve his fantasy and make a full comeback.

To someone obsessed, when another person gets in the way, the solution is to roll right over him. It makes no difference who that person is; the fact that it was I who had openly admired what Steve Jobs had done at Apple, NeXT, and Pixar, I who had courageously fought to make an honorable deal with him, was of no concern. The success I was creating threatened to get in the way of his plans. Betrayal, assassination, trashing of reputations are all part of the everyday tool kit of a person obsessed with power, control, or revenge.

I was in Steve's way and had to be eliminated.

o   o   o

During an interview, a member of the press asked me if I thought the media had been an unknowing accomplice in my being fired.

They would deny it if you asked, but just as movie critics secretly enjoy their power to make and break new films while denying they have or want such influence, no business reporter would admit out loud wanting to manipulate events through their writing.

I'll never know if the article in *Fortune* was read by Apple board members or whether the stinging words might have had any subtle, gnawing impact, but the magazine had not long before stuck it to the board by calling them a "passive group of mostly inexperienced observers," and went on to throw down a gauntlet: They were "unlikely to push for a change as drastic as asking Jobs to replace Amelio. Other boards might, but not this one. While it stands by, Apple looks more and more like a corpse."

Fortune would, I'm sure, love to think they goaded the board to action. I'd love to think they didn't. Since any board member who might have been influenced is highly unlikely to admit it (under the circumstances, would *you?*), neither of us will ever know.

o   o   o

Larry Ellison, on the other hand, had a lot to gain by Steve taking over Apple. Months earlier, he had been prepared to pay billions of dollars for Apple; with me out of the picture and Steve in control, Ellison could expect, and got, a seat on the board, surrounded by familiar, friendly new faces.

So Larry Ellison, Apple board member, seated with other members that he and Steve hand-picked, is now in a position to acquire whatever portions of the Apple technology he wants, at a much more attractive price than having to buy the entire company.

o   o   o

The ego does not recover readily from an episode like mine. Personal rejection was only a surface injury; I thought often about the Herculean effort to stop the downward spiral that had used up the time and energy of so many people working under excessive strain, the waste of emotional and intellectual resources, the hopes and dreams and new relationships that were dashed—essentially a waste of 500 days unless there was follow-through.

During the ignominious days following my dismissal, I worked out of my regular office in City Center 3 while a new CEO's office neared completion in the R&D complex—an office I never occupied and have never seen. My final days were filled with wrapping up, preparing reports for the board, and letting others know the status of the efforts in progress.

Writers of business case studies will likely debate my 500 days, raking it over the coals just as the John Sculley years have been—praising me for some things, debasing me for others, and giving me some kind of final grade for overall performance. But what will truly count is whether my decisions for Apple prove valid . . . and those can only be evaluated if the next CEO is allowed to accept the strength of my efforts. I had helped Apple survive and left the company primed and ready to take advantage of the next big wave of technology.

Apple can survive. Apple can regain its vaunted stature as a leader, a giant, a company worth revering. Apple can achieve these things; whether it will is now in other hands.

o   o   o

As soon as the break was clean and word was out, requests for interviews and speeches began to flood in. One speech I gave soon after leaving was to an advisory board of the consulting firm Booz Allen Hamilton, and I was delighted to find myself seated next to another of the speakers, Henry Kissinger. After my talk, in a dynamic gesture of approval, Kissinger grabbed my arm and said, "You're a classy guy. After what you've been through, a lot of people wouldn't have even shown up."

I thought to myself as I nodded to this exceptional man, *A lot of people wouldn't have accepted the job as CEO of a company in such bad shape as Apple. But I wouldn't have missed the experience—not for anything.*

o   o   o

I have worked through my disappointment in the way Steve Jobs treated me, but shall never forget the pain of it. Perhaps returning to control at Apple will finally melt the ice cube in his heart that has caused him so much pain since 1985.

Along with many other Apple people who had been let go because of the company's many failures, I had taken my turn on the firing line. Some may call that a failure, but, as Kissinger implied, that's not the only way to see it.

When I arrived, Apple was manufacturing the wrong products, with the wrong features, in the wrong quantities, marred with severe quality problems. The warehouses were stuffed with $600 million worth of unsaleable computers. The hard cash reserves were so low that the company could not survive more than another four months. Executives made decisions based on what was right for their own operation, not on what was right for the company. And the culture stressed the individual and freedom of action instead of cooperation and working toward a set of common goals.

When I left, every executive I inherited had been replaced. Apple had $1.5 billion in the bank. A string of stunning new products had begun to appear. A market research organization was producing valid market data for projecting sales revenues, essential for writing a sensible budget. And the executives and managers were showing early signs of beginning to pull together in the same direction, toward common goals. In short, the company had made an excellent start on the road to transformation and recovery; it was headed in the right direction, and there was every reason to expect success by continuing on that course.

My 500 days at Apple were valuable, enlightening, even entertaining. I had the ride of my life and now, in retrospect, I can say—I hardly felt the bullet.

The interactions between intense people, the complicated subplots of greed and glory, corridor intrigue, corporate politics, Hollywood stars, and character assassinations that included revenge and control were beyond any reality I had ever seen up close. The costuming, the haranguing, the creativity, and the characters were all made for high drama.

My 500 days—in Shakespearean terms, neither a comedy nor a tragedy. Let's call it a romance.

Epilogue
TOMORROW AND TOMORROW
AND ALAS, POOR APPLE

Steve Jobs was enthroned at Apple, issuing executive orders and letting Ellen Hancock know she wasn't wanted any longer, even before the press release announcing my departure had been issued.

Eager for a dramatic move, he called Bill Gates and gave him the deal I wouldn't, handing over everything Gates had been pestering me for. But he failed to get in return the one essential element—a commitment that Microsoft would develop applications to run on the new Mac operating system based on Steve's NeXT software. Instead he settled for cash, a sum Microsoft could write a check for without blinking. Bill got everything he wanted in a deal fashioned out of what *Fortune* called "Gates' Machiavellian largess and Jobs's self-aggrandizing salesmanship."

Steve was rewarded with a cover photo on the next issue of *Time*.

After my departure, Steve Jobs replayed the role of Apple messiah, risen again to re-create the original religion of Apple-in-the-Garage.

But within the corridors and offices of Apple, the epic of the hero's return was marred by disastrous outbursts of Steve's temper; his erratic, manic style of dealing with people; and his decide-on-the-spot, don't-confuse-me-with-facts approach to decision-making. He canceled major projects, launched new ones, tied a rock to the incredible Spartacus and drowned it in the ocean because it wasn't his idea, did away with employee sabbaticals, fired most of the successful executives and senior managers I had put in place, took away the autonomy of the Newton group, and bringing his own computer into the executive suite, did the unthinkable: apparently more interested in using NeXT operating system than in what Apple loyalists might think, Steve's machine was not a Mac but an IBM clone!

He drove himself to work, just as I had done . . . but in the largest, most expensive Mercedes Benz, the S600; faced with the same problem of finding places to park, he solved it by using spaces reserved for the handicapped.

He quickly canceled the clone licenses, which—never before revealed till now—triggered a Department of Justice investigation.

And he took credit for the brilliant new products, for creating a program to market Apple products directly to end users over the Internet, and for the many other achievements that had all been initiated without his input—all started long before he took over. It bristled me no end to read in the newspapers about Steve making a deal with Bill Gates, as if no groundwork had been laid; Steve bringing out new computers, which were already in the pipeline; and Steve introducing Macs that can run Windows. These are all things that Ellen Hancock had everything to do with and Steve had virtually nothing to do with. And the fact that she received no credit from him was, I think, grossly unfair.

Despite their handshake months earlier, Steve still burned at the memory of Mike Markkula's role in getting him fired from his own company in 1984. As acting CEO, Steve finally got his revenge, forcing Markkula off the board. He had settled one score and had in mind to settle another.

Jobs wouldn't even talk to Steve Wozniak; he fingered CFO Fred Anderson to tell Woz that his services as an advisor to Apple were no longer needed. Since Woz didn't want to work with Steve Jobs and wasn't receiving any money for his services, it hardly caused a ripple. The company didn't even have the grace to issue a press release.

Even though it was intended by my pretend-friend to belittle me, I still had a good laugh on hearing of the new parameter scale that Steve started using to ridicule any unfortunate Apple person who just said something Steve considered stupid. He tells them the remark was a "one-Gil" or a "two-Gil," or worse.

I rank that as a three-Steve.

o   o   o

Jobs had at last fulfilled the dream he revealed when he had paid me that visit at National Semiconductor and asked me to help him become Apple's CEO.

I believe that men like Larry Ellison and Jon Rubinstein have recognized his genius and tried to help him see through his need for revenge; perhaps that's part of what it means to be a friend.

But instead of achieving peace, contentment, or fulfillment, Steve now found himself struggling with Hamletlike indecision. He had manipulated himself back into the seat of power at the company he had cofounded and built. He was being asked to take over as CEO and chairman. Did he want it . . . or didn't he want it? I remembered his tortured indecision about the role he would play once NeXT was merged into Apple.

He had demanded and fought for his vindication and must have wondered why it didn't feel as wonderful as he thought it would. He had been thoroughly honest when he had told people his heart was at Pixar. And without the experience, management skills, or discipline to lead a Fortune 500 company, why would he want to risk presiding over Apple's decline?

Though the board thrice offered him the crown, which he did thrice refuse, Steve was still running Apple eight months later—apparently unable to find anyone willing to take the CEO job and live every day in an atmosphere of Steve-trums, with Steve still expecting to make all the decisions.

But count on it, if Apple survives and succeeds, Steve will lay claim to the credit; if the company doesn't make it, Steve will find someone else—probably John Sculley or me—to blame.

One can only hope that this talented man will find inner peace now that he has lived out his fantasy, unfortunately at my expense. The problem is that fantasies don't go away—they become living nightmares.

I predict Steve will one day conquer Hollywood as dramatically as he conquered Silicon Valley. Michael Eisner, watch out; Steve Jobs now has a new talent on his résumé: displacing the CEO. The Walt Disney Company could be next.

o o o

Businessmen seem quite capable of conducting autopsies of other businessmen's performances, but are seemingly incapable of analyzing their own. Finally, I was in control of my schedule, and with time set aside for reflection, I decided to review and analyze in an orderly way what appeared to be my mistakes.

In my 500 days at Apple, we managed to get the transformation process well under way, and I'm proud of the success on several fronts. The biggest mistake I had made—I would list it as the *fatal* mistake— was allowing myself to be hammered into predicting when Apple would become profitable. I knew better. I continue to wonder who I was at that moment in time to let people like Ed Woolard convince me to do what I had never done before.

I shouldn't have made a commitment; the company was not yet the well-oiled machine that could carry us forward with any assurance. By yielding to pressure from the board, I set in place a false expectation and an inaccurate yardstick to measure my performance; I would be judged according to a false forecast instead of on my transformation of product quality, organization, and the system software solution. By yielding to the board's pressure, I had created the beginning of the end.

My list of mistakes also includes the delayed launch of a much-needed, aggressive ad campaign that I should have started months earlier; I should have pushed much harder against the board's resistance for budget to support it.

I should have moved much earlier to tackle the deep underlying management problems—the passivity, insubordination, and the rest. We had begun a mid-management training effort of a kind I had used successfully at previous companies, but it had taken too long to design, had started too late, and even then we weren't doing it well enough to have much impact.

And I berate myself, as well, over the fact that I never found an effective way to halt the loss of irreplaceable talent.

My failure to recognize the growing discontent of the board—even if the seeds of that discontent were being intentionally sown by Steve Jobs—was something I still haven't come to terms with. These were all people I trusted, yet not one of them was willing to pick up the phone and say, "Gil, there's something going on here that you should know about." Candidly, if I had this to do over, I do not know what I might have done differently in my relations with the board members.

Another error I made, a major one, was in frankly misjudging where the bottom was. The personal computer industry was growing between 15 and 20 percent a year. What was the likelihood that Apple, despite all its troubles, would have a decline of 30 percent? I failed to see that coming and made decisions based on Apple being able to hold its own or at least keep its revenue to a modest decline. And I was wrong.

Predicting bottom is at best an educated guess. A company in a downward spiral cannot predict with any accuracy or assurance where bottom will be; it requires the ability to forecast sales and adjust expenses to suit. We didn't know where the bottom was when I left, and Steve still didn't know as of this writing, eight months later.

On this list of mistakes, one I do *not* include is the purchase of NeXT; it was the right decision for Apple, and it was bought at a fair price. But the people who warned me about the dangers of including Steve in the deal were absolutely right; I had made a serious mistake by putting such unrestrained, unqualified trust in him.

o o o

"If you make a better product, people will buy it." Somehow that business axiom didn't apply at Apple during my 500 days. We improved the performance of our desktop models by a factor of ten, an achievement that even in an industry with such improbably short product cycles is unheard of.

Yet sales were lower at the end than they were in the beginning. How do you explain that? After chewing over this question from every angle, my only answer was that there's a subjective element in the way people react to Apple having very little to do with how good the products are, and a lot to do with what they read in the newspapers and how comfortable they are with the state of the company.

The problem can be overcome if the company continues pushing ahead in the right directions and making the right demands on its people. Apple was just beginning to grow up and managers were learning to make thoughtful decisions. I had observed improvement in a few situations and it was beginning to spread. When someone said to a manager, "Here's a great idea," the manager would ask for the facts in order to make an informed judgment. How hard I had worked to achieve this level of mature decision-making.

But Steve sets the example of gut-level decision-making, dragging his managers back into the murky quagmire of the Apple culture just after the Big Bang of creation—an outmoded culture that was appropriate for an embryo company, but as unsuitable for a grown-up company as tantrums from an adult.

There was a time when Apple was on a roll and mistakes were an acceptable part of being young, innovative, nimble and quick—it was a new industry in a new era. Times change, markets change, people change . . . and Apple can't survive using innocent methods of leadership and management. Talent alone takes people just so far. Planning, process, and orderly function, though boring to children, are the tools of mature businesses and business leaders.

My three-year timetable is still on target—Apple has until the beginning of 1999 to get its act together. But each day that goes by where some of the urgent matters remain unaddressed moves the date out and makes survival less likely.

o   o   o

There are those who are sure that they know what went wrong: "Amelio came in from the outside, didn't understand the Apple culture, and made the mistake of trying to change it." Part of this diagnosis is accurate: I found I was trying to steer an out-of-control vehicle that was about to crash. It would be the height of folly to think a crash could be avoided without change.

But I never expected the functioning styles of managers to be remade immediately; I had warned the board that this core problem would take time to set right. And there were many people within the company who recognized the need for process and follow-through and were eager to see me succeed.

Apple needed to grow up to take its place alongside other awesomely competitive organizations such as Intel and Microsoft. Intel is an incredibly creative company, and phenomenally well-disciplined, proving that those qualities are not mutually exclusive. I wanted Apple people—such very creative people—to enjoy the benefits of working within a disciplined business structure. I never wanted to kill the culture; I wanted to help it grow up to enjoy a richer future.

The intrinsic behavior problems that forced Apple into a downward spiral had, at the end of my 500 days, not yet been fundamentally changed. I left knowing that until those fundamentals are addressed and repaired, the company would be in trouble.

Apple needs to get over operating like a dysfunctional family and go much further in developing the ability to react as an integrated organization in which people align their individual efforts for their common good. It needs to set higher expectations and help managers become developmental leaders instead of accommodating parents.

I came to realize too late that if the platform was to survive, we were going to have to play one game in the hardware world and another in the software world. My plans included a complete face-lift in structure, splitting the company into two separate units—hardware and software. I was building toward that day when I could have told Jon Rubinstein in hardware, "Do whatever it is you must to compete; if that means making Windows computers and you can create a better version than anyone else has, then do it." The message to the software people through Avie Tevanian would have been, "Rhapsody will run on Windows machines and everywhere else—go sell it as a better operating system for *everybody*."

Despite the efforts under John Sculley, a key problem that Apple never solved was the company's inability to break down the doors of major corporations. I was committed to establishing a secure beachhead for Apple in the enterprise. And Rhapsody was being built with that as its main function. The appealing, platform-agnostic message that lets users "have it all" would be the understructure of an aggressive sales campaign: "Rhapsody will run on any machine—buy our software and you can have the advantages of a Macintosh and still keep using the same computer and running all of your current applications." Business users are not going to throw out their Windows machines and convert to the Macintosh, but a great many people would chose the Mac user advantage if they could run it on their present hardware.

Apple is well on the way to being a major player in this new paradigm.

And thinking beyond Rhapsody, I realized that the stage was being set for an uncertain future in which Apple—and Microsoft as well—would become less important. I could only hope that Apple's new leadership and the board of directors would be sensitive to the future and would remain nimble.

o   o   o

I had a rude awakening on the issue of my severance. The terms were precisely spelled out in my hiring agreement—I still had over three years of salary and bonus due on my five-year contract, plus stock and options, and the unwritten understanding was that I would get the remainder of the million shares of restricted stock. As I might have expected, given my experience with the hiring negotiations, settling the terms did not prove to be straightforward.

After seeing the way things were going, I sheepishly reminded Mike Markkula of the side deal he had made with me—that if Apple reneged on the million shares the board had originally agreed to, he would personally make up the difference from his own pocket. But I told him, "If the board gives me what I've earned, then I won't hold you to your promise."

Customarily, companies prefer to get this kind of obligation off their books by making a lump-sum payment rather than issuing monthly checks. How much did I end up putting in the bank? A generous sum, but much, much less than the $9.2 million that the newspapers reported.

My severance check, when it finally came on November 7, four months after my departure, represented an all-in settlement for the remainder of the five-year term in the amount of $7.7 million. What I actually kept, after taxes and other government deductions and after paying off part of my "loan" to Apple, was about $2 million. I still owe $2.5 million on this loan, so my net was actually negative by about $500,000. The 130,960 shares of Apple stock I received—plus another 50,000 shares promised but still not received as of this writing—is far under the million shares spelled out in the original terms I had signed on to that fateful January evening in New York. Nonetheless, I told Mike that I would not hold him to his magnanimous offer.

If I had stayed at National Semiconductor, beyond not having my reputation tarnished, I would have continued to accumulate wealth at roughly $5 million a year and would have clearly been ahead. Had money been the only motivation, I made a bad decision for myself and my family. But like the majority of major-company CEOs, I'm a risk-taker; most of the time the risks pay off. Sometimes they don't.

But I have few regrets. It was a hell of an experience.

o   o   o

An old and reassuring nugget of wisdom promises that "When God closes a door, He opens a window." In my case, a number of windows have been opened.

As life in Web-time speeds people forward, there's a danger of letting the choices happen rather than making considered decisions. I decided not to rely on the advice of one-time baseball player and malapropist Yogi Berra: "If you come to a fork in the road, take it."

A number of plum offers for other CEO jobs were put to me, but I believed the time had come for me to design my own future. I chose three roles based on my past, preferences, and pride.

First, as a new-age venture capitalist. My original goal to become a teacher had over the years combined with my experience at management, evolving into a style that can best be described as mentoring. Many people who start new companies need exactly the kind of advice and mentoring I'm equipped to offer. As an equity capitalist, my approach would be different from the organizations that traditionally back new businesses.

The typical venture fund is a cash play, looking for investments with the potential for an appreciation on the order of 500 percent, so that each successful play more than makes up for others that will fail.

I was fortunate to connect with two former CEOs I had known for a number of years, Chuck Frank and Barry Schneider, who had arrived at opinions about equity capital that were very similar to mine. And these were men who, like me, had through the years been dedicated to civic affairs and service to the community. Since we shared similar outlooks and similar goals, I agreed to join them in the San Francisco-based Parkside Group, a venture fund with both unusual operational aspects and innovative goals.

Our fund aims at helping innovative and motivated people get their ideas launched and helping companies that are underperforming their potential. We take a highly unusual approach, very hands-on and involved.

One of the sadder parts of my experiences at Apple lay in finding myself more than once with a person who was dealing from the bottom of the deck. Part of the happy ending is moving on to a situation where I will be dealing with two people who have lived their lives to a standard of integrity and community service—a refreshing change.

In my view, there aren't enough political philosophers involved in government, and there aren't enough technological philosophers in technology. There's a clear distinction between the observer who's adept at predicting the future and the visionary who defines the future, especially when he has the ability to influence it. The true visionary is closer to being a philosopher, because he or she will take care to bring into balance human values, ethics, and a knowledge of history.

Science and philosophy are not more than kissing cousins . . . but as a physicist, I see myself moving closer to the world of metaphysics than to the world of engineers, even while I continue to play an active role in the world of business. In this vein, another role I have carved out is as a futurist, and I will work to help scientists innovate for the good of mankind.

The third road I will travel springboards off those contributions as a futurist. There was in an earlier age of this country the view that once the head of a family had struggled, succeeded, and accumulated wealth, the next generation would gain education, and the members of the third generation would then dedicate themselves to public service. Today, when the education typically comes before the wealth, it's not unusual for those three generations of effort to be folded into a single individual.

I have accepted the responsibility to contribute through a particular form of public service: not by seeking office, but by expanding my work as a member of public policy groups and as an advisor to political leaders—helping to shape policies, clarify issues, and apply my experience, emphasizing those topics related to my main interests of science, technology, and higher education.

The obligation was best described by the famed French poet, writer, and aviator Antoine de Saint-Exupéry: "To be a man is to be responsible, to believe that by placing one stone, you contribute to the building of the world."

I am blessed by a life that allows me the freedom, position, and opportunity of placing other stones. Maybe I won't choose one out of three, maybe I'll do all three; or, as it's currently in fashion to say, maybe I'll just listen to what the universe has in store for me.

Acknowledgments

 From Bill Simon

The contributions by my wife, Arynne, to my life and my writing include her generous willingness for me to freely "borrow" her original concepts and use them as though they were my own. We have worked together for as long as we've been married—over thirty years—and our ideas are so closely intertwined that it's impossible to take credit or attribute a word, an idea, or a perception to either one of us. Her contributions to this book go far beyond any typical efforts of editing and advice.

Arynne has been a management consultant and communications consultant to Silicon Valley companies since 1984, when Apple brought her in to coach and mentor executives and top managers; she has supported Apple at corporate headquarters and in the field without interruption ever since. Through the experience, she has come to believe that Apple has nurtured an exceptional kind of independent, maverick intelligence which should become a new definition of excellence, even though it's difficult for most managers to understand or cope with.

It's a reward for any writer to work with a talented, perceptive editor who has the style to add to the work with editorial insights right on target, but without making the kind of demands that dampen a writer's tender ego. Adrian Zackheim fits that description and, in addition, he was an eager champion for this book from the first. A great combination.

My thanks to those who consented to read early drafts and help me with their reactions on content and style—my daughter Victoria, my stepson Sheldon Bermont, my brother David, and longtime friends Bill and Renée Jenkins.

Josie Rodriguez, who has for twenty-four years maintained our home, leaving us free to focus on work, did extra duty, pampering Gil and me with refreshments and lunches to keep us working longer.

A young computer whiz, Kee Wilcox, helped keep distractions at bay by showing up whenever a technology problem appeared and successfully slaying the dragons.

And thanks to Steve Aby, whose help on a previous book I never remembered to acknowledge.

Authors don't often share their research sources, but I want to acknowledge three. My thanks to Apple alumna Joanne Carroll, who plowed through a ton of documents to locate the key items I needed.

The other two may come as something of a surprise. One is electronic—the online files of the *New York Times,* a service that's both free and comprehensive. Even though the system often returns a load of articles having no apparent connection to the key words entered, it does provide the desired wheat among the chaff. I applaud the *Times* and hope their Web site will prove profitable to them, as well as to their appreciative visitors.

Big-city writers have the luxury of being able to call on the services of a huge library with a large research staff. While the central San Diego library is only thirty miles from my home, I instead turn to the research librarians in the little town of Vista, California, where the staff never ceases to surprise by coming up with obscure facts. My gratitude in particular to Kathie Sharp, Sandy Housley, and Jane E. Romita.

Many Silicon Valley friends provided invaluable anecdotes, perceptions, opinions, and observations without realizing that, after checking the details, their input might appear in print. Only in a few cases, and with their permission, have I mentioned names.

This book was based largely on over 100 hours of conversation with Gil Amelio, and might have been months later in reaching the bookstores but for the yeoman services of Marianne Stuber, who put in unreasonable hours transcribing the interview tapes fast enough to stay ahead of my needs.

A special thanks to Charlene Amelio for putting up with more trips, visits, and phone calls than she bargained for, and for her patience with my demands on her husband's time . . . especially through the 1997 Christmas/New Year's season.

My long established friendship with Gil Amelio could have been dashed over my writing his Apple memoir. In my effort to keep this history accurate, I was again impressed with Gil's strength and courage; he allowed me to question his memory, his attitudes, his version of events, and his purposes. He found many of my probing questions very personal as I delved into painful events he would rather not have relived. But he flinched only occasionally, shirked no questions, and shared the emotions as well as the facts.

I admire and respect him even more than before, having witnessed his courage to use this project as a way of holding up a mirror and accepting appropriate responsibility for failures.

Gil and I emerge from this project as even better friends—a rare and highly unlikely outcome when a book project covers the scope of so many emotional highs and lows. Though I'm not sure he would again be willing to relive painful memories that hadn't yet had a chance to heal, he came through like a champion.

I hope the experiences in these pages may prove enlightening to many who wonder what goes on behind the curtain and to those who hope one day to carry an executive title themselves.

 From Gil Amelio

The writing of this book was unexpectedly difficult, because it demanded that I relive an almost singularly stressful period of my life. Seeing it through was only possible because of the loving support of my wife, Charlene, who understood my need to capture the experience in writing. Her quiet encouragement and reminders to tell it from the heart made the task lighter. My children, Todd, Lisa, and Ryan, stepchildren, Brent and Tina, and children-in-law, Mandy and Dan, were all constant sources of support and love. Grandchildren like Logan, Griffin, and Alyssa make all efforts worthwhile. True to form, my mom and dad, Anthony and Elizabeth Amelio—who thankfully are still able to express their 100 percent loyalty—felt that the Apple directors must surely have lost their minds to relieve their son of command.

The task was also made easier by my collaboration with Bill and Arynne Simon. Bill, a frequent speechwriter for me, and Arynne, who is a writer and incomparable speech coach, have been my friends for more than a dozen years. The days at Apple—because of the enormous pressure I felt—were trying on our relationship, and I lacked the time to properly nurture our friendship. With infinite patience, they waited out this period; the writing of this book served to re-ignite our deep respect for one another.

Bill questioned me about my time at Apple with sensitivity, but would not allow me to shy away from the tough moments. He helped me understand what I was feeling and made the experience more real. While the story is mine, it was Bill's talent as a storyteller that helped bring it to life on the written page. The future is, as always, a mystery, but I hope that Bill and Arynne can continue to be an important part of my life.

There were also friends too numerous to list both inside and outside of Apple who understood what I was attempting to do with the company and never flinched in their support. I'm especially thankful to my office staff—Jim Oliver, my aide; Aggie Pagnillo, my executive assistant; Victoria Nielsen and Fran Mottie, secretarial support—for their steadfast loyalty through an experience not of their making. Only one remains at Apple, but they all remain my friends. I also owe a debt of gratitude to George Scalise, who left a perfectly good job at National Semiconductor to join me at Apple. He worked as hard as anyone could have possibly asked and he never had a discouraging word. He and his wife, Dot, remain among my dearest of friends. No acknowledgment would be complete without recognizing longtime friends Professor Bob Miles and his wife, Jane, as well as Mike Townsend, a gifted strategy consultant, all of whom were there with wise counsel when we were in need.

One of the experiences a pilot dreads is that of getting "behind the airplane," with a situation developing faster than the brain can process. It is a terrifying feeling, which I've experienced twice in twenty years of flying. Thankfully, on both occasions, I was able to catch up in thought and action in time to avoid tragedy. But at Apple, I sensed myself behind the situation for months on end. Ironically, during my last several months I was finally beginning to feel in control of events.

My fervent hope is that this book will serve as a foundation for learning and growth, while offering a panoramic view of business as seen from the top.

By reliving many painful experiences and "telling it from the heart," I hope these pages also successfully convey the challenges, emotions, and pitfalls of a CEO when his company is in serious trouble.

Many days at Apple were lonely, frustrating, and stressful, but in total, the experience offered an extraordinary journey that was often thrilling. I am aware of complaints that I was overpaid; from my point of view the contract was written at bargain-basement prices. The reader will find I've taken the opportunity to explore the disconnect of opinions on this sensitive matter.

Both life and business expose us to extremes of human behavior—from selfless devotion to unethical greed—and we are forced to confront the essence of who we really are. Somehow I managed to survive the Apple challenge and have emerged with a renewed and expanded appreciation both of business and of life.

I am frequently asked if I would I do it over again. In *Profit from Experience,* I wrote about the importance of pushing oneself beyond the comfort zone; at Apple, because of many unforeseen conflicting pressures, I was forced to function beyond my comfort level. Admittedly it was frightening, but I've grown as a result.

Would I do it over again? In a minute!

Index